THE GREAT AMERICAN COMMUNICATION CATALOGUE

Theodore Lownik Library
Illinois Benedictine College
Lisle, Illinois 60532

PRENTICE-HALL SERIES IN SPEECH COMMUNICATION
Larry L. Barker and Robert J. Kibler, Consulting Editors

IRVING J. REIN

Northwestern University

PRENTICE-HALL, INC., Englewood Cliffs, New Jersey

the Great American Communication Catalogue

Library of Congress Cataloging in Publication Data

REIN, IRVING J.
 The great American communication catalogue.

 (Prentice-Hall series in speech communication)
 Bibliography: p. 214
  1. Communication—Social aspects—United States.
2. Consumers—United States. 3. Selling. I. Title.
HM258.R347   301.14'0973   75-20461
ISBN 0-13-363598-8
ISBN 0-13-363580-5 pbk.

THE GREAT AMERICAN COMMUNICATION CATALOGUE
Irving J. Rein

© 1976 by PRENTICE-HALL, INC., Englewood Cliffs, New Jersey 07632

*All rights reserved. No part of this book
may be reproduced in any form or by any means
without permission in writing from the publisher.*

Printed in the United States of America.

10 9 8 7 6 5 4 3 2

PRENTICE-HALL INTERNATIONAL, INC., *London*
PRENTICE-HALL OF AUSTRALIA, PTY. LTD., *Sydney*
PRENTICE-HALL OF CANADA, LTD., *Toronto*
PRENTICE-HALL OF INDIA PRIVATE LTD., *New Delhi*
PRENTICE-HALL OF JAPAN, INC., *Tokyo*
PRENTICE-HALL OF SOUTHEAST ASIA (PTE.) LTD., *Singapore*

CONTENTS

PREFACE *xv*

ACKNOWLEDGMENTS *xvii*

1

introduction: the great american communication catalogue *1*

    Institutional Rhetoric *3*
    The Reaction *5*

SECTION ONE
GAMESMAN STRATEGIES *6*

2

an introduction to gamesmanship *8*

    Benign Games *11*
    Murderous Games *13*
    Feint Games *14*
    Dating Games *15*
    Seduction Games *16*
    Corporatemanship *17*
    Marrymanship *18*
    Buymanship *18*
    Other-ships *20*
    Endsmanship *21*

3

the student as consumer: teachers and students playing together *23*

    A Great American Teacher Opening Line *27*
    A Great American Student Line *29*
    All The Chickens Come Home to Roost *30*
    The Last Word *31*

4

the rhetoric of complaining *32*

    The Event *35*
    Consumer Diary *35*
    The Games Played *39*
    The Games You Can Play *41*
    Talk Hooks *42*
    Shootout at Willy's *44*
    Winning and Losing Complaints *45*
    Caught With The Hand In The Till *47*

5

a real game: the rhetoric of pinball *48*

    The Strategy of Pinball *51*
    Winning At Pinball *52*
    A Plea For Abstinence From Pinball *53*

viii

SECTION TWO
INSTANT IMAGE STRATEGIES *54*

6

the great american supermarket *56*

Super Talk *59*
The Supermarket as a Communication Environment *60*
The Great American Supermarket Tour *64*
A Meat Supermarket Vignette *67*

7

the encyclopedia of restaurant strategies *75*

Advertising *77*
Ambiance *77*
Big Mac *77*
Chicken *77*
Cleanliness *78*
Customers *78*
Decor *79*
Dream Meal *79*
Menu *79*
Eating In The Car *80*
Eating Manners (Slobmanship) *80*
Food (Types) *81*
Getting Sloshed (Drunkmanship) *81*
Great American Restaurant Awards *82*

Great American Restaurant Names *82*
Host or Hostess *82*
Ketchup *83*
Lunchmanship *83*
Menus *84*
Eighteen Great American Restaurant Words and Phrases Suitable for Menu Use *84*
Music *85*
Sandwich Making *85*
Sundae Making *85*
Tips *85*
Waiter *86*
Waitress *86*
Universities *87*
Water Glasses *87*
The Whopper *87*
Wine *87*
XYZ *88*

SECTION THREE
MEDIA STRATEGIES *92*

8

the rhetoric of cheap mail order *94*

Mail Order Strategies *96*
Fantastic Claims Strategies *99*
Hard Sell Strategies *102*

Visual Strategies *103*
Naming Strategies *104*
The World's Greatest Perspective *105*
Phone Magic: Need A Magazine? *106*
Handy Household Telephone Put-Downs *107*

9
the greeting cards: super environments *108*

The Slang Plan *110*

10
the media and the cereal bowl *113*

Television *115*
The Shelf *116*
Gimmick Premiums *117*
The Cereal Counter *118*
The Great American Adult Cereal Recipe *119*

11
four quick money-making media specials *120*

Making Money Chatting On The Telephone: Confessions of a Call-In Host *121*
Great American Click-Off Lines *122*
The Great American Cookbook: Fast Print Dough *125*
Beyond Cookbooks *128*
A Perfect Soap Opera Script... *129*
Jefferson Carpet TV Ad *129*

SECTION FOUR
STYLISTIC STRATEGIES *130*

12

the great american princess: a stylistic myth *132*

> *The Princess Game* *133*
> Her Stereotype *135*
> Great Beginnings *136*
> *The GAP Test* *136*
> Princess Putdowns *137*
> The Princess and Sex *140*
> How Do Males Really Land Princesses? *142*
> *Great American Stop Lines* *144*
> Conquest Strategies *146*
> The Rewards *149*
> The Last Great American Princess *151*
> *The Princess Game Game Board* *152*

13

the rhetoric of the bridal salon *154*

> The Sale I *156*
> The Beginning *156*
> The Sale II *157*
> Great American Bridal Shop Counters *158*
> Why Bother *159*
> *General Strategies of Weddingship* *159*
> *The Greatest American Style: The Coke Bottle* *160*

14

two stylistic strategies: doctors and taxicab drivers 162

        Communication Contact *165*
        The Doctor and The Phone *165*
        The Waiting Room *166*
        The Delivery of the Service *168*
        Advice to Pre-Meds: What Should You Look Like 169
        A Problem of Identity *170*
        The Great American Doctor Counter *171*
        Great Doctors' Bedside Manners 172
        The Taxicab Driver and The Hustle *173*
        What Should A Cab Driver Look Like? 175
        Taxicabs As Waiting Rooms *175*
        The Great American Cab Driver Hustles *177*
        Doctors and Taxi Drivers *177*
        The Sudden Communicator 179

SECTION FIVE
PROGRAM STRATEGIES *180*

15

how to make one million bucks in a free society 182

        Will You Settle For 39¢? 186
        How To Run Your Clinic *190*
        Pyramid Sales *191*
        How About $1.39? 193
        Win $100,000 Cash. . . 194
        Vignettes of Programmed Instruction 195

16

nobody's perfect: strategies in delivering new cars *199*

> The Delivery *202*
> The Delivery Con *205*
> Breaking The Program *207*
> The Close *208*

17

the great american finale *209*

> Ignorance of Strategies *211*
> Fear *211*
> Convenience *211*
> Fantasy *212*
> Risk *212*
> Frustration *212*
> The Next Catalogue *213*

the final clearance bibliography *214*

PREFACE

The beginnings of a book frequently are difficult to trace.
I was walking down Aberdeen, South Dakota's main drag on a
hot summer night, counting the lox and bagel stands, when a
pock-marked Army sergeant approached me and asked a simple
question: "Did you see the new Kelindest shotguns on page
43 of Monky Wards' new catalogue?" "No," I responded simply.
Too simply, I discovered, when he suddenly bolted off for
the nearest tavern—the Last Cowboy Bar and Grill.
"Hey," I thought to myself, "I was going to write this book
on glacial eskers, but why not write a book on cultural
communication, instead—with the catalogue as a logo?"

  Well, I'm glad to say it's over. My wife left me for a pipe
fitter with a cabin in northern Wisconsin. My health, once as
steady as the American dollar, wavers between acid indigestion
and tics in my eye (which a window washer in my building
refers to as the writing fellow's squint). I lost three inches in height,
gained twenty-three pounds in girth, wear eyeglasses
for the first time, and bought a pair of Scholl's orthopedic shoes.
My psoriasis continues to plague me—heartbreakingly.

  But I am through suffering, because I now am
unleashing this book on the public. You thought my playing
miniature golf for 135 days straight was a sign of a crack-up.
Well, I got that free game on the eighteenth hole, and the
manager now calls me by my first name.

And, finally, this catalogue is dedicated to an English girl, Mordette Bailey, who—when I was down and out and flying cases of JuJu Fruits to toothless members of Parliament in World War II—gave me some advice. Mordette did not have much, and while munching gooey JuJu's between puffed lips, she said simply, "Buy cheap, sell high."

My new Mercedes-Benz 450 SCL is dedicated to you, Mordette.

Irving J. Rein
Northwestern University

ACKNOWLEDGMENTS

My debt for assistance in *The Great American Communication Catalogue* must begin with my wife, Lynn Miller Rein, who in this project, as in others, has served as the principal critic and editor.

I continue to be surprised and delighted by the rich insights Tim Skelly brings to the book.

My association with Northwestern University students and staff, as always, stimulates and enriches my work. I am grateful to Susan Tick and Susan Weiss for research on greeting cards. Tim Bengston was particularly helpful in the manuscript's latter stages. Mary Ralston was always helpful with friendly assistance. The Northwestern administration has continued to allow me the freedom to experiment and innovate in my teaching and research.

I am also indebted for the research ideas gained from a wonderful summer spent teaching students at California State University at Los Angeles.

In addition, I am grateful to the Advanced Management Institute at Lake Forest College for providing typing assistance for a tired writer in the homestretch of a manuscript.

I owe a special thanks to Dick Cosme of Prentice-Hall, who listened to my ideas and made insightful suggestions. I am also appreciative of the cheerful assistance of

acknowledgments

Ted Arnold, and his efficient assistant, Shirley Chlopak.
The patience and advice of the production editor,
Kitty Woringer, and the designer, Judy Winthrop, were crucial
to the creative design of the book. Arthur Rittenberg
of Prentice-Hall was the original supporter of the book,
and his good sense of humor, hopefully, runs throughout it.

THE GREAT AMERICAN COMMUNICATION CATALOGUE

introduction: the great american communication catalogue

If ever a group of people was prime for one activity, it has to be American consumers. Training in the Art of Consumption begins from the time we are children. Social scientist David Riesman considers consumerism our single greatest activity and cautions of its ever-increasing hold on American values and ideals.[1] In a sense, consumerism is another revival of an old tradition of questioning and battling the seller of goods. There have been few periods when the buyers have not grown restive under the thumbs of aggressive sellers—the moneychangers were chased from the temple, the large landowners of England frequently found a maverick Robin Hood poaching fowl or quarreling about land rights, thousands of nineteenth-century midwestern farmers sent the land-greedy railroaders into the night with buckshot, and early in this century there were strikes against unscrupulous landlords and boycotts of spoiled meat products. But you know what, folks? The moneychangers now are selling cocoa short,[2] the large landowners have subdivided their forests into four-bedroom, three-bath, New Orleans-style Colonials from $58,900 up, the railroaders now are working downtown buying slum property for condominiums, and the meat barons are into antihistamines, saccharin, black market hexachlorophene, and frozen, deep-dish, blueberry pies with SS99. The seller-consumer game has not changed much superficially—except for the players, who now wear doubleknit slacks, eat ice cream sundaes from plastic coated containers, and drive 450-cube, eight-cylinder, 227-inch-long wagons with 40,000-mile, nonskid, radial tires. The old-time customer with his untreated sack-cloth had many of the same problems. Is it the cheapest price?

---

[1] David Riesman, *Abundance for What?* (Garden City: N. Y., Doubleday, Inc., 1964), pp. 113-37.

[2] Adam Smith, *The Money Game* (New York: Random House, Inc., 1967), pp. 251-65. Chapter 18 describes a small group of money manipulators trying to control the world cocoa market and being wiped out by large multinational corporations.

introduction: the great american communication catalogue

Can I trust the seller? Is the merchandise fresh, unmarred, and clean? And finally, how do I get it home?

In many cases the older consumers had an advantage over today's buyer. There were few goods of which the consumer did not have at least a little firsthand knowledge or understanding: camel sellers did not offer three-speed automatic transmissions, and not many camels came with axle ratio choices. Today, in contrast, the majority of buyers are far removed from the place and source of manufacture of most products. The consumer buying a washing machine probably has little idea of how it works, who really manufactured it,[3] or how it is repaired. The product is bought from a manufacturer's fictitious list price which may have no relationship to its true worth. If it works, then you got a bargain. If it fails, then you junk, trade, or endure.

This catalogue investigates only one facet of the ever-increasing consumer game: the quality of the communication between producers and consumers. The producer is the person who has the product or service, and the consumer is the intended recipient of the producer's message. The producer can be the manager of a store, the head of the IRS branch in your neighborhood, your teacher, or employer. The consumer is in the position of being *defined* by the producer's communication, even while wanting what the producer can offer. For example, a customer returning a dress to a store is at the mercy of the manager who will determine whether the item is exchanged or the money returned. Customers in this situation are basically controlled through a large number of institutional strategies.

INSTITUTIONAL RHETORIC

An *institutional rhetoric* is a communication program that the *institution* uses to inculcate its philosophy and values on its workers, products, and customers. For example, the selling pamphlet that J.C. Penney distributes to its sales clerks detailing the Penney's method of selling, and McDonald's Golden Arches—which communicate the presence of a standardized hamburger—are tangible pieces of institutional rhetoric.

Institutions always have had trademarks such as the Coca-Cola hourglass bottle shape, the NBC peacock, or the Heinz 57 Variety slogan. However, the trademark is a small part of a company's institutional rhetoric. A company has training programs, sales meetings, even group therapy sessions—all calculated to produce a company way of doing business. The model for doing business with people is spread throughout the stores, large and small, then imitated and further disseminated throughout the country. There is as much an IBM way of doing business as there is a Harvard image and a New York Yankee rhetoric. The small dry goods merchant from Ohio can fly to New York and find out how Macy's sells napkins and then recreate a similar system in his home town.

In a real sense, most consumer communication is between the institution and us. We may be talking to real people, but their responses are conditioned by the exigencies of a corporate outlook. The undergraduate secretary in the junior college's dean's office may not know that her every response to you is simply an extension of the institution's

---

[3] Many famous store brand name products actually are manufactured by other companies. For example, Sears' washers and dryers often are Whirlpool; Penney's color televisions frequently are Panasonic; and Ward's tires at last look were Firestone.

introduction: the great american communication catalogue

philosophy. "I'm sorry, but we require two more letters of recommendation." The secretary might have accepted one letter when she was fifteen and going to high school; but upon entering that higher educational environment, the right way of handling people became apparent. Always get verification. Two are better than one; three are better than two.

Whether we go to work for someone else or become self-employed, we are forced to see the world through the occupations we decide to enter. Suspending our original attitudes, we often begin seeing through the eyes of a doctor or a plumber. More often than not, we adopt a whole new set of attitudes, philosophies, and a corresponding communication program—an institutional rhetoric (IR). The result of the institutional program often is an unfair contest between the institution and the consumer. The person acting on behalf of an institution is likely to be more self-assured than the consumer. Institutional representatives are only extensions of the institution's corporate personality. They usually are operating on their own turf, facing someone who not only wants something from them, but who is even unaware of how the institution's rhetoric or product operates. Essentially we have created an unfair communication situation in which the producer communicates his message *downward* to the consumer. In Figure A a traditional system is diagrammed with the producer communicating *across* (horizontally) with the consumer and the producer in turn receiving feedback on the quality of the message. Figure B is merely the system turned downward (vertically) with the consumer's feedback blocked by a number of producer strategies. The consumer's attempts to feed back discontentment to the producer often are thwarted by fatigue caused by the producer's inaccessibility and stalling tactics. In addition, the producers create illusions of feedback by such campaigns as Ford's "We listen better," and other "We-know-what-you-folks-out-there-want" strategies. Probably the lack of true feedback and corresponding producer acknowledgment and change have created consumer movements designed to break through the feedback blocks.

There is a popular misconception that institutional rhetoric is confined to large corporations. It simply is not so. There are many activities and life styles in our society in which the characters have become institutionalized—the student—the complainer—the Great American Princess. Even though these people are not part of a corporation under one roof, they represent an Institutional Rhetoric. That is, many of the Princesses in the world share an IR, but they received their training in separate homes, streets, neighborhoods, and towns. Through the magic of a culture in which ideas are transmitted swiftly and reinforced via media, budding Princesses in Topeka can watch Princess Anne on international television; and, if the Princess is wearing a stunning creation of crisp, white taffeta, they all can relate. The same media that brings us NCAA basketball games and "I Love Lucy" reruns deliver to consumers packages of cultural behavior that easily can be imitated. We can learn how to love elegantly from Princess Anne's wedding, how to grieve publicly

Figure A:
A Traditional Feedback System

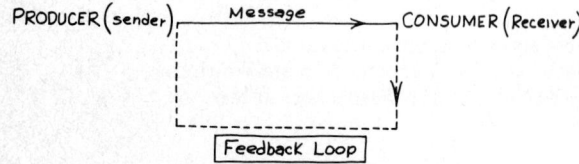

Figure B:
An Institutional Rhetoric Adaptation

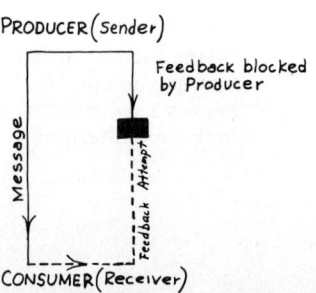

introduction: the great american communication catalogue

from President Pompidou's funeral, and how to accept victory humbly from Howard Cosell's interview with Muhammad Ali.

The real question is how to deal with and understand IR on a daily basis in order both to reduce anxiety and to enrich a consumer's life. Why shouldn't a consumer be in a position to enjoy an IR rather than to suffer from it? When the telephone company bills you sporadically and you begin trying to work through the labyrinth of its computer, why not enjoy each step? Why not be in a position to counter each Bell strategy with ridiculous aplomb—not to manipulate, cheat, or gain financially—but to play and understand the game beautifully, to become objective through knowledge of the strategies and to achieve enjoyment by watching them be enacted.

It would be wise to observe that it is unfair to blame institutions for all our failures in communication; corporations are made up of people who, despite good intentions, are as frustrated by poor communication as the consumer is. We have traveled the road from small mama-and-papa stores to multinational corporations and franchise industries within this century. As business has centralized, simultaneously becoming philosophically more tightly structured, institutional programs have become more dominant. The little shopkeeper who knew his customers by name has given way to companies who do not know a customer's name except by computer but who are recognizable to the customers by symbols, slogans, and catchy jingles. In a migrant population, many citizens find McDonald's Golden Arches a familiar symbol under which to find comfort, food, and reassurance that home is anywhere you make it. Still the people at McDonald's are not familiar, and that is probably a quality of American life that continues to frustrate us. That the McDonald's people are not familiar is not their fault but rather a natural extension of our national drive toward mobility and corporate efficiency.

When we talk about Institutional Rhetoric there is little attempt to discriminate between money-making corporations and institutions that exist for nonprofit motives. A large university is as much a part of the institutionalized producer-consumer relationship as an Arby's Roast Beef sandwich shop. Each in its way has its own rhetoric—manipulative, peopleless, and frustrating to those producing and consuming within it.

THE REACTION

The result of the producer's manipulation is that the consumer fails to respond intelligently to communication situations. Some consumers claim they "got a great deal" when they were truly bamboozled; others make hasty decisions when unusual pressure is applied; and others freeze and fail to make any decision at all. The consumer, instead of proceeding rationally, finds buying decisions too difficult and may end up screaming at the top of his voice or exiting without product adjustment or satisfaction—both conclusions this catalogue would hope to remedy.

The purpose of *The Great American Communication Catalogue* is to analyze producer-consumer communication strategies in a number of situations. The catalogue will demonstrate strategies of both the institutions and the consumers involved. My hope is that exposure of the strategies and counter-strategies of both sides will give choices to the communicators. With these choices, hopefully, the obnoxious strategies will abate, and newer, less manipulative alternatives will evolve.

SECTION ONE
GAMESMAN STRATEGIES

The ability to be a gamesman is a prized possession
in America. When a communication system becomes impersonal,
the need for games to facilitate interaction necessarily arises.
To play games is to see life as a series of moves
and countermoves. A game strategy can be used to protect systems,
to stay noninvolved, or to hurt people. In this section we view
various game strategies as an overall life principle as it occurs
in educational institutions, in the frustrating exchanges
in complaining, even in pinball - a real game.
The focus is to demonstrate the game strategies
of both producers and consumers.

an introduction to gamesmanship

Only a few seconds remained in a brilliant football duel with undefeated Notre Dame desperately driving to tie the score against Iowa University in the fading seconds of the game. Since the clock was racing and the Irish had used all their time outs, defeat seemed certain. Suddenly, a large Notre Dame tackle fell to the turf mysteriously injured, and the referees called an official's time out to allow medical aid to the faking, stricken athlete. The time out allowed Notre Dame to conserve time, regroup, and finally tie the score on a last-second play. A number of American citizens, irate at the uncivil action of the tackle, carped about sportsmanship; but as early as 1953, in South Bend, Indiana, this powerful blocker was the harbinger of the growing art of gamesmanship—a sport that the late, fabled gamesman, Stephen Potter, defined as "The Art of Winning Games Without Actually Cheating."[1] His is a crass definition, but it is as useful a place as any to begin a discussion of the salient strategies of *The Great American Communication Catalogue.*

    Many of our producer-consumer relationships are really forms of gamesmanship with the idea of winning paramount. Noting the relationship between games and life, sportswriter Leonard Shecter observed,

> We play our games, or watch them contested, with the same tenacious ferocity with which we fight a war in Vietnam and with as little reason or sense. We are taught

---

[1] Stephen Potter, *The Theory and Practice Of Gamesmanship* (New York: Bantam, 1965), p. 4. I apologize to Potter for stealing his splendid idea of gamesmanship. But having studied his work, I decided that this gambit is sticky wicket, and, if he still were alive, he would recognize it as a rare example of booksmanship.

from the cradle that we have never lost a war, and that winning is everything, tying is like kissing your sister, and losing is nothing.[2]

The accuracy of Shecter's statement can be confirmed by observing a group of first graders competing for their teacher's attention or watching bargain shoppers battle for the 8 A.M. door-opener specials.

BENIGN GAMES

There are two basic types of gamesmanship strategies important to this chapter.
The first type has tactics in which both sides are aware of the game interaction. In a sense, this really is an equal situation, since both participants know a game is in progress and are playing it openly.

Typical of two-person gamesmanship equality are teen-agers role-playing Romeo and Juliet on the telephone.

"Wherefore art thou, Melody?"

"In the game room, watching TV, Tod."

If later in the conversation the boy is turned down for a date, he needn't feel too ego-involved, since he was only playing a game. The game structure also allows the girl to refuse the boy without feeling she is crushing him or terminating a relationship.
In some cases, the game allows a shy boy to adopt a persona more acceptable to him than his own personality and makes it easier for him to pursue the date in question.

A variation of two-party equality allows the participants to enact different roles while directing their manipulation toward a third party. Occasionally, poverty-stricken professors can be seen at subway and train stations, role-playing their fellow commuters—the affluent business executives they overhear every day.

How's business?

We sold to Esmark.

No kidding.

Well, our interests total 21.5 million, give or take a few hundred thousand.

The beauty of this type of gamesmanship is that the participants are disguising their financially inferior positions. An alternative would be to turn to the waiting executives and tell them that the life of a professor is slow and not materially remunerative but that professors do have the prospect of earning tenure.
However, this kind of direct action is unlikely to receive much attention or sympathy.

---

[2] Leonard Shecter, *The Jocks* (New York: Bobbs-Merrill, 1969), p. 4.
Reprinted by permission of the publisher.

THE Two-Man Professorial Gamesman Ship

The gamesmanship strategy may create so much uncertainty among the executives confronted by the two "millionaires," that they cease their own bragging. A $500 stock climb isn't much when the other person is talking about $21.5 million.

GAIN

............So what has this gamesmanship strategy really profited the two playing professors? Not much to you or me—but to them, a one-point advantage, an edge, a score; and in a win society, what else is there? No one wants to be put down every day of his life because he teaches kids. And in football terms, you outmaneuvered your opponent and forced him off your territory.

A variation of equality gamesmanship is the affluent complaining to one another. Little is more perverse than watching two elegantly dressed middle-aged citizens trying to outscore each other in the game of *Depression*. *Depression* is played by two or more people each trying to establish how he suffered more than the other(s) during the 1929-39 economic holocaust.

an introduction to gamesmanship

He 1: You know, I sold papers to keep the apartment warm.

He 2: WARM? At least you had an apartment. We lived in the back of an unheated store.

He 1: At least you were near food. We ate rats.

He 2: RATS! Who had rats? We ate ROACHES.

GAIN

In this case, each participant eagerly can relive that part of his background of which he is proud. To have money in America is good, but to have money and also to have risen from squalor is even more delicious. A crucial portion of the game is the unlikelihood that any participant will admit the other's victory. More likely, the players eventually will simply bore each other to death.

MURDEROUS GAMES

The second category of gamesmanship is more combative and manipulative, a variation of legalized murder wherein one of the players either is unaware of the action or is aware of it but is helpless to pursue any reasonable solution. This type of game is played by communicators who find straightforward communication not as bendable to their ends as more circuitous strategies. Some of its gamesmen are drawn into play as a defense against manipulation, others for the exhilarating thrill of dominance, and some by the competitive desire to win at all costs. In any case the consumer who understands the strategies has the best chance of blocking an unethical gamesman.

Tennis is a sport that lends itself to immediate examination and illustration of some of the more important tactics of *murderous games.* Like many other sports, tennis has certain rituals, the abuse of which constitutes neither rule violation nor penalty points. What makes tennis so interesting is that proper strokes and agile footwork may produce victory, but a player with mediocre strokes and footwork still may dominate as long as she uses guile. A clever gamesman quickly learns to hesitate before serving, to tie her shoelaces, or to scan the sky for jets. Other more venturesome players may let the racket slip, inadvertently caving in an opponent's face—"I'm terribly sorry—you're not hurt?" Other workable gambits include irritating an opponent by effusively applauding her bad shots and cooly ignoring good ones, stopping action to admire players on an adjacent court, arriving with a two-year-old who wails at courtside, or advising an opponent to straighten an elbow when hitting—"According to my pro. . ."

Who Picks up the Tennis Ball

For the fledgling strategist, we now turn to the most potentially manipulative area of a tennis match. The world knows that balls that land on your side of the net should be fetched by you and not your opponent. A clever gamesman may ignore the balls on her side of the net, forcing an opponent to remind her constantly of the obligation—"Would you mind. . ." "Why, of course." Since concentration is crucial in tennis, the badgered

may begin to slip in this vital area and become exasperated at her own loss of poise. A variation, and only for hardened gamesmen, is to allow adjoining players' tennis balls to lie idly on the court while the adversary serves. The excess number of balls cluttering the court will often distress the server, causing hesitation and uncoordination in a normally smooth service. This tactic is for the hardened gamesman because of the personal risk of stumbling on a stray tennis ball or the danger of players from adjoining courts assaulting you for tardy ball returning. If the shrill for returning becomes too obvious, simply slam errant balls over the fence.

GAIN

.... The object, of course, is to win by forcing a superior player to clutch up and become unnerved by your outrageous behavior. And what have you really gained? Well, no one likes to lose; and once you start losing in life, complaint departments dismiss your problems, beach bullies kick sand in your face, and the whole Great American Dream becomes a nightmare.

FEINT GAMES

The maddening distraction is only one aspect of gamesmanship. A wily player can benefit from studying pool hustling, which features the *feint* as a means to create a setup for a lucrative end. A skilled pool player looking for an opponent to skin must disguise his own skills. The disguise usually includes the hustler's pretending to be a poorer player than he really is. A hustler will move around the table with the clumsiness of one just not skilled enough to beat the onlooking marks, but who nevertheless is earnest. The feint must appear authentic, because too good an act may scare away potential adversaries sensing a come-on. A further risk of a bad fake is that after defeat, the mark may suspect he was conned. Since most hustles are committed in other people's territory, the hustler's style must be elegant enough to avoid disaster. So the feint must be balanced with enough skill to suggest that the hustler is making a legitimate effort while letting the adversary feel he can win. When the game begins, a further enticement for the pigeon may well be a loss or two; then comes a suggestion of raising the stakes, and finally the full repertoire of sensational shots on the gulled victim. An effective hustler will carry out the fake until the entire game is completed, leaving the mark believing the con artist got incredibly lucky.

GAIN

............M-O-N-E-Y—But even if money wasn't involved, there would be great satisfaction in impersonating someone else and then turning loose a surprise attack featuring your real identity. What of the timid teacher who springs loose a blockbuster exam; the crippled newsboy who becomes a comic superhero; the discount store that opens a stylish boutique; the mother who works nights as a topless go-go dancer? Each is like the pool hustler, feinting in one direction, usually indicating timidity or ineptness, and then suddenly— flamboyant SUCCESS.

DATING GAMES

Moving to gamesmanship of a more earnest and decadent nature, we turn to dating and courtship. For many participants, by its very nature, dating is a test of skills. After all, who you end up with for your spouse can influence your sex life for forty years, your general health, how fast you move up the job ladder, and certainly how long you will live. The suitor who finds out too late that Elizabeth Hammershort is not a sweet, malleable, giving philanthropist but a nervy, neurotic, fat-prone opportunist has only himself to blame.

an introduction to gamesmanship

The same can be said for the suitee who thought she was marrying an up-and-coming, athletic, well-dressed accountant who instead turns into a beer-swilling television fanatic who considers embezzling a worthwhile hobby. A man or woman can produce the image of charm or beauty all too easily in a society full of products of deception. Whether by using a padded bra, a toupee, diction lessons, TOPS (Take Off Pounds Sensibly), or vitamin E, a person can temporarily deceive any unwary potential mate. It is clear that the wonders of our technological age create multiple opportunities for dating duplicity as well as the necessity for the sadistic gamesman to develop unmasking games.

The first aspect of dating gamesmanship is unmasking the poor-risk marriages. A few gamesmen like the *Unexpected Pleasures* gambit. In this strategy, the gamesman informs the victim that she is to be taken to America's Number One restaurant. The datee is taken to a local meat packing plant to watch the brutal slaughter of animals, and next she is treated to dinner in the company cafeteria. If she eats the food, chances are you have either a woman of great character or a latent killer. Another game fanatic had each of his prospective dates given a medical inspection by his company's doctor under the guise that it was company policy. He feared that underneath his date's healthy appearance lurked a diabetic interior or worse yet, a serious dental problem. If none of these gambits appeals, a desperate date might try the *Miss America Beauty Contest adaptation,* which requires spilling a plate of food on the date to test for poise. The danger in using this particular brand of gamesmanship is that you could lose a true love in this manner. So the gamesman had better feel strongly that bizarre testing is worth the risk of driving off a promising mate.

GAIN

.... Years of contentment—beautiful, quiet children—avoiding the needless heartbreak of divorce—and other bonuses mentioned above.

SEDUCTION GAMES

A variation of the preceding detectivemanship is using the dating situation as an opportunity for seduction. Using nothing illegal and little that is moral, a seducer promises marriage but insists on elopement that very night. Naturally, the trip cannot be made in one evening, a motel room is secured, and since marriage is imminent. . . . The next day the seducer develops cold feet, and they return home to singleship. Other gamesmen resort to buying twenty-five-cent engagement rings from Woolworth's as lures, manufacturing fatal illnesses as promises, or contriving intricate weather circumstances for delays. It is possible in all these variations of seduction that the seductee is aware of the strategy and finds the script interesting to play out—"What's this dummy going to do next?" And some gamesmen actually find their consciences bothering them after a number of years of this behavior.

GAIN

.... A feeling that once again a trick, a ploy, bested someone unaware. Then, of course, there also is gained a certain amount of sexual pleasure for both parties.

CORPORATEMANSHIP

Moving to highly serious gamesmanship, we find ourselves blocked at making it up the corporate ladder. No one is saying that you shouldn't elect to swing up the job ladder through your incredible drive, mathematical skill, or efficiency. But for every energetic, qualified citizen there are legions of unqualified citizens who annually fill thousands of lucrative positions. Since I assume that working hard is not appealing, I am suggesting that with a few lessons in corporatemanship any boob can rise in an organization.
One possibility for the unprincipled gamesman is to create the illusion of working through a number of carefully planted suggestions. These minigambits were well documented in Robert Morse's film portrayal of the crafty junior executive in *How to Succeed in Business Without Really Trying.* Morse played a character who appeared ambitious by arriving at work every morning just before the boss and feigning having slept at his desk after a hard night's labor. This strategy can be very effective when dueling for promotion with a colleague who needs eight hours of sleep. His futile attempts to beat the gamesman to the office will exhaust the poor fellow and reduce his efficiency to that of a graduate of a low stature college (see *collegemanship*). When the adversary is reeling from lack of sleep, the gamesman informs him repeatedly that, unlike his victim, *he* needs a maximum of three hours' sleep. The other gambits—such as becoming drinking friends with influential superiors and ingratiating yourself with the president by appearing at his church Sunday mornings—seem hardly worth mentioning.

However, it would be untidy not to mention *telephonemanship* as a prerequisite for corporatemanship. It is important for a callee never to be in a situation where the caller has him in a one-down position. It is imperative that the gamesman always selects the time and place of the call for comfort and control. *Rule One for the gamesman:* Never accept a call from anyone; always insist on calling back when you are receptive and in position to manipulate. *Rule Two:* If you want authorization for a project always call your superiors when they are sure to be preoccupied. If 3:00 o'clock is time for a dalliance, 3:08 is perfect. *Rule Three:* When calling subordinates do as doctors do—call at dinner time or just before bed. When the underling answers, do not identify yourself, but forcefully bark your orders and hang up. *Rule Four:* Never make a major decision on the

an introduction to gamesmanship

phone; always insist on lunch (see *lunchmanship* in "Encyclopedia of Restaurant Strategies"). Who knows what effects liquor and Oysters Rockefeller will have on your opponent?

GAIN

............Warm trips to the Bahamas, Mercedes-Benz 450 SCL, American Express card—maybe even the front cover of *Business Week*.

MARRYMANSHIP

I'm sure you're wondering when I will get around to marrying the boss's daughter as a strategy for the up-and-coming cad. Well, I feel the whole matter is too risky for a true gamesman, as evidenced by the following anecdote. T. F. was a greasy lout who looked as if he'd been wrung from a sewer. Though shiftless and brainless, he had the good fortune and apparent presence of mind to marry the dopey, handsome daughter of a large catalogue firm magnate. A flock of envious males saw the greaser whisk away millions of dollars worth of toasters and coaster sets. Unfortunately, in a bit of double gamesmanship, poor T. F. is now working himself to the bone as vice-president of Asian development. His Mercedes-Benz is small consolation when, after a sixteen-hour-day under the watchful, vindictive eye of his father-in-law, he returns to a wife of such ignorance and docility that *Search for Tomorrow* is too intellectually challenging for her. So, I can hardly recommend his gambit as worthy; but if you must, at least be sure it is *old* money.

GAIN

............A rich, sleepless, boring life.

BUYMANSHIP

I have told you how to make it up the ladder to riches—now a discussion of the proper method of spending it. Anyone can walk into a store, plunk down a credit card, and exit with a product. This behavior runs counter to the ethics and spirit of gamesmanship. The store is not simply a place to purchase goods but an arena in which combatants of various hues and stripes duel rhetorically over candlesticks and Italian provincial bedposts. Not to savor every moment of the struggle is simple-minded, as exasperating to an aficionado of *buymanship* as a Japanese pocket radio without batteries, a Sheffield stainless steel knife made of aluminum, a batch of fresh, unwritten checks at closing time. Besides, once you have financial success, what else is there but the hassle over soft goods, hard goods, and piece goods?

A true buymanship gambit begins with an attitude of disdain toward the clerk and his time. The object is to busy the clerk with complicated questions to establish a relationship of master to servant:

an introduction to gamesmanship

19

Customer: Do you have any 100 percent llama undershorts?

Clerk: Well, we have some silk dealies with red ants crawling on the seat.

Customer: I was in New York last week, and the better stores were all carrying llama undershorts.

Clerk: Gee, I never even heard of them.

Customer: **MANAGER! MANAGER!** I've had enough of your insolence!

In truth, if the clerk had llama undershorts the customer wouldn't have bought them anyway since they look tacky[3] and probably would scratch. The customer counters the clerk by launching into an attack on the poor quality of merchandise in comparison to that carried in New York, or in desperate times, the customer attacks the clerk's dirty fingernails.

GAIN

. . . . It was stated most beautifully in the thoughts of a Mrs. Halpern:

What a delight to ask for something they don't have, to see the brazen salesmen cringe as she enters a high class, conservative men's store and asks for a flowery sport shirt, to drift into Tiffany's and describe a spray of zircons, to visit a costume jewelry stand and demand rubies.[4]

Then, of course, there is an interesting variation of buymanship called *return-return,* practiced by only the most steely-nerved of all gamesmen. Need a dress for a special party? A tie for a confirmation? A garter for a debauchery? Haven't any money? The strategist buys the item on a charge, wears it grandly, and then return-return.

A return situation is fraught with danger only in the event that you show timidity or breathe far too heavily for the time of year. (A full discussion will follow in "The Rhetoric of Complaining.")

Returner: I wish to return this dress which does not please me.

Accepter: But there is catsup all over it.

Returner: **ARE YOU MAD?** The dress is a catsup decoupage by Cardin. **MY GOD,** the impertinence!

Accepter: Well, okay, but I've never heard of it before.

Returner: Thank you, dear.

It goes without saying that the great returners have set records that will be hard to match. Who can forget Lewis K. who successfully returned a box of assorted,

---

[3] TACKY—as in those citizens with the inability to distinguish between sleaziness and class. Late night television commercials are tacky.

[4] From *How Much?* by Burt Blechman © 1961. Reprinted by permission of Astor-Honor, Inc., New York, N.Y. 10017.

an introduction to gamesmanship

ten-year-old Dunkin' Donuts, claiming they were stale; or L. Roloff, who kept his Midas Muffler guarantee through eighteen cars and $912 worth of free replacements. These legendary gamesmen mastered the rattled voice gambit, the calculated bellow, and the World War II limp. In return-return, anything goes; and this includes attempting suicide in front of the complaint counter. To a true gamesman, a failed return is a call to death.

GAIN

Returner: A SPECIAL. Two pounds for how much. What do you think I paid?
Fan: Oh, for cream-filled chocolates, about $4.25.
Returner: NOTHING! I ate the filberts and returned the rest!

OTHER-SHIPS

The areas of gamesmanship could go on and on:

Collegemanship

The real question is not what you learned in high school, but how you snowed the college recruiter. How many wily kids do you know who ended up in a third rate teacher's college? What are recruiters looking for? Honesty, real intellectuality, cleanliness, well-contained personal drive?

Question: HOW DO YOU FEEL ABOUT ATTENDING HARVARD?
Answer (wrong): *I want it desperately enough to kill my mother. (My God!)*
Answer (right): You get out of college what you put in. (And of course YOU will put in.)

Question: WHO ARE YOUR IDOLS?
Answer (wrong): *John Wayne (forget it); Bob Hope (nope).*
Answer (right): Martin Buber (big); any Foreign Film-Maker (sure thing).

Question: HOW DO YOU FEEL ABOUT GRADES?
Answer (wrong): *They are the passport to the world's goodies.*
Answer (right): Ideas transcend grades; thoughts come not in A's and B's.

If all these strategies fail with the recruiter, there is one variation that—while not sure-fire—may turn the tide. Attack the recruiter as bigoted toward your minority group (whatever), and you might get lucky.

Childrenship

How to score through your kids. "So Danny made it to Amherst. Congrats, Phyllis, congrats. Jimmy turned down Amherst—not that it's a bad school—but he wants to specialize in neurosurgery; and between that and his football career, stamp collecting, and the gift of a new car from his generous father, he's thinking of working a year at the Post Office."

Decoratorship

Who in the neighborhood has the best decorator. "Oh, my dear, I love your rattan wallpaper. I'm sure you'll enjoy living with it. My decorator used it in our rec room three years ago and we still adore it."

Lunchmanship

Well, let's see, you had a cheese sandwich and coffee, and I had a salad, lobster, broccoli, steamed potatoes, 1966 Taittinger, and dessert. Hmm...that's $15.80 apiece not including the tip."

ENDSMANSHIP

Certainly from a philosophical point of view, one could question the morals of gamesmanship. In addition, a reasonable case could be made that America is being poisoned by an easy and promiscuous use of strategies to wallop the unsuspecting. A better means of expression and transaction would be elimination of subterfuge and a retreat to straightforward communication. The trouble is that some gamesmanship is fun, entertaining, and probably as good for you as fidelity.

It is clear in modern American communication that the intensity and number of games have increased. Possibly this increase is because as our society becomes more centralized, more complex, and less personal, the intimate relations inevitably become infrequent; and gamesmanship thrives on anonymity. A return-return is easier at Dunkin' Donuts than a similar attempt in a small-town coffee shop. Once people begin to know each other it becomes difficult to play unequal gamesmanship.

So do you play or watch? If you are desperate to succeed there are some areas of life that demand gamesmanship. It is hard to imagine a junior executive not playing along with the typical institutional gamesmanship of large companies. The penalty for not playing is often far greater than a junior executive could endure financially. *To-play-for-financial-reasons* many people call the *real world* as opposed to the *school world,* which, by its alleged openness, is false. The next chapter will examine that myth.

One alternative to desperately playing is to become detached and objective about the nature of gamesmanship. A consumer can adopt complete understanding of the

an introduction to gamesmanship

strategic nature of communication games and act accordingly. If a game is being played, *enjoy it* if you find it amusing. *Stop it* if you find it appalling. *Applaud it* if you find it brilliant. *Win it* if you cannot stand defeat. The danger for the knowledgeable player is that such pragmatism may result in abusive treatment of innocent or less capable participants. Another alternative to desperately playing is to produce a generation of knowledgeable gamesmen who can stop manipulative communication through their ability to recognize and counter the more unfortunate manifestations. Armed with an understanding of gamesmanship, the consumer can play superbly when the object is enjoyment or relaxation and refuse to play when the signal callers turn to communication violence. Was it at the Notre Dame-Iowa football game that a confused spectator coined the phrase, "You can't tell the players without their numbers"? Or was it the Iowa football coach who lamented, "Why didn't I bring my rule book?"

the student as consumer: teachers and students playing together

3

One of the favorite sports in American games is *going to see the instructor about a lousy grade.* Offended students offer wildly varied reasons to justify a grade change. A common complaint is that the student wrote a brilliant essay exam, but the reader failed to appreciate its point of view, humor, sarcasm, ethics, or role play. Another common student complaint is that the reader counted off for a few spelling or grammatical errors. Instructors counter with the charge of 143 spelling errors in a twelve-page paper and syntax rivaling the incoherent babblings of radio and television baseball announcers.

Steve: You know, Jeff, a good hitter is the world's greatest athlete, bar none.

Jeff: Is that so, Steve?...I guess Ted Williams is poetic testimony to the dominance of the grand old game.

Steve: Of course, Jeff, some people think that hitting a baseball is easy; but a baseball is throwed [sic] at speeds of 98 miles an hour and that's plenty fast.

Jeff: Right you are, Steve, and now in beautiful San Diego our southpaw lefthander [sic] spins a strike two.

For whatever reason the student feels disgruntled, the student (consumer) feels hostility toward the educational institution; and between the institution's sophomoric faith in the workability of grades and the student's realistic belief in their negotiability, an oft-repeated class struggle ensues.

The teacher who gave the grade feels a number of pressures to which she must respond. She must grade because everyone expects them—including students, parents, admissions officers, medical schools, and employers. A student with a 3.85 out of a 4.0 grade point average has our society's equivalent of Aladdin's Magic Lamp.

the student as consumer: teachers and students playing together
. . . .
25

The teacher who has the power to change a *C* to a *B*, a *B* to an *A*, or a *C* to a *D* is the bestower of that Lamp. This degree of power in a meritocracy is roughly counterpart to being the chancellor of the exchequer in King Arthur's Court or controlling the water rights in eastern Texas in 1876. If the teacher votes a low grade for the student, that consumer's options for a happy life are diminished. "You bum," cries the mother. "A failure," agonizes Dad. "Our engagement is terminated," snaps the campus leader. "Unmotivated," thinks the employer.

The result of the importance of grades often is a confrontation between two of society's heaviest players—the Educator and the Learner. Each of the participants has innate advantages and disadvantages. For the complaining student, there are a number of rhetorical advantages. One is his youth, which in case of a shouting match might carry the student through a strenuous exchange. An American Council on Education Study found that 59 per cent of American college and university faculty members are over forty years of age ("ACE Faculty and Staff Survey Newsletter," August 1973, p. 2). For most students this means that the teacher adversary is twice as old as they; and, given the blandness of American diets and the sedentary nature of teaching, a fist fight undoubtedly would result in a resounding student victory. However, a rough and tumble brawl with a teacher is going to get the student only a one-way ticket to the blast furnaces at United States Steel, a job turning the self-tapping screw into the right fenders of Chevrolet Vegas, or a life waiting on tables at the home-town cafe. The teacher may even get lucky and put you into the hospital where your hemorrhaging mind can reconsider the use of fisticuffs as a solution to your problem.

However, age can be a positive factor if the student is a lovely or handsome twenty and the teacher is a decrepit forty-five:

the student as consumer: teachers and students playing together

What makes this tactic work is the congruity of the directness of the "love" hustle with the directness of the college and university environment. In the apparently open society of schools where conventional standards of behavior are not necessarily expected, the direct confrontation approach is not a bad risk. The downside risk for the student is not great, since most teachers are not going to become involved in punishing for a hustle; and there is always an outside chance of acceptance (if the student really wants that). It should also be stressed that this tactic is not designed for operation on the district supervisor for International Business Machines or in other business environments where the behavior codes are more conventional.

It is fairly obvious that the Ms. Orwell dialogue is strictly time-bound for the practitioner. As age deteriorates the face and body, other less pleasurable strategies are forced upon the now wrinkled and graying.

Since we are discussing appearance, a word about proper clothes for the teacher-student encounter (*clothesmanship*). For the student there are two divergent schools of thought. The conservative school advocates that dark, somber clothing is appropriate to reinforce the image of somber purpose and industriousness. The liberal school recommends clingy, wildly hued clothes symbolic of high spirit and freedom. The clothing strategy the student chooses rests on his or her ability to analyze the faculty member and on the specific excuse being employed. A funeral obviously calls for dignified clothes and a seduction attempt for brazen dress. Yet, a genius of the game might dramatically switch apparels—shattering the instructor's expectations and using this temporary bafflement to win the grade change. Still, a crucial error, a misjudgment, a halter when a peasant dress would do—and the best of verbal strategies is awash. This battle strategy necessarily employs important weapons of both the verbal and nonverbal variety.

From the teachers' point of view, their natural advantages are tied to the institutions they represent. An educational institution should offer the student some kind of lifetime negotiability:

> "Yes, I have a B.A. from Stanford."
>
> "Well, I've graduated from the Wadena Cosmetology Institute."
>
> "I've taken an M.A. in math from Boston University and have a supervisor's certificate from Virginia."

The importance of higher education is that it remains with students for the rest of their lives; forever more they are a Michigan M.B.A. or a Swarthmore B.A., and this may mean money, prestige, and negotiability, talent notwithstanding. There are students, of course, who confuse the real worth of the institution by disregarding the negotiability of a degree and concentrating on the quality of the education they receive. These academic innocents are potentially dangerous for schools and teachers, since they fail to recognize the institutional structure and the instructor's role as middleman. They will not submit to

the student as consumer: teachers and students playing together

shabby treatment in order to be knighted; and feeling somewhat free, they may be difficult to manipulate. For most students the teacher who is part of the lifetime accrediting process has power—so much power, in fact, that proper use of institutional prestige can overcome most student attempts at reversing authority.

For the teacher the most profitable strategies, therefore, are those that use the natural advantages of the institution. A most effective opening ploy takes the form of a personal interrogation that most students find threatening:

What's your name?

Where are you from?

What's your father do?

Why did you come here?

It's important that the teacher offers these questions with good nature. The impact of the questions accompanied without even a sneer is sufficient, since many students hate to reveal their background to an institutional representative. If the teacher meets suspicious retorts, such as, "Why do you want to know?" the counter-response is complete openness. "You know where I'm from, don't you? Why shouldn't I know where you're from?" The reasonableness of this kind of answer often will force the student to tell you he is Harry Kimmelhauser from Salt Creek Lane in Hinsdale, and his father makes combat boots for the Chilean Army, and he came to Ponderous U. because he couldn't get accepted at his first- and second-choice schools because of low SAT scores. Then, of course, you've got him—having now a large number of openings to attack. Does he mind being called Harry? Does he mind living in a lily-white suburb? Does he mind having a father who contributes to war? Does he mind going to his third-choice school?
Any advantage that the complaining student might have had is blown away by the series of questions. If he, for example, could not get accepted at his top college choices, he probably is not exceptionally bright; and since he is not very bright, why should the exam reader have found his work of high quality? The implication is that a low SAT scorer from the suburbs who has a father whose contribution to the Chilean Army is 14,222 blisters isn't much of a bet to write brilliant exams.

A GREAT AMERICAN TEACHER OPENING LINE

Student: Mr. Jones, I'd like to speak with you.

Mr. Jones: You're not going to **BITCH** about a grade, are you?

Student: (hesitatingly) No, I've come to find out what you're teaching spring term.

Mr. Jones: THANK GOD, I'm so **DAMN** tired of talking to weak-kneed grade-grubbers.

DOING POORLY IN SCHOOL?
Ooo.o.o.o.o..
YOUR TROUBLE MAY NOT BE CLASSROOM PERFORMANCE, BUT DYNAMISM IN TEACHER'S OFFICES! A STUDY BY A GROUP OF COLLEGE ADMINISTRATORS FOUND THAT STUDENTS FAILED TO CONTROL THE TEACHER IN 7 OUT OF 10 ATTEMPTS AT GRADE MANIPULATION!*
THE ANSWER?
FREE!
WITH EVERY NEW SUBSCRIPTION TO THE STRATEGIST MAGAZINE
THE POCKET LIVE STRATEGIST
I'M A DUMMY--A REAL DUMMY--I SPENT 3 YEARS IN COLLEGE GETTING DIRTY D'S AND CLOUDY C'S. AFTER TWO WEEKS WITH THE PLS I CHANGED 6 OF MY GRADES INTO A'S. HE NOT ONLY CHANGED MY D TO AN A—BUT ALSO LET ME SLEEP WITH HIS WIFE! I'M CONVINCED.
— SOLOMON ORFIS
I'M PREGNANT, BUT I'M IN MEDICAL SCHOOL. I NOW HAVE 3 ILLEGITIMATE CHILDREN-BUT I ALSO HAVE A 4.0 AVERAGE, AND LOTS OF PH.D. FRIENDS. GOD LOVE YOU, PLS!
—MS. RUTH LES
ACT NOW!
WIRE, CALL, WRITE
P.L.S.
419 SOUTH PERSUASION
RED CLOUD, NEBRASKA
44454
*STUDY AVAILABLE UPON WRITTEN REQUEST

the student as consumer: teachers and students playing together

The student is now forced to accept defeat or to move to the attack. A clever (yet overworked) tactic is to claim unusually poor performance because of a family calamity. The father who suffered a heart attack or a business failure has some utility with certain bleeding-heart professors. A mother who had a nervous breakdown or recently miscarried also is very effective, if not overplayed. An artful gesture when reciting a piteous tale of woe is to appear on the edge of tears, yet to have the gumption not to fall victim to a complete breakdown. In most cases, the professor is so irritated with the inefficiency of campus counseling services that she will fail to check the credibility of your story. And, if she checks and finds that you lied, what can be done? The penalty is that the grade stays the same and the instructor no longer respects you. In this producer-consumer game hyperbole is a crime—but rarely punishable by death.

A variation of the family misery tactic is the "I need an *A* for grad school—this class breaks my back" appeal. This plea is one of the most common student tactics and the least likely to work—hang a big "I'm a dummy" sign on your chest. The teacher is going to surmise that if you need the grade that badly you must be slow. He's probably teaching the biggest "mick"[1] in school, and you need to be mentally retarded or a screw-off (which you probably are) to get less than a *B*. There is little chance that a grade change is going to be put into effect to propel a simpleton into graduate school.

A far better tactic is for the student to claim that this *D* is the only one in an otherwise *A* career and that the Yale Law School is excited about his admission but will throw the application into the academic ash heap if it includes even a *C*. This argument can trigger the teacher's anxiety about negative peer evaluation. "Why should I have given this Plato a *D* when the whole damn school is giving him *A*'s?" And if he has any notion of Judeo-Christian brotherhood and fair play, he might genuinely feel contrite. Again, given most teachers' antipathy toward registrars, he probably will fail to check whether you are indeed an *A* student. In fact, if you attend a large state institution, the two of you may never meet again.

A GREAT AMERICAN STUDENT LINE

Student: Mr. Jones, I received your grade when leaving to see **my hospitalized girl friend** in Albany.

Mr. Jones: Well, there must be a point, Todd!

Student: (tearfully) My day was **ruined** by the low grade and so was **my vacation.** My girl was **so upset** she had a **SETBACK**.

The teacher can fight this flurry of appeals with a number of strategies. A very effective tactic is to instruct a secretary to screen the applicants on suitability for seeing the professor. A suitable student is one who doesn't want to complain about grades. If the secretary is malleable, the professor can induce her to ward off complainants with dire warnings of previous professor-student encounters. Most effective is the story

---

[1] A universal student term for an easy course. In some institutions the term is "gut."
In some cases beware that a "mick" refers to an easy *C* or *B* and an unattainable *A*.

the student as consumer: teachers and students playing together

about the student who came in with a *B* and so antagonized the professor that his negotiations ended in a *D*. A clever student can counter the professor's evasion attempts by posing as a college textbook representative who brings free books and seeks unpublished manuscripts. Probably the student will be ushered eagerly into the office of the hungry-for-attention instructor. Once there, the student's explanation had better be good, for the professor was expecting some giveaway books or an expense account lunch.

. . .which brings us to an explanation of a teacher's most effective counterattack. . . .

ALL THE CHICKENS COME HOME TO ROOST

Student: I feel that my grade was unfairly given.

Professor: Well, I treat students without discrimination.
I will therefore be glad to read your exam again,
but your grade can then go *up* or come **DOWN!!!**

Now the professor has injected the element of high risk; the student must creatively respond or retreat to the Dodge Dart assembly line. The student may perceive the adversary as having escalated to a level of combativeness and risk that is too steep—better to accept a law school of lesser reputation than none at all. The teacher is the final decision maker on the papers or exams and conceivably could decide any way she pleases. The student came into the situation falsely assuming that the grade either could go up or, at minimum, stay the same. The professor's move toward a *complete* grade reevaluation destroys the student's assumptions as to what he or she saw as dominant in the situation—that the grade could only go up.

In most interactions someone frames a situation during the opening remarks that determines how the game will be played. In a teacher-student encounter, a student had better be equipped to counter the unexpected. A swift professor may establish a framework of reality so dangerous that the student is boxed into a corner.

What makes the teacher-student encounter an interesting metaphor for many observers of high-stakes games is its uncanny relationship to events later in life. A successful student in a grade change maneuver probably cannot tough it out by threats and bullying gestures. Instead, what is demanded is a role play acted out with stock lines and scenery. Imagination, creativity, intelligence, and gall are prerequisite to the encounter.

The student dressed in mourning clothes enters during office hours of the teacher who is seated behind a desk provided by the institution. The teacher asks the nature of the visit (all the while knowing) and, if he is feeling charitable, may gesture to a chair. The student, role-playing subservience, hating every minute, haltingly, excitedly, or anxiously spins the tale of woe. If the story of death does not move the teacher perhaps the promise to major in that department will. "I had hoped to switch majors to Classics, but a *D* washes out that hope." A flicker on the teacher's face encourages a move to a final plea. "Grades mean nothing; I know that, but I felt I learned as I have never learned before," he laments. "Why deny me, teacher?" he continues. Why let a small indiscretion damage the future of a sniveling child (perhaps a natural tear in the corner of any eye)

the student as consumer: teachers and students playing together

whose grandmother passed away, who stands perilously close to Yale Law School, who now wishes to major in Classics, and who—if you only say the word—will dance for joy. The hair is brushed aside from the eyes and the closing plea is finished. And how many closing pleas will follow in asking for a raise, a day off for a fishing trip, or a discount on a doctor bill?

THE LAST WORD

And what of the final plea of the teacher, the person instructed by the institution to preserve its integrity from shirkers and nonacademics. He, too, is role-playing, as the institution has vested in him an official position that he must defend.
He can always fall back on the argument that rules forbid grade changes.
Or, if intimidation fails, the instructor can nonverbally roll his eyes and arch his eyebrow to indicate skepticism. He can saw off the legs of his office chair to lower the occupant's height and attempt to dominate through altitude. But the teacher knows his advantages are merely extensions of the institution's prerogatives. If the student loses the teacher does not necessarily win. No one wins teacher-student grade encounters,
because a student victory defeats the system and a teacher's triumph only sustains it.

In a sense, the teacher-student encounter is one of those societal dances between participants who know little of what causes their very motion. A student reacts to the pressures of grades—perhaps he is ignoring one class to attend to others, or is too bored to stay awake at lectures, or simply is ill-equipped to compete in the grade marketplace. But a student either earns high grades or is condemned to completing lesser life ambitions and subsequent roles. Against this backdrop, what are a few moments of subservience to the authority figure?

The teacher is set in motion by his role as grader and life-authenticator. He defends a system that is fundamentally irrational, and he probably knows it. This teacher may have taught a course poorly this term, or he may have been unclear in making assignments, or the class may have met in a room of substandard quality. But the teacher must ignore weaknesses and limitations and complete the inevitable dance between institutions and consumers.

the rhetoric of complaining

4

SHAKE! YOU SINNERS!

THOSE WERE THE WORDS THAT FILLED MY HEAD AS I ENDURED THE LIVING **HELL** BEQUEATHED TO EVERY CONSUMER ON THIS EARTH. LET MY **TRUE** STORY LIGHT THE WAY TO **SALVATION** FOR **YOU** AND **YOURS**!

CUSTOMER SERVICE DEPT.

In America nothing is so fraught with anxiety as buying the goods so expertly sold by our manufacturers and marketers. The once simple act of exchanging our earned dollars for television sets, houses, Barbie dolls, and automobile tires has grown complex. In our search for fair treatment, honest merchants, and good buys, the consumer's sometimes helpless cry crescendos. He wants to know how to counter simple cheating; or, how does he fight shoddy goods? How does he complain and still maintain his dignity? How does he communicate to corporation management a feeling of product discomfort and a desire for producer-consumer change? In brief, how does a customer complain about defective merchandise—and win?

In all fairness, however, a word should be said about the chronic complainer aptly christened the "mooch" by long-suffering complaint department personnel. There are people who enjoy turning stores into rummage sales by buying new merchandise and later returning it out of spite or for personal gain. For example, a chronic complaining customer may buy the cheapest model of a television set and, dissatisfied with picture quality, insist on repair or replacement of the set. The customer then demands a deluxe set at no extra charge because of inconvenience. Another complaining customer may pay for a tune-up at an automobile dealer, later insist the carburetor was damaged during servicing, and demand a complete engine overhaul. The Great American Mooches read discount advertisements, hunt down bargains, and then—after the sale is over—try to return the item for full list price.

In this discussion, we explicitly ignore those situations in which a complaining customer is without fair cause. Since the chronic complainer is often the customer who just preceded you and upset the manager, he is, often as not, a contributor to your plight.

the rhetoric of complaining

However, in this analysis, we look only at those complaint situations where a legitimate complaint is repulsed by a producer.

The situation described in this chapter is an example of a problem in returning a poorly manufactured product. In this case, the victim is followed during a three-month period through the purchase and return of two related products—automobile tires and shock absorbers. Most of the aggressive, interpersonal strategies used by salesmen and customers are detailed in the ninety-day chronology.

THE EVENT

The automobile business is a major force not only on the new and used-car level but in its handling of replacement parts. In fact, for the major American automobile manufacturers, the replacement parts business is far more lucrative than selling the whole car. Automobile owners periodically need tires, shock absorbers, batteries, mufflers, ball joints, and other normally deteriorating parts. When the time comes for replacements, a large number of companies—dealers, discounters, and chain stores—fight for this profitable business.

On occasion, the replacement part is defective, and the customer may return and attempt to gain satisfaction in the form of credit or a new part. In this example, the return was prolonged and painful because the complaint was something difficult for the customer to verify—the tires purchased were out-of-round. If the tire making mold is not truly round or if the tire is defective in some way, it probably will not roll smoothly on pavement, causing the automobile to vibrate—a malady felt particularly in the steering wheel. The customer finds himself lurching up and down to every nuance of an uncaring road surface. The car analysts call this bobbing trait *busyness,* and you might call it *shaking.*

This customer purchased two tires and four shock absorbers from a large chain discount store in early July. The formerly smooth-riding car immediately began to vibrate and thus began the following saga.

Consumer Diary

July 12th, A.M., CHICAGO Returned to the discount store and politely asked for an explanation of the car's behavior. A mechanic drove the car and upon his return, politely informed me that the car either had a bad rear end, or the competing discount store's tires—which spun sarcastically on the rear—were out-of-round. It was also advised to ride on the new tires for a while, since they might flatten out. I suppose tires are like souffles.

July 12, P.M., EVANSTON, ILLINOIS At the competing discount store, after a visual inspection by a moonlighting airline mechanic, the rear tires were judged "perfect." The present, newly purchased shocks were pronounced too stiff and needed his replacement shocks, which would make my low-priced undulator ride "like a Cadillac." I escaped.

July 12th, P.M., EVANSTON At a service station the car's tires were rebalanced.
The service station manager then drove the car around the block and pronounced it perfect.
I agreed that the car seemed to ride better.

July 13th OFF FOR VACATION. THE CAR SHOOK.
WHO WAS TO BLAME?–
MY WIFE AND KIDS BLAMED DADDY.

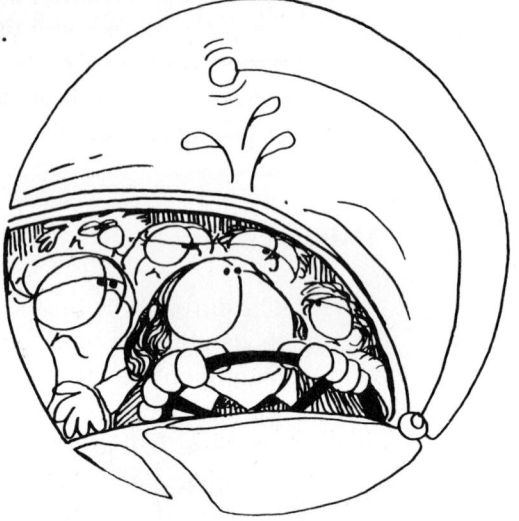

July 14th, NEW YORK MILLS, MINNESOTA A service station operator in Minnesota rebalanced the tires,
and said, "Try that for a while."

July 15th, NEW YORK MILLS The same service station operator rebalanced the tires,
and we went for a ride. He said the road wasn't perfect but suggested I place my hand on
the dashboard to feel for excessive vibration. I did. We agreed the car rode "not too bad."

July 16th, NEW YORK MILLS The tires were electronically evaluated at an automobile dealer and
pronounced "hopelessly out-of-round."

July 17th, WADENA, MINNESOTA At a small branch franchised store of the discount chain the
manager argued that there was nothing in the tire universe known as "out-of-round."
The manager had gone to tire school, and the instructor, using visual aids,
had demonstrated scientifically that tires cannot be out-of-round.
The manager did offer to send the tires to headquarters (200 miles away), and if
the factory inspectors cried "out-of-round" he would replace the tires.
Since this tire pilgrimage was supposed to be only
a portion of a vacation and since the return process
took at least a week, I declined.
Somehow the prospect of delaying my vacation
and putting my car on blocks to await a missive
from headquarters was not appealing.
Do you think the manager knew that?

July 18th, BRAINERD, MINNESOTA   At a medium-sized branch of the discount chain, the tires finally were measured after a wait of an hour and a half. The tires were found to be more than one-quarter inch out-of-round and were replaced. The sales people thought it hilarious that any tire could be that misshapen and still roll.

July 18th-25th   THE CAR SHAKES.
VACATION FURTHER DISINTEGRATES.
WHO'S AT FAULT?

July 25th, DULUTH, MINNESOTA   The trip is interrupted to find another branch of the chain store to adjust the tires. The Duluth store is downtown, and after driving around the block numerous times I find a spot in which to park. Personnel are very sorry; but the automobile service section is closed forever, and the nearest functioning branch is in Superior, Wisconsin.

July 25th, SUPERIOR, WISCONSIN   After a long wait, the manager sullenly measures the tires with a gauge, finds two tires on a shelf, orders a worker to replace the tires, and abruptly departs. He never looks at me or exchanges one word with me.

> "Gee, I'm sorry, Sir."
> "Golly, what an inconvenience."
> "It's no bother."

Whatever happened to these simple expressions of empathy?

July 26th, NEW YORK MILLS   A service station operator says the tires were not balanced by the discount store personnel, and they need balancing. In fact, the chain store worker left on the original balancing weights when the tires were mounted, thereby purposely making the tires unbalanced.

July 27th, NEW YORK MILLS   The manager of a service center drives the car and pronounces the tires perfect. He takes his hand and depresses the front of my car and it bobs. He says the shocks are not stiff enough. All four new discount chain store shock absorbers are replaced by four new service center superior brand shocks.

July 28th   Home from vacation. THE CAR SHOOK.

August 3rd, CHICAGO   The service manager at the original discount chain store says my problem is out-of-round *wheels.* Furthermore, he claims, the New York Mills service center superior brand shocks were the same shocks as the discount chain's that they replaced.
The discount chain simply uses their own brand name. The tires are nevertheless electronically rebalanced, and we shake out.

August 4th, ARLINGTON HEIGHTS, ILLINOIS   The new, new shock absorber manufacturer is queried, and their service manager recommends their top-of-the-line, road leveler shock absorber to solve the problem. They would give me a full $52 retail credit for my weak shock absorbers in a trade for the more sophisticated $102 road levelers. I say okay, if they work; and if not, the personnel would remove them. We go for a test ride and the mechanic evaluates the car as the worst riding of that make he's ever encountered. The sophisticated road levelers come on and off in thirty minutes.

August 5th, EVANSTON   An auto alignment company expert pronounces that the badly out-of-round tires can be salvaged through his astute, electronically aided, rebalancing skills. He guarantees his work.

August 12th, EVANSTON   The auto alignment expert finds that the performance of all four tires still reflects their out-of-roundness, and he rebalances them.
He tells me to never come back.

August 13th, CHICAGO   I call the discount chain's main office and find the appropriate supervisor shocked. After an appropriate meeting at the discount service center, the manager claims the trouble was internal. He recommends a rear end job.

August 14th, HOME   Decide to suspend search for in-round tires and smooth-riding shocks until next summer. Sometimes shaking is better than the battle.

June 15th, LOS ANGELES, CALIFORNIA   The following year the engine lurches forward during a gas stop. The twisting engine jams the accelerator and the car bolts uncontrollably. Much of the shaking stops when the engine's motor mounts are securely replaced.

THE GAMES PLAYED

The situation in a consumer return is fairly well structured. The company has a product, the return of which results in additional handling costs for each person involved. Obviously, this amount could be spent more profitably in shipping and handling new merchandise, waiting on new customers, and in promotional activities. Little wonder that the store attempts to minimize those returns through a number of manipulative communication strategies.

The most opportune strategy for the store management was for the salesman to redefine the situation. In the first encounter of July 14th, as in the last encounter of August 13th, the problem was diagnosed as a rear end malfunction. If the consumer buys the diagnosis and spends $250 for a refurbished rear end the salesman has, in effect, created gold from dust. The customer's return was simply another opportunity to add new sales. The rhetorical skill involved is to convince the customer that the problem is something other than the return of the merchandise. In fact, one of the two salesmen who tried to sell shock absorbers as a solution succeeded.

In many return situations, the problem with the product can be explained from a number of viewpoints. Most cars can benefit if even marginally from premium road levelers—just as many women who return tightly fitting dresses can benefit from a reducing course, and a large number of men who find their jigsaw shorting out can benefit from a double-duty, UAL-approved safety cord. In other words, the add-ons cannot hurt; that is the philosophy of the store. That the redefined situation fails to address the immediate grievance of the consumer must be ignored, since that attitude runs counter to the American mercantile spirit! The add-on is as American as apple pie, as Christian as multicolored Biblical lamps,[1] as necessary to our economy as cream-filled Hostess cupcakes.

A variation of the add-on sales opportunity is to redefine the problem as lodging in the customer's head and not in any actual product malady. In two examples, the mechanic drove the customer's car and claimed the ride was smooth. To deny the accuracy of the mechanic's judgment is contrary to the American system of observation.

---

[1] Lamps are sold door-to-door by allegedly in-training Bible students who purport that each bulb color has scriptural significance. For example, the red bulb is for the blood of Christ, and the yellow bulb symbolizes His resurrection.

the rhetoric of complaining

We hire experts for everything—ball bearings, urinary tracts, and wet basements. The man must know, since he works with cars all the time. This respectful feeling often is coupled with an interpersonal closeness with the mechanic caused by his leaving his company environment to join you in testing your car in the live world. It is far easier to be unreasonable to a service manager working behind a service counter than to disagree with a mechanic sitting inches away in your car's front seat. He is now a real live human being, and you must interact with him in the same setting you usually reserve for friends and acquaintances. Since he is doing you a favor by testing your car's wobble, staging an argument over his judgment would be uncivil.

    Another strategy of the producer was to make the complainer wait long periods of time for service. At the branch franchise store in Wadena, the manager was sluggish about waiting on the customer, and the proposed adjustment would have taken at least a week to enable the nomadic tires to wend their way to headquarters and back. The manager of the Superior store kept the customer waiting for two and a half hours while he performed a number of other duties. The tasks that prevented the manager or salesman from adjusting the complaint were anything that came along—a phone call, a salesman's inquiry, another customer's question, and—in one case—a coffee break.

    The waiting strategy is effective because many customers have limited time. If the customer is complaining on a lunch break, or has his children out with him after 8:00 P.M., the complaint might be terminated because of a deadline. Also implicit in the waiting time is the system's disapproval of your activities. Returning merchandise for adjustment is deviant behavior and consequently is treated only when time is available. No one likes a whiner or complainer. Take the stuff and shut up.

    The most frequently used strategy was to subject the customer to harassment that at times deteriorated into abuse. It was a rare occurrence for the customer to be treated courteously. He was screamed at (Wadena, July 17th; and Chicago, August 3rd), denied eye contact (Superior, July 25th), and told never to return (Evanston, August 12th). In all these examples, it was difficult for the complainer even to institute a normal, reasonable pattern of communication.

> "This blender shorts out."
>
> *"It does?"*
>
> "Every time I turn the switch, sparks fly."
>
> *"My, my."*
>
> "My chocolate cake became a gelatinous sponge."
>
> *"Why don't you stick your head in it? Maybe you'll get pineapple upside-down cake."*

    From a practical point of view, maintaining pressure to return the merchandise amidst abuse is very difficult. It sometimes is more pleasurable simply to terminate the argument or to seek another channel of satisfaction when a clerk is sarcastic or screaming. Only a rare person can sustain or is willing to endure verbal abuse in a public place. The scene is usually grim, with two strangers standing head-to-head, screaming at one another over a misshapen tire or a plastic blender. Most passing customers are going to find the entire performance disgusting. And inevitably, your boss, girl friend, or family

the rhetoric of complaining

clergyman happens by at the very instant the argument reaches the foul language stage. Or you may have an inhibiting fantasy that the police will arrest you for disturbing the peace. The best course of action seems to be immediate withdrawal. There is something very unsettling about encountering abuse in an unfamiliar environment. Under these circumstance, many producers seem to recognize the effect of cold, discourteous treatment on a consumer.

A profitable device used by some producers is indignation. To be indignant can be effective, because this stance implies a strong moral position. The manager who believes in his product despite your shabby evidence to the contrary is in a potentially impregnable position, communicatively. The Wadena manager said his integrity was at stake, and the Chicago manager offered to return the money. Though these positions were somewhat compromised when the customer challenged them, the effect on store morale often was stunning. The manager's sales personnel often seemed impressed by the argument of integrity; perhaps they were the real audience, anyway. The manager may have been using the complaint situation to educate employees in the basics of company loyalty. To maintain status. . .not to back down. . .to rub noses in the dirt. . .these expressions are not just the rhetoric of a football coach. The stand-up salesman is every bit in this tradition. If we are a culture bound to money, then the act most heroic is to defend monetary expenditure, even for defective goods.

THE GAMES YOU CAN PLAY

There are a number of strategies you can employ to win the game of complaining. An easy ploy is to search a metropolitan area for an outlet that cheerfully will adjust the problem. Somewhere in this great land there is a manager who finds out-of-round tires a national disgrace and is launching a personal campaign to remove them from our highways. This gambit is not only time consuming for the customer but for some purists it represents an unfortunate cop-out. The point of complaining often seems to be to take the product and shove it down the throat of the corporate devils. The purist never runs from a good battle—he gives as good as he got—he answers a rifle shot with a cannon. He bandages his wounds with stickum and dirt as he inflicts massive hemorrhages on his opponent. He walks from the encounter with not only new tires and shock absorbers but with the voice box of the manager dragging from his tail pipe. The customer complaint is the twentieth-century counterpart of *Gunfight at the OK Corral.*

One obvious tactic in handling producers is to return the abuse. A nasty salesman is put in his place by similar strong language from the consumer. In most cases, unfortunately, the result of heightened abuse is more abuse and—as discussed earlier—potential embarrassment for the consumer, who may win the merchandise return but lose face by being forced to resort to shouting and vituperation.

The same weakness is evident in going berserk or breaking down in tears. If the tactics fail, the consumer has exhausted his strategical choices. Where do you go after suffering a complete emotional breakdown in a department store? The consumer is standing in front of a sales counter, surrounded by gawking thrill seekers, watching

the rhetoric of complaining

himself play Butch Cavendish going down in a swirl of verbal bullets. If you do not mind risking a simpering, sniveling retreat, then shout, go crazy, or break down in tears. If the effort is unsuccessful, you are standing in the middle of a crowded store with foam running down your chin, eyes rolled back in a daze, arms twisted askew; and where do you go from this position? "Sorry, folks, I'm not really a raving madman."

Some complainers feel that love and understanding can disarm a reluctant producer. In many scripts, a complainer praises great service, efforts previously rendered, and, claiming understanding for the store's problems in dealing with a manufacturer's defect, demonstrates patience by encouraging the producer to wait on customers with more urgent problems. Many consumers reinforce their "relentless love" approach by smiling at the producer, leaning forward for intimate conversation, and joking about the whole situation—"I never thought tires would affect my life style." The advantage of this approach is considerable since the producer may welcome a respite from nasty complainers. Moreover, rather than going berserk or breaking down in tears, the complainer can always escalate to a more subtle level of hostility. "I've been nice, but now you're getting to me." The chief disadvantage of this approach is the importance of establishing control over the producer at the outset of the interaction. In an earlier chapter on teachers and students the point was emphasized that seizing the initiative early is important in dominating a relationship. The producer may feel she has control of the situation while being cajoled and loved, so that the consumer's ultimate hostility and threats are ineffective.

A better idea is to seek privileged, special lines of communication available in any complaint situation. In most situations, there is an unhappy or simply talkative member of the department.

Talk Hooks

"This just has to be a really tough job."

"I hear you got lots of tires back there."

"The guy who runs this place is unbelievable."

On two separate occasions, tire changers in the Brainerd and Superior stores revealed large numbers of returned, out-of-round tires. This type of information can be devastating when used to confront the Wadena tire school graduate or the Chicago rear end specialist.

"What about that back room loaded with rejects?"
"What are you talking about?"
"I'M TALKING ABOUT ACRES OF LOPSIDED TIRES."

This type of interchange often can be used to rearrange the communication hierarchy, ending with you in a commanding position. The customer now has special information about the tire business transaction and potentially has a weapon with which

the rhetoric of complaining

to control the producer. The producer ought to be convinced she is negotiating with someone extraordinarily informed about the chain store's tire problem. And if the consumer can follow the charge with some carefully gleaned facts about tire separation, adhesion, and stability, he should be rolling on new tires quickly. This inside-person strategy works, because information is a form of consumer control; and a steady stream of inside-product information can turn a situation around. In addition, the knowledge that her store security has been breached is unsettling to the producer. She possibly never discusses security silence about product defects with her staff, but now she must turn her attention to that reality. At this point in your confrontation, she is fast becoming preoccupied with calling a meeting with Janice and Roy about their big mouths. The important priority is to get you out the door so she can deal with the air whistling through her porous security system.

> "Would you put two new belted 8:45:15 whites on this wagon, Roy?
> ... And when you're finished, come into my office."

A problem with countering manipulative strategies is the danger that consumers will manufacture strategies that escalate beyond reasonable limits. For example, another strategy that is effective when properly counter-applied is to play the consumers against the producer. An obvious strategy the producers used was to force the consumer to wait unreasonably long periods of time for adjustment. The counter to this uncivilized behavior can find the consumer resorting to a form of communication violence not unlike tactics noted earlier in *gamesmanship*. To force this interaction the desperate consumer begins a discussion about the store and the service with fellow customers.

"Have you ever seen service like this?"

"This place is driving me out of my mind."

"Have you ever heard of out-of-round tires?"

With any kind of luck, the other customers will begin to share their problems.
The strategy is for the consumer to turn from the manager and create a small, transient group, a group of people discussing the quality of the store and its employees impromptu.
An effective conversation might be sustained in this fashion.

Complainer: (To adjoining customers) "I can't believe this place. I've been waiting forty-five minutes for service and they don't wait on me."

Customer: "That's really tough."

Complainer: "Listen, I've been riding on two out-of-round tires till my teeth jiggle! Have you ever had that kind of trouble?"

Customer: "Are you kidding? I've been riding on out-of-rounds from these people for 32,000 miles."

Complainer: "You, too! What a shame." (Turning to other customers) "Unbelievable! CAN YOU BELIEVE IT?"

the rhetoric of complaining
....

Customer 2: "I CAN believe it. They botched my tune-up."

Complainer: "YEAH!" (Seeking to include as many customers as possible) "What are WE going to do about it?"

When this move was used in the Chicago store (August 3rd), the manager—fearing a large-scale revolution—pleaded to the complainer, "Talk to me. I'm the one who can do you some good!" The effective complainer, now sensing that he dominated, hesitated, then turned slowly from his new friends to the manager. "Oh, you want to talk to me?" Then, a line for only the most unmerciful counter strategist: "We were just talking about the fraudulent automobile accessories you sell here." The word *fraudulent,* coupled with group pressure (ten or eleven formerly friendly, now screaming customers), got those tires off his car fast. He was now a plague; and in lieu of a cure for the disease, the best remedy is isolation—out the door.

The only problem is that the consumer has now become as unpalatable to the human race as the producers he controlled. Any rational complainer wishing to remedy a complaint has to set personal limits. Otherwise, the complainer—inflamed by the success of a tire store victory—finds using the strategy more fun than making simple requests.

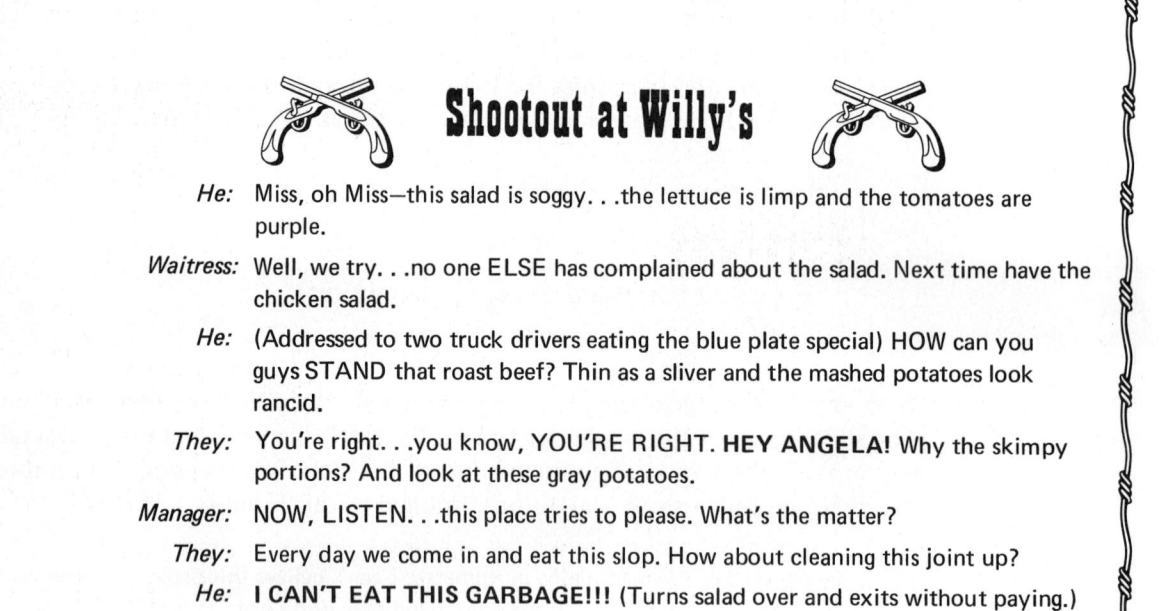

Shootout at Willy's

He: Miss, oh Miss—this salad is soggy...the lettuce is limp and the tomatoes are purple.

Waitress: Well, we try...no one ELSE has complained about the salad. Next time have the chicken salad.

He: (Addressed to two truck drivers eating the blue plate special) HOW can you guys STAND that roast beef? Thin as a sliver and the mashed potatoes look rancid.

They: You're right...you know, YOU'RE RIGHT. **HEY ANGELA!** Why the skimpy portions? And look at these gray potatoes.

Manager: NOW, LISTEN...this place tries to please. What's the matter?

They: Every day we come in and eat this slop. How about cleaning this joint up?

He: **I CAN'T EAT THIS GARBAGE!!!** (Turns salad over and exits without paying.)

There are other less obnoxious methods for handling the return situation, but they still demand an element of risk. If the customer doesn't like the way the car performs or is serviced, he can leave it.

the rhetoric of complaining

"IT'S YOURS."

"What do you mean, it's mine?"

"I don't want it any more the way it runs, SO KEEP IT."

Besides the satisfaction of watching the producer's face tighten in disbelief, the consumer is in a strategically strong position. The complaint system rarely anticipates the citizen who shrewdly recognizes that brashly giving up merchandise is an ultimate weapon. Few multimillion-dollar companies want "stolen" merchandise on their property. Technically, since the car's title card remains in the consumer's hands, the company is going to look silly with a strange car in its possession. Obviously, no one is going to jail a service manager for housing a distraught complainer's car, but the potential aggravation is not worth it for him. If I were the manager, I would repair the car and get that menace out of my shop.

WINNING AND LOSING COMPLAINTS

What makes any counter-strategy effective is a willingness on the part of the consumer to take a risk—engage in small talk with the staff, rile up fellow customers, abandon merchandise. It is a bold act to abandon a car or a television set to a company—an unexpected, shattering break with normal (average) behavior and expectations. In a sense, the behavior the consumer is exhibiting is deviant if not insane. But since the producer has no legal or professional right to institutionalize him, he can cope with only the surface problem. His stance is to reduce the stress the customer poses by relenting to his demands, because ultimately this solution is the easiest.

A producer has only so many options to exercise before succumbing to the path of least resistance. He can add on products by redefining the problem, he can attack the customer's perception of the problem, he can make him wait long periods, treat him verbally or nonverbally with discourtesy, or he can become indignant. All these producer strategies are fairly predictable. However, fears of sudden unemployment prevent a producer from acting totally irresponsibly. The consumer has no fear of this sort of retaliation from a superior; so if he can transcend hang-ups over property, he is free to be strategically effective.

Unfortunately, some of the more effective counters find the consumer contributing to the sum total of communication violence. The product is returned; yet somehow the consumer has further weakened the quality of our Institutional Rhetoric. One alternative for those consumers unwilling to struggle with a face-to-face confrontation is to write or call someone with administrative power in the company. A consumer often will find that the problem is a long-standing customer grievance and that company officials are eager for solutions. If this is not the case, the consumer will have to move up the chain of command to the power authority who can resolve the problem. This strategy requires that consumers can spend some time researching how the company is organized and can

the rhetoric of complaining
. . . .
46

afford a waiting period for a resolution or adjustment. A consumer quarreling over an overpriced dress can afford to wait; but the beleaguered traveler in Wadena, Minnesota— faced with a bouncing ride versus adjustment— moves reluctantly to his strategic weapons.

A producer-consumer complaint is an old fashioned shoot-out. In John Wayne films, the hero searched for years to find the outlaws who kidnaped his best friend's children. The odyssey of the consumer's diary has the same doggedness and self-righteousness. Some day the tires will roll as effortlessly as a Rolls Royce gearbox shifting into third, and the consumer and his vehicle will retire to Wyoming.

Caught with the hand in the till

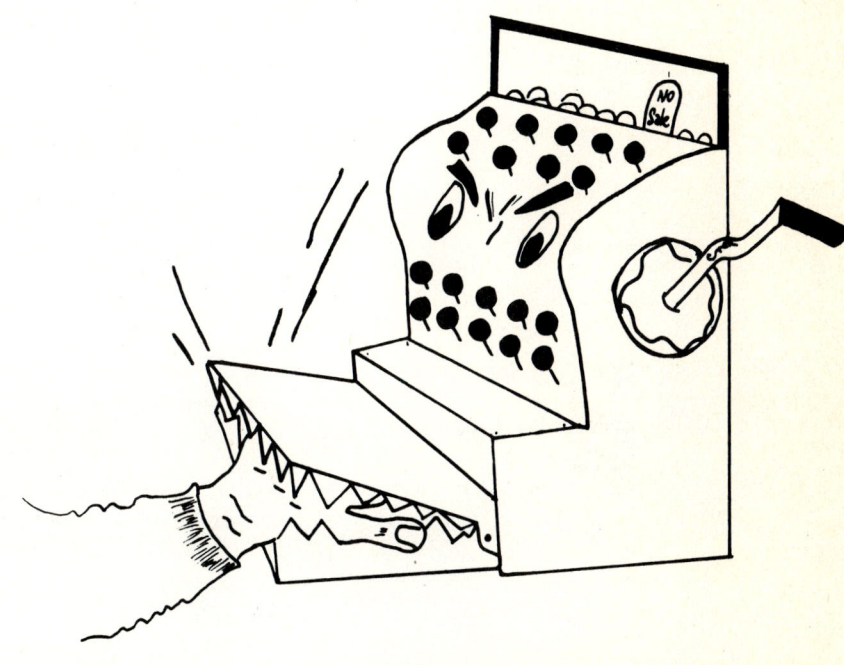

"O.K. O.K. You got me in that one. But it's still cheaper than Bruno's."
. . . . . .
"I didn't say it's cheaper. I said for a couple of bucks less you get a brass holder."
. . . . . .
"Listen, do you think I get rich here? No way. . .I'll stand behind what I said, **only**. . . ."
. . . . . .
"Boy, did you catch me!"
. . . . . .
"Will the boss holler at me!"
. . . . . .
"I said for one day—not one year."

a real game: the rhetoric of pinball

5

A true game ought to re-create the tensions of success and failure in everyday life's events. A game ought to be risk-oriented, yet offer a contestant a certain amount of gratification—monetary or symbolic—for different degrees of effort and success. The game of pinball offers players these characteristics and is worth examining as a preparation for real-life games.

The first American pinball machine boom occurred in 1931 and was made possible by the introduction of inexpensive, primitive machines.[1] A number of innovations altered those early pinball machines until we had the modern version used today. Today most machines are independent pieces of furniture, 23 inches wide and 53 inches long, containing a number of flippers and holes. The object of the game is to score the maximum number of points and hopefully to earn free replays. The original game cost one cent for seven balls; today's game usually costs twenty-five cents, and the cost is climbing with the rate of inflation.

The main strategy to attract players is the illuminated back cabinet that records the score. As the balls are shot into the holes, the score is tallied noisily and energetically on the back cabinet. The player's ego is massaged as the score mounts—impressing not only himself but anyone else caught in the amusement area environment. The player's scoring combined with others playing on nearby machines creates a noisy, discordant sound—clatter, bang, clatter, clatter, bang, clatter. Anyone who plays pinball in this atmosphere is competing with people for highest tallies and replays while contributing to a musical group effort that becomes an absorbing part of the game.

---

[1] For an interesting discussion of the introduction of pinball, see a Bally-sponsored book by Herbert B. Jones, *Coin-Operated Amusement,* Bally Manufacturing Company, Chicago.

a real game: the rhetoric of pinball

In a room full of machines, the various games must compete with each other for playing time. A rarely played machine is carted off and replaced by a newer, more seductive model. Most pinball machines compete for play through their brightly colored designs; there are some classical designs of successful pinball machines. A good example is Bally's famous "Fireball," with a bright red superhero who seems to be hurling flaming balls at the player from the back cabinet. The same company features "El Toro," a purple-clad matador surrounded by a number of ferocious looking bulls. Why play pinball games such as "Fireball" and "El Toro"? The answer lies partially in the technological advances of the game.

When the first portable pinball machines were introduced, an unbelievable 50,000 Ballyhoo[2] games were sold in the first seven months to thousands of unemployed men and women looking for income during the Depression. The first machines were battery powered, countertop sized and ideal for crowded cigar stores, candy shops, and ice cream parlors. This machine flourished in an economy where money was scarce and people sought cheap amusement.

In 1933, when economic conditions were improving slightly, a machine called "Skyscraper" was introduced, featuring illumination and automatic scoring. These innovations greatly enhanced the game's appeal by creating bright lights for attention and effortless scoring instead of requiring the player to tabulate mentally—a point not overlooked by anti-pinball lobbies, who had felt all along that pinball players were not smart enough to add. Two years later, the back cabinet was added to the machines, allowing more advertising and providing the successful player with more ego gratification as his score mounted on a large, clanging, illuminated glass sheet.

A problem that vexed the industry for years was devising a meaningful reward system that fell short of gambling. During the early years of pinball, many stores used the games as a form of slot machine with high, cash payoffs. Pinball was labeled a "bad boy's game," and "decent" citizens protested America's youth lolling about bowling alleys and pool halls gambling on the infernal contraption. Ironically, one of the appeals for pinball has been the delicious joy of playing one of society's devil devices in full view of passing Main Street.

In 1941, a major principle of pinball machines was added with the introduction of a replay mechanism.[3] The replay allowed the producers a satisfactory method in which to reward a diligent player without causing themselves an undue economic hardship...although nothing is as satisfying to the player as hard cash. A replay means the player gets a free game without depositing an additional coin, and the hope of a replay may keep a player feeding coins into the owner's coffers all night.

The discovery of the illuminated back cabinet enabled designers to produce the most elaborately detailed persuasive element in pinball. A successful pinball machine must catch the eye of a prospective player to entice play. The enticement first was suggested when "Skyscraper" was introduced (without a back cabinet), featuring a large building on the surface of the play field. The subsequently added back cabinets allowed

[2] Trademark of early Bally pinball machines.
[3] Jones, *op. cit.*, p. 26.

a real game: the rhetoric of pinball

more surface for the motif appeals, and the producers have become more proficient in their designs. The designs and motifs of machines differ greatly, and they often refer to events in the era during which the games were designed. In the 1940s many back cabinets featured warplanes and ships; in the 1950s partially naked women were popular; and during the 1960s space race, an oft-played game was "Moonshot." Many modern designers now try to appeal to sports-minded Americans by re-creating football gridirons, baseball diamonds, and hockey rinks. The back cabinet design has something for everyone—be he soldier, pervert, adventurer, or athlete.

THE STRATEGY OF PINBALL

The main element of pinball action seems to be the wildly gyrating ball careening down a mined play field. Pinball, by any stretch of the imagination, seems to be an energetic, swiftly played game of suspense and movement. Although the pinball designer would not disavow the fast-paced action, the primary focus is upon refining three basic principles of play.

The first principle is to achieve *balance*; the pinball designer strives to create a game that is not too easy and not too hard.[4] A casual player may find a tough machine too difficult and forsake the game after repeated defeats. Similarly, if victory is a common occurrence, a skillful player may abandon the machine, since it provides no challenge. The designer must create a machine that satisfies the less talented player's need for an occasional win and at the same time challenges the veteran, skilled player. In most machines, the balance is achieved by building a bank of "tricky" shots into the action that, according to pinball historian Herbert B. Jones, "are accomplished not by skill alone, but by skill and the 'breaks'—the gentle assistance of Fortuna, who impartially smiles—or frowns—in turn on the champion or the duffer."[5] A typical example of a balance shot is the *kicker,* which violently kicks the ball into action—scoring quickly and dramatically when illuminated—by either random selection or skill.

A key strategy in pinball design is to allow the player the thrill of *almost winning* to promote continuous play. If a player ends his game on the verge of victory, he often finds this a satisfying experience and an inducement to keep inserting more quarters. A method to heighten near success is the additional bonus score, introduced to give the player additional points for hitting a special target. A player doing poorly knows a bonus hit means a possible replay, and this hope constantly tantalizes him in anticipation of possible success.

In the pinball industry, designers are aware that close failure often will result in continued play, and for one who makes a living from pinball, that is a life line.

The last strategy designed into the game involves the *scoring action of either the ball about to exit the out-hole, or the movement of the last ball available for play.*[6]

---

[4] For a detailed analysis of how a pinball machine works, see Jones, pp. 20-35.
[5] *Ibid.,* p. 35.
[6] *Ibid.*

a real game: the rhetoric of pinball

It would be poor game strategy for the designers to permit a hapless player to be out of the action after the first ball or two. Most players enjoy the tension of knowing that a poor score can suddenly be lifted to an astronomical point total by hitting a special target in late game. The most common device used to trigger a late hit is the "Collect Bonus," which, though accumulated throughout the game, cannot be collected until a special target is hit. An effective Collect Bonus placement can occur just as all seems lost and the last ball is heading for the out-hole. BLAM!—1,000, 2,000, 3,000, 4,000, 5,000....!

WINNING AT PINBALL

A player controls only three segments of the game that he can use to counter the basic principles built into pinball. The first element is the *spring-loaded ball shooter,* which initiates play when pulled, catapulting a ball into the play field. By trial and error, an effective player learns the tension on the ball shooter necessary to produce a ball trajectory yielding a potentially high score. The object for the pinball player is to create a profitable groove that can be repeated over and over again. A good ball shooter acquires a shooting touch not unlike that of a proficient jump shooter in basketball.

Once the ball is in play, the next player control element is his ability to *tilt the machine* to change the course of the ball without activating the "tilt" mechanism. A clever player knows just how much pounding and twisting a machine can take before it will break down. The player practices a form of "brinkmanship"[7] with the machine's tilt mechanism as his enemy. He pushes and massages the wooden cabinet until the glass top rattles from the pressure of his cupped hands. The higher the risk (degree of tilting), the greater the possible point totals and subsequent replays. A misreading of the tilt mechanism results in a loss of the ball; or, in some machines the termination of action and the loss of the player's quarter. The situation of risk is not unlike many of the producer-consumer relationships outlined in this catalogue.

The final player control element is the flipper, a three-inch-long, rubberized plastic arm activated by a side button in the machine.[8] The purpose of the flipper is to allow a player multiple chances to score points; the mechanism acts as a bat to propel the ball. Most pinball manufacturers place flippers at the exit of the central out-hole of a play field, allowing dexterous players the sensation of a retrieve from a near out. A good player is adept with the button, since he must allow the ball to rest on the flipper at the proper angle before letting fly. An occasional player invariably will strike the ball too soon or—hesitating—will watch it exit and slither off into the ignominious out-hole.
The only answer is to try again.

To win at pinball, a player must take high risks—successfully. If he fails to take mounting degrees of risk, the game is boring, since the ball merely follows a random course,

---

[7] Jones uses this term, which stems from political gamesmanship, to describe a pinball movement. See p. 31.
[8] The button-operated flipper was designed by D. Gottlieb and Co., the world's largest manufacturer of pinball machines.

a real game: the rhetoric of pinball

then exits through the out-hole. To enjoy pinball, a player must take the risks; even if he loses, he has had the pleasure of the challenge, the chase, and the eventual denouement. This string of events is not unlike that experienced by the energetic, high-rolling citizens who lead exciting lives that many people envy. In real life, most of us minimize our risks and use games as a harmless outlet for our fantasies. Marshall McLuhan's position on games is consistent with this interpretation when he observes "that games are a sort of artificial paradise like Disneyland, or some Utopian vision by which we interpret and complete the meaning of our daily lives."[9] We need games for those moments when playing *real* games becomes too personal and we need the release.

A Plea for Abstinence From Pinball

Kids! Stay away from pinball.
It is evil—wicked—and causes warts.
I know!! I have a split marriage.
My family deserted me because
I couldn't stay away from pinball.
I started with one game a week—
then two—you know the rest.
I'll do anything for a quarter.
Last week I played 1250 games,
robbed two food stores,
and didn't wash before supper once.
If you want information on
PINBALL ANONYMOUS (PA)— write:

OTIS CRIMPHAND, National President
Box 402—*or* BONUS SCORE 850,000
Touch, WA., 100, 050, 642, 81648

---

[9] Marshall McLuhan, *Understanding Media.* Copyright © 1964 by Marshall McLuhan. Used with permission of McGraw-Hill Book Co.

SECTION TWO INSTANT IMAGE STRATEGIES

In the beginning, Americans enjoyed large amounts of land,
water, and clean air. America was a land of abundance
with great mountains, an enormous farm belt, and massive
stands of trees. In this century the shopping centers and land
developers confiscated great amounts of the open spaces.
However, the Americans used to nature and abundance,
were not ready to purchase products from concrete expanses.

The *Instant Image Strategies* were developed
to provide Americans with an illusion of nature,
without returning to the undeveloped days.
In the two chapters in this section, we find two food
institutions seeking to create atmospheres conducive
to joyous purchasing and eating. The merchants tried
to create images that were stimulating and would imitate
the real thing-the elegantly landscaped shopping centers,
the supermarket's fruit in old-time pushcarts, the restaurant's
Old West motif...all saying - "We're like the real thing,
Come buy with us." All a producer needs for an instant image
is an idea and money. But the "real thing" is gone.

the great american supermarket

6

ORDER NOW FROM THE G.A.C.C. AND RECEIVE

FREE!! THE FAMOUS GROCERS' SCHOOL TALENT TEST!

DO YOU LIKE TO MANIPULATE? DO YOU HATE PEOPLE WHO SQUEEZE FRUITS AND VEGETABLES? IF SO, YOU MAY HAVE THE SORT OF TALENT WE'RE LOOKING FOR! ANSWER THE SAMPLE QUESTIONS ON THE NEXT FEW PAGES, AND IF YOU SCORE WELL WE'LL MAIL YOU THE FULL "GROCERS' TALENT TEST," WHICH COULD START YOU ON THE ROAD TO AN EXCITING CAREER AS A GROCER!!

FOUNDERS OF THE FAMOUS GROCERS' SCHOOL

OSKAR LEE DINK
GEORGE WHIPPLE
CARL DENHAM
MARY JANE McHENRY
GEORGE ARTHUR PINCH

Tomatoes are cheaper
Potatoes are cheaper
Now's the Time to Fall in Love. [1]

When popular radio comedian Eddie Cantor sang these catchy phrases from the Depression, tomatoes were indeed cheaper—a nickel a pound. Of course, wages were very low, and there was a question of whether or not you had a nickel. And often people spent their nickel in a small, crowded corner grocery store where the owner waited on each customer personally. The store didn't need a parking lot, because most people simply walked from within the neighborhood. It was a high-interaction environment, because the owner was in close contact with his customers and their complaints. If you didn't like the Smithfield Grocery Store's beets, you merely walked across the street to the Monroe Street Store and knew old Smithfield was watching every step.

"Well, Joe, long time no see...Haven't seen ya' around for a few weeks."

"Yeah, I've been sick."

"Oh, I hope you feel better."

"Give me a pound of beets, will ya', Smitty."

---

[1] "Now's the Time to Fall in Love," words and music by Al Sherman and Al Lewis, copyright 1931 by De Sylva, Brown, & Henderson, Inc. Copyright renewed, assigned to Chappell & Co., Inc., 609 5th Ave., N.Y. Used by permission.

the great american supermarket

This discussion is no advertisement for the small, corner grocery store, because I recognize its liabilities. It lacked stock, kept limited hours, and sometimes overpriced its merchandise; and often that merchandise was old. But the small grocery store was a personal communication environment that reacted to every nuance in the neighborhood. Most store owners kept charge customers and were lenient in bad times. If you sent Mary with a note to Mr. Smithfield for a can of coffee, 2 carrots, 1/2# of ground sausage, and a 32-oz. bottle of strawberry soda, you expected her to return with the items and the change in a little brown paper sack. And most of the time, Smithfield gave Mary a penny piece of candy for her effort and threw in a soup bone for good measure. There was stress about prices and quality then, as there is today; but the customer had the satisfaction of knowing he was dealing with the proprietor or his wife.

Today, the thought of sending Mary to the supermarket is laughable. How would she get across the highway? Who would fetch the merchandise for her once she arrived? Who would open the transparent, plastic film packages to give her 2 carrots and 1/2# of ground sausage?—and a free piece of candy? Little Mary would be lucky not to be arrested for shoplifting.

The modern supermarket didn't rise from the ashes of the corner grocery store; it lit the fire. The supermarket—with its wide aisles, enormous selection, and football fields of parking—captured the imagination of shoppers. Mr. Smithfield and his accessibility gave way to ingenuity, cleanliness, and technology as expressed in the supermarket.

SUPER TALK

"What's the latest in frozen food?"

"A great new individual serving of Cordon Bleu— the same Cordon Bleu offered in New Orlean's finest restaurants. *Defrost, heat,* and *serve.*"

"What else is new?"

"Hey, the ecology thing is forcing a return to glass bottles. Just like U.S. Steel and the other biggies were converting to ecology."

The supermarket is an excellent example of a producer-dominated situation resulting from advancing technology and consumer greed. The automobile enabled the consumer to seek larger, less convenient outlets for merchandise, and a seemingly low regard for intimate, interpersonal relationships fueled the conversion. As for the small grocer, his future was limited not only by his dwindling market but by his inability to

the great american supermarket

buy at the same prices as the large chain. In a sense, the supermarket take-over was a perfect example of the twentieth-century drive toward more efficiency and less interpersonal contact. The fault was not with the nasty money barons, the international Zionist conspiracy, or Wall Street moneychangers, but with the realities of superior technology. That some qualities of life were lost in the transition was inevitable, and the supermarket serves as an example of the cost we have paid.

THE SUPERMARKET AS A COMMUNICATION ENVIRONMENT

The supermarket, in its strange way, fairly bristles with communication. Its communication, however, usually is one-way—enticing, not reflective. Perhaps it is too much to expect a supermarket to reflect the more subtle nature of a sensitive communication environment. The object is to move food items through the store at as furious a pace as is legally allowable, without regard as to whether Brand A is better then Brand Y. The question is whether the product moves fast enough to warrant shelf space and, in some cases, whether the manufacturer is paying for space. In this sense, supermarket advertising reflects a money-to-item relationship startlingly devoid of the complex psychological appeals of even a motor additive advertisement. Do you want it? There is little need for four-color layouts with a dozen typefaces if the product is the same as in the other food markets and the only variable is price.

2 pks 99¢   3 rolls $1.19

6 pts $1.28   59¢ Limit-One

There is a penchant in supermarket strategy to price items at a penny or two less than a number ending in zero. The supers think that 39¢ sounds cheaper than 40¢, and in truth it does.

The majority of supermarket advertising consists of price offers accompanied by mundane pictures of the product. Sometimes the advertising copy is varied by claims of cents off or a new variation on an old product—wide necks on ketchup bottles.

the great american supermarket
....
61

But for the most part, supermarket advertising is stark black and white with terse, unappetizing descriptions of services and products.

[Advertisement: "18¢ A POUND LESS THAN A YEAR AGO! FRESH WHOLE FRYERS"]

What an ugly pile of chicken! The description of the chicken is honest only if you know little about fowl. Special chemicals are used to grow most chickens quickly on scientific breeding farms. The chickens are then ice-packed in wooden crates, and their remains are shipped to supermarkets. In this ad "fresh" means never frozen; it does *not* mean "wholesome, pure, and nutritious." The ad's description of the chicken is irrelevant, since the producer in most cases is now selling price and not quality. A chicken to most shoppers is a chicken. If ours is 49¢ a lb. and yours is 53¢, you lose. But just remember that force-fed, waterlogged fowl for 49¢ may be not as good as that 53¢, happy, fully matured, "together" chicken from an old-fashioned farmer. How does the consumer know? Easy. Get in the car, run down, and look at the chicken.

SAMPLE QUESTION 1.

WHICH IS THE "TOGETHER" CHICKEN?

[Illustration: A) a live chicken saying "OOOG..."; B) packaged "CUT WHOLE FRYERS" saying "AW REET!"]

the great american supermarket

62

Into your car—BAMM...The door used to say SLAM...We're off to the supermarket—BUZZ...Buckle up, we're off to the supermarket—BEEP...when a guy in a Volkswagen cuts in front of you...The nerve of people in small cars...GLUMP GLUMP ...What do you expect a car to sound like while idling in traffic?...Shut up, will ya—I know I'm supposed to be in the right lane...If you don't like it, walk.

The supermarket has signs telling you that it's Safeway, A & P, Jewel, or Grand Union—impersonal messages with large, block letters that turn to bright neon signs at night, lighting up the sky like plastic stars. They are not cute, warm signs:

> Hi - I'm A & P. Who are you?

> NATIONAL TEA LOVES YOU

The signs simply say SAFEWAY, not SAFEWAY FEELS GOOD TODAY—just SAFEWAY. The standardization of the signs reassures the consumer that the supermarket experience will be consistent with his expectations of conformity and efficiency.

> FREE PARKING

SAMPLE QUESTION 2.

THIS SIGN IS...

(A.) TO BE PLACED IN THE NEATLY STRIPED PARKING LOT ADJACENT TO YOUR STORE. THIS MAKES YOUR SUPERMARKET "CONVENIENT."

(B.) A SLOGAN OF THE GROCERS' LIBERATION FRONT. IT REFERS TO ELEANOR PARKING, AN OUTSPOKEN GROCER, WHO, IN LATE 1969, WAS TAKEN PRISONER BY AGENTS OF THE INTERNATIONAL FOOD CO-OP.

the great american supermarket

Turn into the free parking lot, and you find neat rows of striped lanes for easy, neat access. The stripes are not ambiguous. They are six-inch wide, white bands painted on honest, black tar.[2] It is messy and unnatural to straddle a stripe. A house has fenced, exact boundaries, and so should the parking lot. The lot is clean, well manicured, and lacks the brash, urban pushiness. Plenty of acreage, with nothing around except Goodyear Tire outlets and Lum's Restaurants. But, and this is an important *but,* Goodyear and Lum's are also neat, well striped, and not too close. Good neighbors, Goodyear and Lum's.

The walk to the store is pleasant and unsurprising. There are red Buick hardtops next to blue Ford Country Squire wagons with wood applique[3] sides and in used car ad vernacular PW, AT, PS, AC, and LoMis. Where else in America can you find a '62 Chevy Bel Air standing next to a new Jaguar without regard to class difference?

Most supermarkets are one-story ranches with large expanses of glass—heralding prices, prizes, and features.

[Sign: Our Policy IS TO GIVE 1 Rain CHECK ON ALL SALE MERCHANDISE ASK FOR IT!]

[Sign: OUR POLICY IS TO GIVE 2 RAIN CHECKS ON ALL SALE MERCHANDISE ASK FOR 2]

One lamentable window strategy is to mix honest buys with regular prices. When Mr. Smithfield placed a sign advertising butter for 49¢ on his window it usually was a bargain. Now, many supermarkets—knowing that consumers expect bargains on the window—will mix in regularly priced merchandise. If you're that dumb. . . .

---

[2] A standard formula for parking is 3.5 square feet for every 1/2 square foot of store frontage.

[3] American station wagons, for about 250 extra dollars, come equipped with plastic side panel decals that are supposed to look like wood. Real wood, of course, rots. But to pull into the supermarket parking lot looking like a country squire or an estate baron is *class.*

the great american supermarket
. . . .
64

Whoosh—into the store, and now let's play a game. I assume every reader of this book has frequented supermarkets. In many cases the number of visits ranges in the thousands. Now the questions: What does this communication environment look like? Where are the high-volume perishables? How does the floor plan move you through the supermarket? What are the communication strategies in this everyday environment?

THE GREAT AMERICAN SUPERMARKET TOUR

The first point to notice in any supermarket structure is that the most frequently shopped-for food items—dairy, meat, produce, and bread—are on the perimeter of the store. Most consumers enter the store for these four basics, and their placement insures a tour of at least the store's outer aisle. The considerable distance of the four basics from the checkout counter also contributes to the possibility that consumers will discover additional products both coming and going. By forcing consumers to tour the store for needed basics, the layout insures that pickled relish and potato chips may be seen and purchased. And, as will be discussed later, once the consumer is moving around the perimeter of the store, a well-placed special can entice a tour down yet another alluring grocery aisle. An alternative to the perimeter strategy would be to completely facilitate the consumer by placing all the high-volume perishables in the center of the store near the checkout stands. This plan obviously is weak, since it restrains the consumer from impulse spending. In fact, no one in his right mind would put together a store in this fashion.

SAMPLE QUESTION 3.

WHAT IS WRONG WITH THIS STORE?

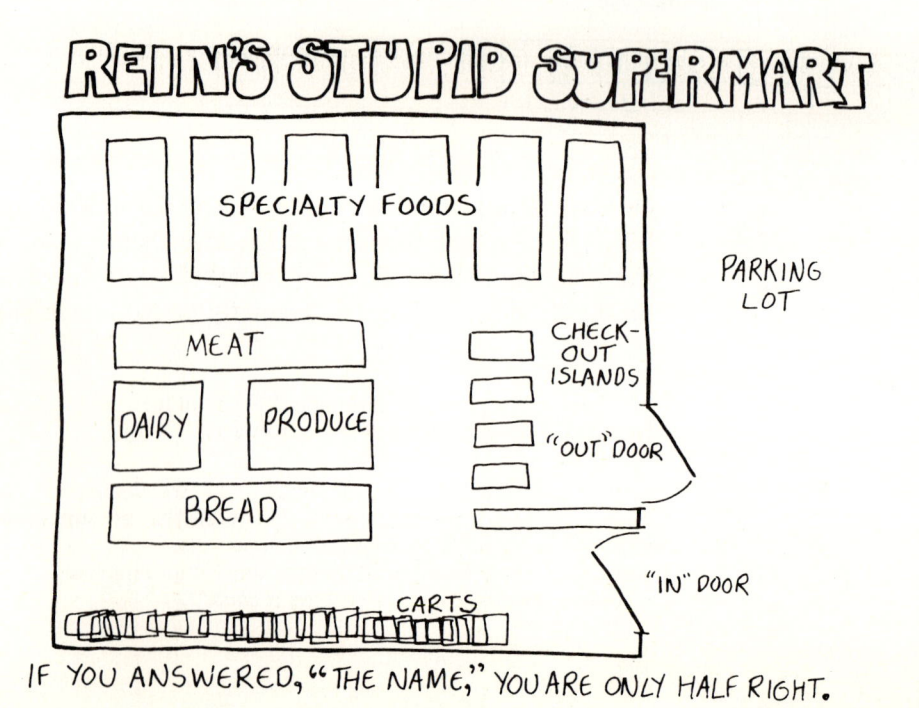

REIN'S STUPID SUPERMART

[Diagram of store layout with SPECIALTY FOODS along top, MEAT, DAIRY, PRODUCE, BREAD in middle, CHECK-OUT ISLANDS, "OUT" DOOR, "IN" DOOR, CARTS, PARKING LOT]

IF YOU ANSWERED, "THE NAME," YOU ARE ONLY HALF RIGHT.

the great american supermarket

65

Once the store structure has the consumer moving through, a number of strategies are used to promote additional sales. The specials at the door are remnants of the fast-paced selling of the turn-of-the-century public and flea markets. A buyer was hustled off the street by a salesman who claimed a super bargain of a $5 suit or an $8.50 Omega watch. Once inside the buyer finds that he can have the $5 suit if he doesn't mind that it is a 23-year-old, one-button, gray flannel; and the $8.50 watch is really an Onega. For another $165 he can have the "n" switched to an "m." The supermarket's modern version of this strategy offers a cornucopia of often useless but provocative specials, at the entrance. The implication is that the rest of the store also is brimming with low prices. This use of heavy promotions at the store's entrance is not a particularly devious tactic on the part of a market; still, the implication is not easily missed.

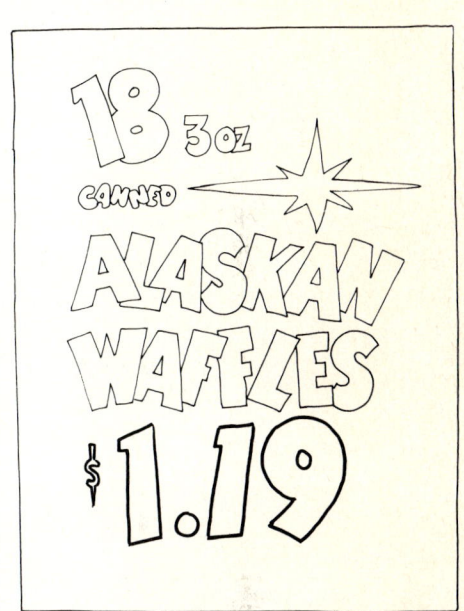

3 MELMAC SOUP DISHES ENGRAVED WITH STATE FLOWER $1.50

5 CANS NO 3 SUCCOTASH $1.00

18 3oz CANNED ALASKAN WAFFLES $1.19

GUM by the case 250 paks $8.99 Black-Strawberry Pineapple

COLA 6 for 79¢ 12 OZ. Sugar Free

the great american supermarket

The next stop is bread—the first staple in many stores and probably the most emotionally powerful. It is a strong stimulus through both its Biblical and sensory appeals. The staff of life has a pleasant odor that—if not dulled by too many preservatives—ought to put the consumer in a pleasant state of mind for the trip through the rest of the store. The smell of frozen food is unlikely to have the same effect. So up the aisle we go, grabbing a couple of gallons of $1.39 low-fat 2% milk, a 16-oz. carton of small-curd cottage cheese with gum stabilizer for 99¢, and some large, white, double A eggs for 96¢ a carton. The end of the outside perimeter aisle is reached, and we turn toward meat, located conveniently at the rear of the store. Are we to buy our meat and produce and skip to the cashier? No—no such luck. There is a sign on the end of the first, inside aisle.

16 oz. KRISPY CRACKERS 24¢ 23¢ SPECIAL!!

The cart, as if equipped by radar, pivots towards the bargain, and after the shopper grabs two boxes of Krispy Crackers he glides down the aisle of pickles, crackers, and cookies. After the shopper picks up a 53¢ box of cream-filled, chocolate star cookies, the end of the aisle is reached. And at the end of the next aisle:

>   REWARD...Reinforcement
>   Up the Maze—Down the Maze
>   Pickles—Special Discount on No. 3 Corn
>   Potato chips—10¢ off

the great american supermarket

Finally, the meat counter where red-, pink-, and beige-colored protein glistens through provocative peek-a-boo packages. In the old days a butcher cut steaks-to-order from beef quarters. If you wanted 1/2-inch thick steaks, he cut it. If you wanted pockets in your pork chops, he cut it. If you wanted your round steak tenderized, he cubed it. The meat counter at the supermarket offers a similar option. If the consumer isn't satisfied with the wide range of precut meats in the counter, he can press a little button—RING...RING...RING...Out comes Howard the butcher.

"What do ya want?"

"WHAT DO YOU WANT!" What I want is some service. But everyone at the service counter is staring at me for ringing the bell, and Howard looks piqued, because he was watering the hamburger and hates to be interrupted during the treatment. So the friendly, available butcher is an illusion, because the system is only apparently, and not realistically, open for producer-consumer communication.

A Meat Supermarket Vignette

"The reason I called you is the beef roast is TOO DAMN fat!"

"So, buy something else."

"I don't WANT something else, Howard, I WANT a lean beef roast."

"Do you see this knife, Complainer?"

"KNIFE OR NOT, BUTCH, YOU CAN CUT ME A LEAN, WELL-MARBLED BEEF ROAST!"

"Ow!"

Into the cart go 2 lbs. of lean ground beef, 6 medium, center-cut pork chops (though I wanted five), a 69¢-a-pound squishy, unhappy chicken, and 1 lb., 8 oz. of sandwich steaks. The sandwich steak used to be labeled cube steak; and before that change, it was tenderized round or flank steak. The old process was to take a relatively tough steak such as round or flank and run it through a machine that perforated the steak fibers and made them soft as butter. In a technological breakthrough, an enterprising corporation invented a machine that will take the good old hamburger and press its shriveled consistency into tenderized steak. It looks like steak, costs like steak, but tastes like pressed hamburger. The name change from hamburger to sandwich steak reflects a simple attempt to imply one thing and sell another.

How do you tell what's in the package?

Ring Howard.

> GROUND FRESH MANY TIMES DAILY TO INSURE FRESHNESS
>
> **FRESH GROUND BEEF 89¢ LB.**
>
> SAMPLE QUESTION 4. *DRAW ME!*

   Supermarket management is not unaware of some of the unfriendly communication meat counters transmit to their customers. In some stores an attempt has been made to upgrade the image by recapturing the good old days. Some stores have a separate meat section, cordoned off with wood paneling, pictures of country scenes, butchers dressed with bow ties and straw hats, and quaint labels on pressed hamburger—"Ye olde sandwich steak." Unfortunately, it's still Howard behind that bow tie, and the meat still is wrapped in plastic film. This strategy becomes "Louie's Fruit Stand" in the produce section, and "The Baker's Dozen" in the bakery section. It usually fails to capture the essence of the turn of the century. This process, known as compartmentalization, is an adaption strategy that could work only if the customer felt that Louie really *owned* the section—not 200,000 A & P stockholders. Most people recognize the incongruity of the supermarket's attempt at ingratiation through nostalgia but probably will ignore the strategy and buy fruit as usual.

   Turning back to the canned food aisle we move toward soup. Soup! The mother laboring over a hot stove, mixing beef stock with beautiful carrots, fresh lima beans, and spring green parsley. The result was a large pot of rich, energy-giving elixir—good for dilating bronchial tubes, relieving constipation, and removing warts. There on the shelf is Heinz's Great American Beef Noodle with Dumplings, brimming with hot goodness. Or, select Campbell's Cream of Chicken, 10 3/4 oz. to a can, containing homespun Monosodium Glutamate and Dehydrated Onions. On top of the Great American soup can it originally said, "Close to homemade." On the back of the label are a couple of mothers rolling dough with ye olde rolling pin and stirring the soup pot on ye quaintly curlicued olde stove.

> Delicious Beef Noodle with Dumplings Soup is like the soup created in the bustling Dutch Kitchens of the Midwest. This hefty soup is characterized by a hearty beef broth, with meaty ground beef, wholesome dumplings and tender golden egg noodles.

the great american supermarket

Who says we can't recapture Mom's soup? I just wonder if Mom put Disodium Inosinate and its apparent brother, Disodium Guonylate, in her broth. And like the nostalgic meat market that attempts to recapture the image of bygone days, the advertising campaign for a nostalgic American soup fails through a simple credibility gap—it tastes like canned soup. Yet, into the cart we pop Great American Chili and Great American Split Pea with Smoked Ham. Mom hasn't made soup since she got a job as a security chief in the French division of the Milani Salad Dressing Company.

Leaving soup, we're off to the frozen food section, where white freezer cases[4] contain the latest in American technology. A galaxy of products offer more free time to the consumer: a TV dinner with golden brown chicken, snowflake potatoes, and corn topped with polyunsaturated margarine; a turkey potpie with golden, hydrolyzed vegetable protein protecting its quivering gelatinous mass; a lemon cream pie with yellow meringue the color of Sherwin-Williams' Finest, topped with a white cloud crust as billowy as shaving cream. These analogies may be appropriate, since the pie has no natural ingredients and may well contain some offspring of turpentine and soap. Well, into the basket we throw a couple of TV dinners—chicken and beef for variety—and a lemon cream pie—your body can't tell if a food is fresh or manufactured, anyway.

A quick 2 cans of 5 oz. chopped, ripe, black olives—regular 33¢ NOW 27¢. . .and I am buying peanut butter.

"Where's the jumbo peanut butter?"

"I don't know."

"What do you mean you don't know?"

"Ask George, he's a regular."

"Hey, George, where's the peanut butter?"

"Aisle 3 down low."

"Down low." The cheaper, large, bulk items such as sugar and flour are usually bottom shelved in a supermarket. Most consumers will reach "down low" for a staple they really need. The slower selling, more expensive products such as anchovy paste, crabmeat, and water crackers are likely to be shelved at eye level for high consumer visibility. Some consumers think that staples and other bulk items are "down low" because they are heavy and might collapse the higher shelves.[5] In most cases the strategy of shelf placement is explained by the dictate, "Unseen is unsold." According to one supermarket study a customer purchases as many as two out of three items on impulse.[6]

---

[4] The original freezer cases looked like white coffins and forced the shopper to open the heavy lid to remove the packages. The association of death and frozen food hampered sales until the mid-forties. I owe this note on refrigeration to M. M. Zimmerman, *The Supermarket* (New York: McGraw-Hill, 1955), p. 148.

[5] Observation made in an unpublished supermarket study completed in 1972 at Northwestern University by Irving J. Rein, Mark Feldman, Richard Kallan, and Robert L. Shuter.

[6] Zimmerman, *op. cit.*, p. 183.

the great american supermarket
. . . .

A tube of anchovy paste is unlikely to be impulsively purchased on a bottom shelf, but sales of bulk staples are constant wherever they repose.

Well, "down low" for a big jar of Skippy—Super Chunk—with Hardened Vegetable Oil [hydrogenated fat], and seasoned with Dextrose, Salt, and Sugar. Some heart researchers claim that hydrogenated fat clogs your arteries and eventually puts you in the hands of the undertaker, a rather gruesome thought while buying God's bounty. Besides, enough of anything will kill you. . .saccharine. . .DES. . .caffeine. So into the cart goes jumbo Skippy—and now for some celery, lettuce, tomatoes, and oranges.

Louie's Fruit Stand looks particularly good today, because summer is upon us and a full complement of fruit and vegetables is displayed. The celery is 2 for 49¢, and you must buy two of these green-gray, natural roughage stalks, since they are coupled irrevocably by a rubber band. The lettuce is shimmering, glowing beneath a clear plastic encasement. As for the tomatoes—we can select from little cherry tomatoes, hothouse tomatoes in cardboard tubes, or unwrapped home-grown tomatoes. The supermarkets used to wrap none of the produce, but they discovered that customers squeezed, mutilated, and tore the tender merchandise. In addition, a customer who wants one lemon will be forced to buy a pkg. of six. Toss in the advantage of packaging all the produce with modern machinery in a central location, and wrapped produce is inevitable. Into the basket goes the wrapped merchandise—and we forgot bread.

The cost of retrieving a product after having traversed the supermarket is considerable. Forgetting means moving against the grain of the maze. Unlike in public streets, there are no patrolmen here to whistle over an offending cart wielder and issue him a ticket. The pressure in the supermarket is often that miserable sense of running against convention, fashion, and good judgment. Apparently it is reprehensible to break the law of designer strategy and many customers endorse this principle enthusiastically.

"PLEASE! GET OUT OF THE WAY."

"Madam, all I want is a loaf of bread."

"MOVE YOUR OWN CART. I WANT BREAD STICKS."

"Okay, okay, get your cart out of my side."

Where are the stock boys, the manager, the police to stop the cart attackers? If someone attacked you on the street with a knife a policeman could make an arrest for assault with a deadly weapon. When attacked by aggressive carters in a supermarket, most victims can only wince in pain or retaliate with a cart counteroffensive.

"BANG!"

"OUCH!"

"Oh, excuse me."

"Listen, say excuse me first, and then I'll get out of the way."

Bang!

Bang! Bang!

Bang! Bang! Bang!

Bang! Bang! Bang! Bang!

Bang! Bang! Bang! Bang! Bang!

the great american supermarket
....

Well, bread is bread and the choice comes down to the difference between natural and unnatural. Unfortunately, the unnatural is much cheaper since air usually costs less than ingredients. So into the cart go 3 lbs. of white enriched bread with some "harmless softners." Add a pkg. of eight hot dog buns of the same enrichment and we're off to the checkout counter.

On the way to the series of four-foot-wide checkout aisles we flip into the cart a few impulse items. We gather a record of Connie Francis singing a duet with Mel Torme about love during the month of March, a formerly $4.95 book (now 39¢) by an ex-homosexual who is now a prominent psychiatrist, two pkgs. of pinochle playing cards with pictures of the chain's founder on the back, a tin of $1.29 salted mixed nuts marked down to 69¢, and four pkgs. of Royal Princess hard candy made in England by ex-members of Parliament. I usually take a shopping list to prevent such extravagances, but shopping is a treasure hunt. I am confronted with wave after wave of super bargains, half-price specials, and closeouts, not to mention new jiffy cooking bags—which recapture the flavor of fresh vegetables. To stick to a shopping list denies not only the supermarket designers' attempts to increase your bill but the whole idea of shopping. To shop is to discover. A bag of Brach's Jube Jels won't hurt, either.

Now let's pay for this stuff. The strategy of the checkout is a delicate one. According to supermarket strategists, the optimum number of people waiting in a line at one time is four, including the person checking out. Like much theory, the actual operation varies a great deal under the pressure of reality. Amidst weekend crowds, if too many people are waiting, they become disenchanted with the store and will not return. If no one is waiting the store creates the illusion of no activity, which implies no turnover—stale bread, rotten fruit, rancid butter. In addition, the heaviest business is concentrated in the weekend hours from Friday 4 P.M. to Saturday 6 P.M. One apparent answer to this checkout problem is for the store management to hire more part-time employees for the weekends. This strategy does facilitate movement through the checkout area, but fails to confront the central problem—quality and frequency of communication.

The complete answer lies in the way in which the checkout help communicates with the customer. The supermarket has developed a system of communication at the checkout that—though super-efficient—prevents any significant verbal exchange. For most consumers, the only live interaction in the store is with checkout help who know and care little about store operation; this live interaction is somewhat less than meaningful for most customers. In an effort to provide the brief exchange with cordiality, most checkers are instructed to hail the customers with a bright smile and, "How are you today?" You are supposed to answer "Okay" or even more desirably, "Fine." If you chattily reply, "My stomach is upset and my teeth are rotted to the gums," most checkers ignore the response and begin the ringing of the prices. If you shout, "Hold it, you asked me a question and I want a response to my answer," the checker would be shocked and probably would call for the manager. No one is supposed to have a meaningful conversation with a checker. We all know the checker is following orders when reciting:

"How are you today?"

"I'm going to vomit."

the great american supermarket

That communication with checkers is simply customer strokes with little interaction expected is no more shocking than similiar communication behavior between neighbors over a back fence. Some neighbors say hello to keep in touch, but don't really want to know about your job problems. Even more interesting is that customers not asked about their state by uncaring checkers consider the store's employees unfriendly.[7] For some people, a programmed stroke is better than no stroke at all. After all, a "How are you today" is better than a grunt, and it's not that the supermarket has singled you out for special inattention. The supermarket is merely saying hello in a manner consistent with technology, programming, and efficiency. A logical extension of this trend is for the checkout clerks to speed up the interaction to allow an even faster flow of customers. The solution is to use compressed speech to say more in less time:

Compressed	*Nostalgic*
"Hello. . . . . ?"	"Hello, how are you today?"
"Fi . . . . "	"Fine, it's a beautiful day."
"Goo . . . . "	"Good, I'm glad you're shopping with us."
"Th . . . . "	"Thanks for the double bag."

A crucial question at the checkout is who unloads the cart. In most areas of the country the customer unloads the cart onto a conveyer belt that moves his selections to the register at the behest of the checker. In some areas, large supermarket chains vary this method by having the checker unload the cart personally, ring the purchase, and call the prices simultaneously.

This friendly method is in contrast to the typical one that has the checker touching the item, ringing it up, and then pushing the item into a gathering area without calling the prices. In most situations the checker doesn't call the prices by item—"Carrots, 19¢; Cheese, 79¢"—but punches the register with alacrity—ring, slap—leaving the customers with no idea of what is being rung unless they resort to fast action. The customers have to unload their carts quickly and bolt forward to share the checker's vantage point of the cash register before she starts ringing. With seven impatient people behind you and an angry, under-surveillance checker ringing bitterly, you had better be sure before:

"Miss, ah, Miss. . ."
"WHAT!"
"The lettuce is on sale for 39¢, not 45¢."
"Charlie, what's lettuce?"
"I don't know—ask Phyllis."
"Phyllis, how much is lettuce?"
"I'll check, honey. . .39¢ today."
"I'll take it off the orange juice."

[7] Rein, et al., Supermarket study.

the great american supermarket

An innovation in checkout is the Universal Products Code (UPC), which is a computerized code stamped on the grocery products. When the checker passes the item over a laser beam scanning machine mounted under the checkout stand, an in-store computer picks up the UPC reading and feeds back to the floor register the item's brand name, product, and price. The items in the grocery store are not individually marked—only "UPC'ed" and that means the customer now must deal with a computer:

"Miss, ah, Miss. . ."
"WHAT!"
"The lettuce is on sale for 39¢, not 45¢."
"Braaaak, Kachung. . . Chung. . . Chung. . ."

The problem with questioning the checker is that it often breaks down store efficiency. People often are waiting longer for service on a weekend and they are in a hurry—everyone is in a hurry. What's 4¢ when you are on your way to play golf or you have to buy grass seed from the hardware store? "Move it. . .Next. . ." It's cheaper this way.

Into the cart again come the purchased groceries. How do you get out? The strategy of leaving supermarkets varies. In most stores the customers wheel their carts on their own power to their own car, unload, then exit. The only hitch is keeping your car door open, grabbing the groceries, and holding on to the cart before it careens into an adjacent auto. A variation is leaving the cart at the door with a loader, driving up, and having this young, virile stock boy lift the groceries into the car. Another variation is placing the groceries into a numbered basket and trundling the whole works out the door on a conveyer belt to loaders and customers' vehicles. The latter sounds like the most efficient method, but it creates monstrous tie-ups as customers' cars line the shopping centers' exit lanes to claim their baskets. The unwieldy process of leaving a store puts into perspective the entire cumbersome system.

The consumer originally enters the store with only checks or money and ends up laden with grocery bags. These groceries are stuffed into the car and taken home and consumed. The leftovers are thrown into the garbage can for disposal, and a few days later the consumer returns with new checks and dollars to renew the cycle—a wasteful system.

The ultimate solution to leaving is never to have left in the first place. The smell of bread (no matter how airified), the stock boy's insolence, and the pushing and banging of the carts could become as quaint as Mom and Poppa stores. In stores of the future the consumer may shop by pictaphone as a camera scans a large warehouse full of products. We hit a set of numbers on our phone, including our bank account number, drive down to a central depot, and pick up our goods. What we now call a cold, sullen supermarket environment could actually be only a step to the final solution—a computerized warehouse. In retrospect that degrading cart duel may seem like a beautiful communication experience.

And what of this step to the final solution? Is the modern supermarket a manipulative communication environment? In a sense, it is the perfect metaphor for what is occurring in our image-conscious society. The supermarket is a large, systematic

the great american supermarket

dispenser of goods, devoted to the interests of the greatest number of people. Most consumers have decided they prefer to trundle carts through massive aisles than to buy from the corner store. Many consumers are aware of problems with this modern distribution system, since it offers many products but little human interaction. Even more subtly, however, the supermarket defines the way we buy our food through its uniform, nation-wide system of operation. High-volume perishables on the outside. . . staples on the bottom shelf. . .wrapped produce. . .checkers who say, "Good morning" and don't mean it. . . .

In addition, the consumer has no sense of the effort made to produce his nourishment. We have gone from buying directly from the farmer, to watching Mr. Smithfield cut a T-bone off a short loin for our dinner, to the modern supermarket's transparent plastic film package containing a defatted, deboned steak. In each advancement, from hormone-injected meat to freeze-dried coffee, we move a little further from understanding the intricacies and hard work of bringing products to market.

True manipulation creates instant images that replace reality—the package instead of a cow, the supermarket layout instead of a farm. Our power to change the supermarket is equally unreal. We can go to the supermarket and argue for health foods and other good things to eat. The supermarket chain can add these products to their shelves under our pressure, but our power is still only illusionary. The supermarket will purvey any product that is legal, turns over rapidly, and offers a decent profit. When the health food fad began to evaporate under the pressure of high prices, the supermarket reduced the variety of items on its shelves.

Though the supermarket structures our perceptions through a carefully designed environment, consumers *can* receive satisfaction on a personal and short-term basis. An effective shopper can arrive at the store with a careful list, convince Howard the butcher to cut succulent T-bones, and insist that Louie separates the coupled celery stalks. In addition, a consumer can ask for rain checks when sale items are out of stock, carefully evaluate the unit pricing tags on the shelves, and insist on seeing the manager when a stockboy gives inaccurate or too flip directions. If the consumer will take the time to attend to such details, money will be saved and the supermarket may be less of a personally aggravating experience. But all these remedies, although rewarding, will not fundamentally change the supermarket's use of environment to control shopping behavior. The supermarket is designed to move goods at the most efficient rate. The rain check request is a power that gives the consumer the illusion that the system will bend to individual needs.

The real consumer power would be to force supermarkets to place the high-volume perishables in the middle of the store where consumers can readily buy them and quickly exit from the store. This will probably happen when tomatoes are again a nickel a pound.

though not necessarily the cheapest, of these places.
the encyclopedia of restaurant strategies

7

Dear Connoisseur,

One common symbol of American affluence is going to a restaurant and having someone else prepare your food. While you sit or stand in relative luxury, people of lower station are busily frying, basting, and scrambling food. In a sense, dining out is not only a symbol of affluence but one of the few remaining acts of positive refinement and joy. When eating in a restaurant, the most uncultured still feel obligated to restrain their belching, slurping, and other piggish habits developed in their own kitchen hideaways.

The restaurant is essentially a kitchen constructed to attract large numbers of people. Because the rhetoric of restaurants is so complicated, and because so many of our readers probably will find the business irresistible, we proudly present the first edition of an encyclopedia landmark. If you have problems with entrees on our menu, feel free to substitute.

Best regards,
THE MANAGEMENT

ADVERTISING

How can you convince people to stop in and eat? Restaurants use many appeals ranging from slashed prices to claims of incomparable quality. If your food is inferior, you might claim your restaurant is a gathering place for movie stars, sports heroes, junkies, cab drivers, or indigent royalty.

If you own a fast food chain you will probably emphasize cacophonous, hyperbolic advertisements featuring dancing French fried, warbling ordertakers, and doltish roast beef slicers. Though fast food chains, like the telephone company, sell their products through consumers' daily use and constant exposure, their ads are unalike in stridency. A monopoly can afford to be tasteful and solicit empathy, while a fast food chain feels compelled to beat competition with pirouetting chicken legs.

AMBIANCE

This term describes the overall atmosphere and enjoyment of an eating establishment. Is it a fun or charming place to eat, despite the quality of food? A proprietor can create ambiance by filling water glasses, allowing eaters to dawdle, adopting a foreign accent, or sprinkling sawdust on the floor.

BIG MAC

The BM is a triple-tiered sandwich featuring two hamburger patties, 1.6 oz. each and containing no more than 19% fat content, lettuce shreds, two pickle slices, chopped onions, cheese, a special sauce vaguely reminiscent of Russian dressing, and one and one-half buns. Whether you are buying a BM in Teaneck, New Jersey, or Christ Church, New Zealand, you get the same ingredients, same portion, and same taste. In fact, the McDonald chain is so effective that for many eaters a hamburger is a McDonald's, and anything less—despite the usual ground beef and bun—is an imitation.

At McDonald's, a consumer is encouraged to purchase the preassembled burger intact. If the consumer wishes a plain hamburger, he is politely told the wait will be five minutes. In a busy McDonald's, there is little room to step aside and wait peacefully while the custom-designed burgers are manufactured on the assembly line. The crowd pushes forward, gobbling up the standardized product as you grimly wait, holding on to a small piece of counter real estate. The temptation is to succumb and eat a ketchup and mustard-coated, onion and pickle-speckled hamburger. (See the Whopper)

CHICKEN

Who is America's Number One Chicken Salesman? Why, the General himself, who with his "chin-greasin' power" chicken tempts the palates of millions of Americans who are too lazy to cook, who want a food vacation, or who are wealthy.

CHICKEN
(AFTER DEEP-FRYING
AND ENCRUSTATION BY
THE GENERAL'S
SECRET RECIPE)

How to Order at General Thompson's:

Customer: I'll have the barrel.
General Thompson: That's $5.95.
Customer: Here's the money and a little extra, because you're so clean.

How Not to Order at General Thompson's:

Customer: I'll have...let's see, mmm...2 chicken legs...a couple of thighs...12 breasts...no mashed potatoes and gravy...2 pecan pies...and I want to see you cook it.
General Thompson: Sir, everything comes in prearranged containers for happy eating. The bucket is the right order for you, since the individual parts are twice as costly, and that doesn't include free mashed potatoes, gravy, and rolls. Sorry, but only the health inspector sees our kitchen. Watch us cook it? We have secret recipes.

If you buy the prearranged containers from the chicken houses, generally you will get an inordinate number of wings. A fifteen-piece bucket, which contains four wings and perhaps two backs, may be a bargain or, then again, a clever piece of manipulation.

CLEANLINESS

The absence of cockroaches, rats, and other food-eating parasites determines the standard of cleanliness. Fortunately, most food, if cooked at 320 degrees, will harbor only dead bacteria. If you run a cheap, well-lighted, dirty restaurant, try doubling the prices on your menu and using candles. If you eat in dirty restaurants, try remembering that the emphasis placed on sanitation is a relatively recent phenomenon. In many ancient cultures, cleanliness was rarely considered a virtue. That their death rates were high hopefully can be attributed to the lack of penicillin, not the persistence of cockroaches.

CUSTOMERS

FOOD! FOOD! FOOD! FOOD! FOOD!
CUSTOMERS

Thank You Loyal Customers

When we first opened our original Orange Blossom Restaurant Deli—on the east corner of Willow Street—we introduced the new concept of eating in renovated horse stalls, twenty-four hours a day, seven days a week. We couldn't believe the response! After a grease fire in the kitchen, an earthquake, a mass murderer marauding in our dining area, and the damn health board closing us periodically, you still eat with us. Without our employees, without you, we are nothing.

YOUR HOSTS
ORANGE AND BLOSSOM BRISKET

DECOR

What the restaurant looks like is far more important than the quality of its food. The elegant restaurant is much like a theatrical performance with the decor serving as a set. One of the leading designers of restaurant equipment has observed:

> "In this competitive age, I fear there exists very little opportunity for the operator who simply offers food without creating an appropriate atmosphere to attract and satisfy his guests. Clientele, traffic patterns, and the like must be carefully studied, and a restaurant created to fit the specific situation."[1]

The number of decors is as varied as are life styles. A possibility is a gay nineties setting with tufted red velvet chairs, brass lanterns, and murals of chubby cherubs. If the nineties decor is not appropriate, a western motif is always comfortable, especially with wagon wheel chandeliers, lots of rich, natural wood, and rooms labeled "Kansas City," "Sioux City," and "Tombstone." If Chinese food doesn't go well in the "Sioux City" room, try bamboo curtains, porcelain figurines, and red, curlicued Chinese symbols. Whatever you select, it must be worth the price of admission.

A List of Decor Naturals:

Potted plants, a plate containing white and black mints, a theatre rope to control crowds, Formica table tops, stainless steel tableware, a rolling cart for dirty dishes, a dollop size ice cream scoop (see Sundae Making), flocked wallpaper, a cigarette machine, a canopy entrance, an assorted selection of Lifesavers, one reluctant toothpick dispenser. (See Ambiance)

DREAM MEAL

The time is short and your funds are low—what's the answer? An evening of fast franchise food. Why spend a fortune at an elegant rip-off when you can have a progressive dinner on the strip?

Menu

Appetizer: *Drive to Orange Julius* for a bracing glass of "Orange Julius" featuring freshly squeezed oranges, simple syrup, crushed ice, and Orange Julius powder or;
Speed to Dairy Queen and nibble at a jumbo Peanut Buster featuring ice milk coated with dark chocolate and sprinkled with nuts.

---

[1] Sam Horowitz, *Chicago Tribune,* Dec. 17, 1973, p. 9.

the encyclopedia of restaurant strategies

80

Entree: Get back in car and *drive to Tico Taco* for some enchiladas "always in season and seasoned to please." *Now motor to Mr. Steak* for a USDA choice top butt steak.

Dessert: Now finish this dream meal by *coasting over to Dunkin' Donuts* for fresh-made-hourly pecan donuts. And, we forgot a beverage. Well, *scoot over to A&W* for a frosted-in-the-mug, cold stein of root beer. Only the phonies eat in old-fashioned restaurants—you eat in your car and eat fast and you will feel better and lose weight.

EATING IN THE CAR

Raise the sandwich to your lips by placing one hand through the steering wheel while the other rests tentatively on the door handle. Now carefully bite down on the sandwich and watch the Thousand Island dressing spray your clothes, seats, and dashboard.

A Special Note on Tipping From Your Car:

Most carhops use the strategy of lingering beside your car to intimidate you into tipping while you pay the check. Since carhops, like most of their ilk, work for a small hourly wage, they should be tipped for decent service. The problem of escaping without tipping if the service is bad is complicated by the tray hanging from your car window. If you bolt out of the drive-in with the tray, you run the risk of imprisonment. It is better to endure the face-to-face stare of an untipped, bitter carhop. It helps, while suffering this indignity, to counter her enmity with your own happy thoughts. Try to think of ocean waves crashing against moonlit beaches, or daydream of walking through a woodsy mountain trail on a clear July morning. The carhop, when viewing your contented, serene expression despite her nasty glare, quickly will remove the tray. (Note—This strategy is excellent when not getting service anywhere. Serene people unnerve employees.)

EATING MANNERS (Slobmanship)

Eating with your hands is not considered indiscreet in some foreign cultures. Before your next experience eating out, research exotic eating habits, and wear another culture's national garb. If the folks in the restaurant have any class, they will eat like you in order to make you feel comfortable.

←----FOOD

FOOD
(POST-MASTICATION)

FOOD (Types)

Food is what restaurants normally serve to patrons. Some critics claim American food is not food but garbage loaded with hazardous additives. Though that probably is true, why worry about empty calories and pesticides in your shrimp en casserole? In a couple of years the air will get you, anyway.

The question of what foods to specialize in is crucial for the area in which you live. There are such American favorites as steak, fried chicken, and chili; or you can move into ethnic foods such as Greek, Italian, Chinese, Japanese, Mexican, and the rest of the world's foods. If you are operating a restaurant in Red Cloud, Nebraska, the ethnic selection really is not viable, and you must move to continental—steak, chicken, hamburgers, veal, and maybe one exotic choice a night, such as weiner schnitzel.

In most cases, it's important to have a chef (in Red Cloud, a *cook*) who can prepare these favorites. But do not fret if the only person you can find can't boil water. A combination of modern technology and centralization brings you the frozen entree. You remember that package of cordon bleu in the supermarket? The chef defrosts the package, puts the pasty mass into an infra-red oven, adds a premixed institutional sauce, and voila!

> *SPECIALTIES*
>
> ---
>
> VEAL CORDEN BLEU...
> A savory and unique eating experience served with Sauce Supreme
> $8.45

If the problem is fish, you can buy crab-stuffed flounder in individual frozen servings. Or for another exotic dish, order frozen breaded patties of beef that—after you defrost—you can label "Milanesa of Beef Espagnole." Food is no problem. The real problem is selling it.

GETTING SLOSHED (Drunkmanship)

Willie, after a few drinks, usually drops his sotted head into his clubhouse sandwich. Wanda usually wakes him and wipes his face and receives a $10 tip. If Willie arrived sloshed at Mr. Neck Bone he would still get a Mr. Neck Bone Bib, a coloring book, a baked potato, and a plastic "well done" stick all for free. It shows you how drunkmanship is tolerated in this country.

GREAT AMERICAN RESTAURANT AWARDS

Normally, haute cuisine awards are given to French restaurants for exotic culinary achievements. For the most part, these cooking feats consist of ladling cream sauce over some otherwise inedible chicken or fish. Therefore, the award this year goes to Jumbo Lou's WEINER CASTLE in Skokie, Illinois—the nation's largest village. Jumbo Lou wins for the best dialogue for humiliating a cook before his customers. "Can't you see the *man* is waiting for a hot dog, Stupid? I'm telling you, Buddy, these half-baked kids drive me nuts," snarls Lou, with rolling eyes. Runner-up award this year goes to all the pancake houses in America, primarily for convincing people to spend $2.50 for three pancakes (25¢ value, tops).

Last year's winner of the award, the plastic order-taking doll of Jack-in-the-Box, is third this year.

> "Order, please."
>
> "Ah . . . three fries . . . two Jack-in-the-Boxes . . . one taco . . . and four Cokes."
>
> "That'sthreefriestwoJacksonetacofourCokes."
>
> "Right."
>
> "Here's your order, $32.50."
>
> "I didn't order 42 Jack-in-the-Boxes."
>
> "Oh, yes, you did."

Fourth and last place goes to the folks from H. Salt, Esq., for their intestinal fortitude in offering Icelandic whitefish, wrapped in a wafer-thin golden crust, to a meat-eating culture.

GREAT AMERICAN RESTAURANT NAMES

1. Dew Drop Inn—*Beer, numbers, good ol' boys.*
2. Flamingo—*Suggests a wild, impetuous air, amidst tropical drinks in hollowed-out pineapple shells.*
3. Goldie's Home-Cooking—*Warm, homey.*
4. La—*Can be combined with any French word, as in La Fontaine, La Touraine, even La Garbagé.*
5. Plantation—*Southern cooking, a doorman.*
6. Racetrack Grill—*Wire chairs, chili eaten at the counter.*

HOST OR HOSTESS

A person who shows you to a table. In a busy restaurant, a host or hostess often can be bribed for preferential seating. The bribe should be tendered with a bill creased between the third and fourth fingers and accompanied with a faintly mumbled, "For you, my

the encyclopedia of restaurant strategies

man" or "my dear." If the bribe is refused, put your right thumb in your mouth and wave the remaining fingers (two, three, four, and five) at the haughty one. If all else fails, tell the host or hostess that Sherman said it was all right. For some reason, the name "Sherman" has clout with restaurateurs. Avoid the names "Ernest" and "Chris"; they have the opposite effect.

KETCHUP

A common American axiom revolves around the notion of quality ketchup in quality restaurants. It is supposed that a restaurant serving Heinz is serving high-quality food and that a lesser establishment is serving cheaper ketchups. A great strategy is to serve a quality ketchup and lousy food. Some people will continue to eat in your restaurant, because axioms die hard. The restaurants that serve ketchup in "Ye Olde Ketchup" squirt bottles often use the containers to camouflage the watered down merchandise. The fast food franchises frequently use little plastic packets of ketchup that defy opening and whose contents frequently splatter eaters. And, finally, the Great American hamburger is now featuring a squirt of ketchup and a squirt of mustard, which— as a combination—may destroy the stomach linings of millions of Americans.

LUNCHMANSHIP

There are many aspects to dining out that are quite different from the at-home experience. At home, most people are familiar with their family members and sometimes tolerate such personal idiosyncrasies as slurping soup, wiping remnants with a sleeve, and eating head down, all of which tend to become part of the family ritual and are accepted. There are only so many times that mother can muster the energy to warn Leonard that he is a slob and that no one will marry him if he doesn't stop eating his mashed potatoes with his hands. The public restaurant is quite different, since not only are you eating but in most cases you are talking as well, usually with people not raised in your family kitchen. Additionally, there are scores of other diners all around you. Up goes the head, off the table go the elbows, onto the lap a napkin, and in a swirl of activity, the cutlery ends up in the proper hand. And in addition to all this unaccustomed activity, you somehow have to get the food to your mouth, down your throat, into the whirling acid that dissolves the food into paté, and finally into the remaining pathways of your body. All this, you recall, is in public before sometimes as many as 300 to 400 people.

A typical problem for many lunchers is swallowing something unpalatable or getting stuck with an item lodged in the esophagus. The inexperienced luncher will struggle with the food—eyes bulged, face flushed—while trying to keep the opposing eater unaware of internal stress. Far better to propel the bit of food across the table toward the startled face of your eating partner than to appear uncomfortable. Accompany the shot with, "Now that feels better"; and if it is a business luncheon, quickly follow with, "Why not sign now and save some postage, Ed?" An experienced luncher will capitalize on his own blunder and use it to his advantage by catching the dining partner off balance.

the encyclopedia of restaurant strategies
....
84

What can the other luncher do? In one exclusive New York City eating club in 1952, this ploy produced a fierce food-spitting battle waged in every nook and cranny of the room.

MENUS

A menu is normally a cardboard list of the food of the eating establishment. Since it is the most direct form of communication in a restaurant, the strategies must be well chosen.

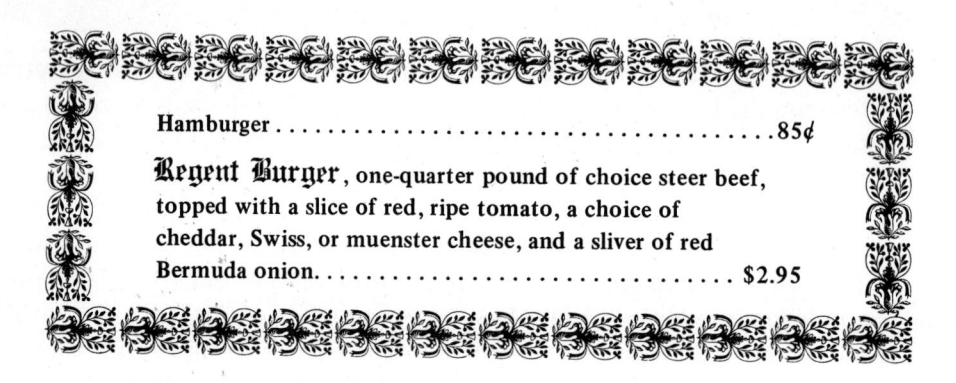

```
Hamburger............................85¢
Regent Burger, one-quarter pound of choice steer beef,
topped with a slice of red, ripe tomato, a choice of
cheddar, Swiss, or muenster cheese, and a sliver of red
Bermuda onion............................$2.95
```

Eighteen Great American Restaurant words and phrases suitable for menu use

1. Famous—*as in famous Reuben sandwich or "Our famous..."*
2. Chef's suggestion—*as in "Try our pies with a scoop of ice cream."*
3. May we suggest—*as in Charlie's Own Grilled Cheese.*
4. Farm Fresh—*as in two eggs, any style, with toast.*
5. Fabulous—*as in Fabulous Pin-Wheel Sundae.*
6. Deluxe—*as in French fries and cole slaw included.*
7. Continental style—*as in French Toast.*
8. A la Carte—*as in paying extra for spinach.*
9. Mother's Finest—*as in a small overhead.*
10. Fixed Price—*as in lots of money.*
11. Coupon—*as in "It entitles you..."*
12. Milk-Fed Beauty—*as in Veal Paprikash.*
13. Birthday—*as in, "If so, prove it and we have a free cake for you."*
14. Monday—*as in Liver with Onions or Bacon.*
15. Tuesday—*as in Family Night—all you can eat fried fish.*
16. Salisbury steak—*as in hamburger.*
17. Corn—*as in canned.*
18. Specialty of the House—*as in...we're long on it.*

the encyclopedia of restaurant strategies

MUSIC

If your restaurant attracts poor conversationalists, get a juke box. If instead you choose programming music into your restaurant, the following rules should be observed:

1. *Rock and Fast Food*—The fast beat aids turnover by making the diner gobble.
2. *Oriental Music and Jewish Food*—Although Jewish food is heavy, Oriental music sounds thin.
3. *Country Western and Steak*—After all, doesn't steak originate in the country?
4. *Gilbert and Sullivan and Fish*—The answer should be obvious to those lovers of *H.M.S. Pinafore*.
5. *Blues and Haute Cuisine*—French food is so expensive.

SANDWICH MAKING

The great sandwich makers discovered long ago that the appearance of a jumbo taste treat is managed by using lots of bread and frilled toothpicks—and topping the ruse by placing all the sandwich filling into the cut middle where eaters can stare at the bounteous portion. Hopefully, by the time the diner has munched through the middle, the barren edges go unnoticed.

SUNDAE MAKING

The sundae is the pièce de résistance of ice cream service as it features the illusion of abundance. The Ph.D.'s of ice cream makers select tulip shaped, narrow bottomed glasses to accept a dollop of ice cream—crowned with a camouflaging cloud of whipped cream, nuts, cherries—and labeled "a two or three scoop sundae."

TIPS

For devious customers, the strategy of tipping is simple: create the instant image of a big tipper. The waitress or waiter will lavish service and find little in return.

Step One—Have a title. "Doctor" is best, but "Colonel" or "Governor" are also acceptable.
Step Two—Call the help "My dear" or "My man" (that implies $10).
Step Three—Using a large denomination bill, occasionally clean your teeth.
Step Four—Announcing loudly that you were offended, leave a paltry five percent.
Step Five—Keep moving; the ploy works only once.

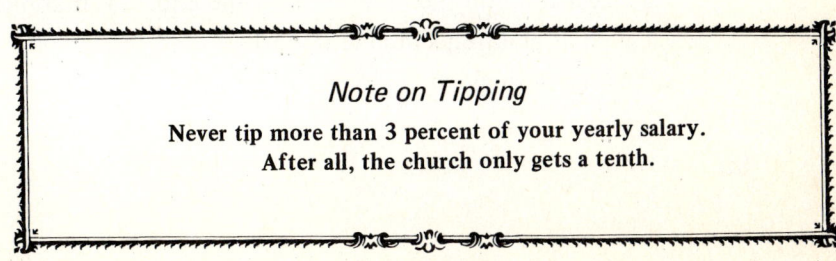

Note on Tipping
Never tip more than 3 percent of your yearly salary.
After all, the church only gets a tenth.

JOKE

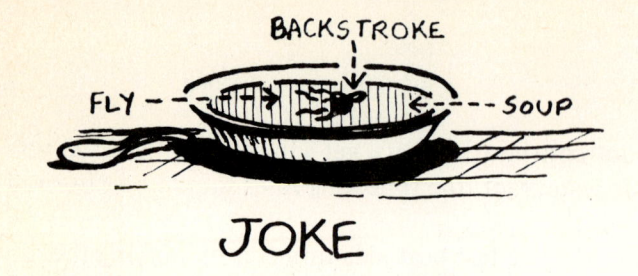

WAITER

A Great American Restaurant Waiter Joke

Customer: *Waiter,* there's a fly in my soup.
Waiter: Yes sir, there is.
Customer: *What are you going to do about it?*
Waiter: It's all right, sir. There's no extra charge for the meat.

WAITRESS

A waitress can be a woman ranging from 4'1" to 7'2", fat or thin, greasy or dry, Jewish or Gentile, mellow-voiced or abrasive. All she needs is skill as a manipulator, since the waitress-customer relationship is concerned with negotiating with a customer for the tip. A tip can range from a turned-over glass of water with a penny under it to 15 to 20 percent of an enormous check. How the waitress conducts herself before the customer is vital, since it is the customer's perception of the waitress that often fetches the tip.

Most waitresses see their relationship with their customers as a problem in image management. In a sense, the waitress analyses the dress, manner, and number of people in a party and then adapts a message to the situation. A rich customer may like having his cigarette lighted, and a poorer customer may appreciate having the waitress suggest a hamburger.

Strategies of Attention:

1. Bustle around the customer filling water glasses:
   a full water glass is a symbol of good service.
2. Continually ask if everything is all right.
3. Remember the steady customer's name and what his favorites are to drink and eat.
4. Suggest food on the menu even if the choice is marginal.
5. Laugh at children's innane remarks.
6. Play up to single men, coddle older folks, leave lovers alone.

the encyclopedia of restaurant strategies

Shakedown Strategies:

1. Fumble in apron for change.
2. Write "Have a nice day—Pat" on check.
3. Hover over table during payment.
4. Throw in a free item—it costs the management but earns you a nice tip.

UNIVERSITIES

If you decide to buy a restaurant franchise, chances are you will matriculate at an institution of higher learning. A beginning student might attend McDonald's Hamburger University, Dog 'N' Suds Grover College, or the Pizza Institution—Shakey U.
Instead of studying Plato and Thucydides, a fledgling student bones up on deep-fat frying, straw management, and floor mopping.

WATER GLASSES

Water is what some people like to drink with meals. A method to discourage this cheap habit is to fill the glasses with warm water. Then sell pitchers of beer and soda pop. The creators of fast food chains don't even offer water. They win this edition's Great Waterless Strategist Award.

THE WHOPPER

This king-size burger creation, which is billed as the "largest of its kind," is placed on a gigantic bun containing "a generous portion" of open-flamed broiled beef, plus crisp lettuce, juicy tomatoes, pickles and onions, a smear of pungent, red ketchup, and a copious lathering of rich mayonnaise. The Whopper was Burger King's two-fisted culinary assault on McDonald's original, puny, single burger. The Whopper staggered the burger world with its generous, eye-popping size. Moreover, the Whoppers were manufactured on an assembly line to the particular order of the customer. This size and versatility threatened to unseat McDonald's strategy of unvarying preassembled burgers.
But McDonald's responded with the Big Mac, followed with a Quarter Pounder, and, as if to mock Burger King, produced a synthesis of breakfast: the Egg McMuffin—a bun, a slice of American cheese, an egg, and Canadian bacon.

WINE

Wine generally is served at the better quality restaurants. If it is served correctly, a good wine can enhance a diner's meal. A real problem is if you wish to impress a date or an

WINE (PRE-BOTTLING)

acquaintance with your ability to order a fine wine and you do not know anything about the product. For openers, memorize the following chant:

> "Let's see...Chenin Blanc is paranoid—can't decide what it wants to be. Maybe a Chardonnay...Ah, an excellent selection if not for the ham-handedness of the vintners in aging...OH, A NICE RED TABLE WINE...medium-aged... reminds me of a good fillet."

Since table wines are cheaper than such varietals as Chenin Blancs and Chardonnays, you got out cheaply and placed your companion in the situation of being grateful. When the wine arrives, sip it and gargle briskly; then, grimacing, spit the remains loudly on the carpet. Inform the wine steward that the wine is plainly wretched, oxidized, contaminated, and chemically unstable. When the second bottle arrives, pronounce it a bit Krautish and quite tannic in odor, but possessed of a light body and a good finish, and—therefore—drinkable. If the wine is quite good, declare that they "ought to tear up the Johannesburg Riesling vines and plant more of these." If you can't afford wine but your date insists, order it, test it, and pronounce, "The rotten egg smell overpowers anything of value in the wine." She will order a Coke.

XYZ

Few people would quarrel with the assertion that the restaurant business is primarily image management. Very few restaurant successes are predicated simply on good food at low prices. Typically, the restaurateur tries some angle—from hot bread to skimpily clad waitresses—to entice customers. Whatever the gimmick, the restaurateur attempts to attract specific audiences to her establishment through some of these tactics.

"Varsity Drag" words and music by De Sylva, Brown and Henderson, copyright 1927 by De Sylva, Brown & Henderson, Inc. Copyright renewed, assigned to Chappell & Co., Inc., 609 5th Ave., N.Y. Used by permission.

the encyclopedia of restaurant strategies

In this encyclopedia we have covered the range of restaurants—from fast food chains to establishments of elegant haute cuisine; from McDonald's and Burger King—with their limited menus, bright colors, and inexpensive prices—to the French and continental restaurants, featuring elegance, fine wine, and servile waiters and waitresses. Though these businesses are far apart in food and serving philosophy, they do share some key *Great American Communication Catalogue* principles. They attempt to control the customer through structured environments. The fast food chains spend a great amount of time and money shaping the customer's experiences. The shaping extends from the arrival in the parking lot to the colors and textures of the serving interiors to the placement of the waste barrels.

In most fast food environments, the consumer's ability to act unhurriedly and to ignore structured influence is essential to fair treatment and good service. A fast food consumer should not hesitate to order a special burger or to return a soggy, inedible Texas steak. The food may be inexpensive, but you still paid for it and have a right to a palatable eating experience.

A fine restaurant also uses environment to influence a consumer. The environmental selections are upgraded to justify the expense and heighten the specialness of the occasion. The more expensive the restaurant, the greater will be the increase in interpersonal attention (from waiters, waitresses, hat checkers, maitres d') to augment the environmental strategies. The personal attention also means that the consumer must cope with ordering options and gratuities. This group of quasi-servants should not prevent the diner from ordering inexpensive wine if desired, checking the bill for accuracy, or reducing the tip if dissatisfied. If only good service is rewarded, the next person buying an environmental food illusion may have a better experience.

In most restaurant strategies a controlling metaphor is used, of which most of the image is a natural consequence. It may be a King Arthur metaphor with an Olde English type motif or a turn-of-the-century coffee shop with white-hatted, elderly waitresses pouring coffee and keeping clean the Spartan decor. In any case, a decor is an instant image, and we've become so insensitive to them that an Arby's seems as organic as home-grown tomatoes—at a nickel a pound.

DO IT AND LEARN IT!

Perform more than a couple of exciting experiments with the G.A.C.C.'s fascinating

1
SLOT A — SLOT B

PUT IDEAS... INTO ACTION!

2 SLOT C, SLOT D

3 SLOT E, SLOT F

You get your own **6** (SLOT G, SLOT H) with authentic components used by the industry!

4 SLOT J, SLOT I

5 SLOT K, SLOT L

LET ME SEND YOU 2 FREE BOOKS

MAIL ORDER LAB PROGRAM!

BREAKFAST CEREAL LAB PROGRAM!

HOME GREETING CARD PROGRAM!

COOK BOOK STUDY PROGRAM!

RADIO AND T.V. TALK PROGRAM!

1

HOW TO BUILD STUFF

HOW TO WRITE STUFF

HOW TO SAY STUFF

HOW TO EAT STUFF

2

HUNK OF CARDBOARD

PEN AND PAPER

MOUTH

6

THE GREAT AMERICAN COMMUNICATION CATALOGUE IS PLEASED TO GIVE YOU THE CHANCE TO CUSTOMIZE YOUR OWN LEARNING EXPERIENCE! FOR MORE BACKGROUND ON EACH OF THESE EXCITING FIELDS PLEASE CONTINUE READING.

DEVELOP YOUR OWN BREAST DEVELOPER

SNAP! CRACKLE! PHUT!

IF YOU WEREN'T STUPID YOU WOULDN'T BE SICK! / DUMMY

3

HOST: "WE'LL BE BACK RIGHT AFTER I THROW UP."

SUCCESS AFTER DEATH by N. BAYH

MOBY DICK by HERMAN MELVILLE

4

YOUR FUTURE IN (UN-) EMPLOYMENT

5

INSERT LETTERED TABS IN CORRESPONDING SLOTS

SECTION THREE
MEDIA STRATEGIES

In this section we examine the full range of media strategies, including such obvious delivery systems as cheap mail order, sleazy carpet advertisements, media attempts to influence children's cereal purchases, and telephone salespitchers, and the more sedate strategies of talk show hosts, cookbook writers, soap opera scripts, and greeting cards. In each example, the message is transmitted through a media outlet, whether oral or written. And in each example, the consumer is manipulated through a wide variety of strategies often peculiar to media exploitation.

the rhetoric of cheap mail order

8

Certain media forms are inherently more manipulative than others. An excellent example of a strongly manipulative form is the cheap mail order advertisements[1] offered in the back sections of such women's magazines as *Glamour* and *Teen Screen*, such men's magazines as *True* and *Argosy*, the Sunday newspaper supplements, and comic books. These advertisements typically are black and white rather than in color, topped by a large, bold headline, and offer a mail order coupon with which the product may be obtained.

    The strategies used to entice buyers must be adroit because on the surface, the advertiser's problems are tremendous. A consumer buys an inexpensive magazine to read some stories and articles and incidentally is confronted by an avalanche of ads claiming a number of remedies for God's or the individual's negligence.

    CREAMS FOR A LARGER BUST
    WIGS FOR RATTY HAIR
    BODY BUILDING FOR PUNY MUSCLES
    FURNACE PILLS FOR BURNING EXCESS FLESH
    SAUNA TOGS FOR LOSING INCHES
    PIMPLE SOLUTIONS THAT WIPE AWAY BLACKHEADS

---

[1] I am indebted here for research on cheap mail order categories to Susan David, Diane Goodrich, Sue Mutchler, and Bobbie Nusser.

the rhetoric of cheap mail order

In most cases, the problem is related to certain norms of society that relate to popularity and desirability. To have a large, firm bust is an important virtue in a society that associates bosoms with sexual allure and daring. If, through a quick miracle of science "You *too* can have a *Big* Bosom," why deny yourself? For a couple of dollars, a flat-chested, miserable loser can add six full inches of firm loveliness the way many successful housewives, career girls, and topless exotic dancers already have been helped. If bulging biceps are preferred, the same couple of dollars can change you from a depressed, bloated sagging pile of blubber to a powerful, he-man type who can lift fifteen-ton-railroad cars and bite the tops off Tab cans. When a sawbuck won't even get you a pair of inflatable shorts anymore, it is reassuring to know that a couple of bucks can still get you a new body.

Even the promise of a restyled body cannot completely solve the seemingly overwhelming problems of mail order sales. In most cases, the advertiser is asking the consumer to purchase a product that is of unknown origin, quality, and usability. A mail order is the proverbial pig-in-the-poke. Only after the consumer drinks the magic elixir, shoves the pellet in some orifice, squeezes the springed muscle developer, or straps the garment onto the protrusion will he know if he's received his money's worth. And the advertisers may need a strong element of consumer fantasy for their wonder workers to appear to slice off fat like a laser beam or blot and dot pimples with amazing alacrity.

Fortunately, even if the products fail, at least they fail in private. If you are a loser and need a new face, or if you suffer from wrinkled throat or hemorrhoids, at least the whole world needn't know of your desperation. It is easy to snip a coupon, place it in a nonreturn-addressed envelope, and send a private correspondence through the nonnoticing postal service. In return, you receive in plain wrapper (pw) a package containing secret formulas to transform a willing but heretofore thwarted body. Late at night, while the family sleeps, you take out that slimming sauna suit and let the furnace effect melt away unneeded flesh. If the suit is nothing but a $10.95 sweat suit, only you know of the seller's duplicity. And, what the hell—for $10.95 you can't even get a decent rubdown.

MAIL ORDER STRATEGIES

A few strategies are unique to the mail order business. The most obvious one is the *money back guarantee,* which is prominent on most mail order coupons. This all-inclusive guarantee is designed to reduce consumers' feelings that mail order products are unreliable or misrepresented. After all, sending money through the mail to a mysterious box number requires unusual faith in human nature. The money back guarantee reassures the anxious and implies that *the buyer has nothing to lose.* "If I am not wholly delighted after ten days, I may return the unused capsules for prompt refund." So the consumer takes a couple of capsules-a-day of hormone-activated, wonder-working, reinforced with BHT, Energy Plus Wooko; and his breath still reeks, his underarms continue to perspire,

the rhetoric of cheap mail order

and friends still call him "Stinky." He decides to mail the unused capsules back—but not before paying the postage and handling for the return and—in the case of the rupture reliever—not finding a suitable box and finally keeping it. Fortunately, most leftover rupture relievers make great slingshots, but three "Tummy Trimmers" fail even as washrags. In some cases, the company lags in returning money or simply changes its address or product name when a sufficient number of complaints accumulate. The beauty of mail order manipulation is that a correspondent cannot see the abandoned garage that serves as international headquarters for the "world's largest" manufacturer of adjustable hairpin lace looms.

***

Dear Action Urgent:

I sent $7.98 on May 1st to the Oriental Express Products Company of NYC for a book entitled *Kai-rate: Save Yourself First*. It is now November 18th and not only have I not received my book, but I've been beaten up three times by street gangs. My letters to the Oriental Express Company have been returned with no address available. Help!

Unprotected,
LDH, LA

***

Dear Unprotected:

We found that the Oriental Express Company is now the Japanese Institute of Scientific Warfare. They claim no relationship to the disbanded firm. The book was examined by an expert and found to be fraudulent—in fact, the illustrations were taken from a WWI US Army calisthenics manual. We have referred your case to the Attorney General of New York, who will contact you as to procedures for a California resident to follow in your complaint.

Action Urgent

***

the rhetoric of cheap mail order

If the money back offer isn't sufficient bait, the companies cram a number of appeals into the ads to hit every need known to Western civilization. If you are cost conscious, a multiple bargain appeals:

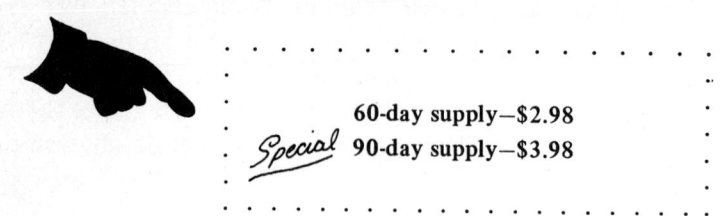

> 60-day supply—$2.98
> *Special* 90-day supply—$3.98

And, of course, it doesn't take a genius to figure out that double nothing is still merely nothing doubled.

The cost conscious buyer also is lured with seemingly free *add-ons* labeled as "A BONUS OFFER" or "INCLUDED AT THE SAME PRICE" to insure a fast response to the ad. "While the supply lasts," if you purchase a $49.95 wig for $19.95 you will also receive a free nail beauty guide. If you buy a rupture truss, you receive free a booklet on rupture care, containing action shots of proper lifting procedures for rupture sufferers. Some mail order firms use the free booklet offers not as an *add-on* incentive to buy a product but as bait to sell a product offered in the booklet or to compile lists of the names of interested consumers to sell to other mail order companies.[2] The bait is often used by homebuilders who use such free booklet offers as *10 Ways to a Dry Basement* to sell liquid foundation sealers. The mail order world, like the real world, seldom offers something for nothing.

Another mail order strategy is the *promise of discretion.* A large number of mail order firms inform the consumer that the product will be shipped in a plain wrapper. The postman will not know that you are trying to expand your chest or to entice a boyfriend with a crotchless panty. However, it says nowhere in the ads that money refunded for returned merchandise will be sent in an unmarked envelope.

> HERE COMES ANOTHER $8.95
> FOR A DISSATISFIED CUSTOMER
> OF THE SEXUALLY STIMULATING
> HAND VIBRATOR LTD.

The tendency for most shoppers is to maintain the bond of discretion even if they become unhappy with the merchandise. This return-return involves too many risks. The rewrapping of the product reminds the buyer of the stupid purchase.

---

[2] An unfortunate side effect of buying by mail is the possibility of getting on mailing lists that companies purchase to advertise products whose material will not only clutter your mail box, but also might be offensive.

the rhetoric of cheap mail order

The money back envelope may reveal the product's name. A failed return-return has the Attorney General's office asking for germane details of the fraud. The complainer often suspects that his fraud claim is bantered about by nosy officials in the state capital.

"I don't believe this one, Ed."

"Another weirdo, Frank?"

"This kook filed a claim because his vibrator shorts out."

"Hey, I know that guy. He's my sister's boyfriend."

For many people, the product is discreetly wrapped in a garbage bag or placed in an attic, far from prying eyes.

FANTASTIC CLAIMS STRATEGIES

The world of mail order has developed its own vocabulary designed to invoke a clipped coupon. The *fantastic claims* strategy often combines the expectations of technology (anything can happen in this age) with simple-minded, blatant language and overstated use of capital letters, hyphens, and large type. Some of the claims are simply comic book clichés hooked to products of questionable merit. Many of these ads claim their product is an "amazing new discovery," which readers can't dispute since they've never seen it before. Other ads promise that readers "will thrill to a smoother skin" by using a "new triple-action" product designed for a "fresh, new look." A thrill of any sort may be worth two dollars, but the key fantastic claim often is "triple-action." Most products can perform one function—wash dishes, clean floors, dry-clean clothes—but mail order products offer triple the action by clearing up skin, reducing large eyelids, *and* bleaching freckles—all with a single pill. It may be worth sending through the mails for a product that can do more than one thing. Some mail order firms use the hyperbolic style of action comic books—"Triple hammer fists"; he-man alliteratives—"bulging biceps"; dramatic analogies to war weapons—"B-L-A-S-T-S AWAY FAT"; or mystical energy-consuming phenomena like "FURNACE IN A TAB." And what are words, if not for exaggeration?

The most interesting of the fantastic claims strategies are the offers for a better life advertised by correspondence schools. Few would argue that an airline mechanic can make a good wage and—given a run of good luck—probably will live happily ever after. However, in exchange for enrolling, the correspondence schools offer an entire new life style. The ad appeal often includes the promise of a gorgeous wife, large and multiple cars, a brick house, and expensive vacations. All these benefits are yours just for mailing the coupon and embarking on a correspondence course.

Some correspondence schools play on the reader's fantasy of telling off Mr. Boss. . . .

Unfortunately, few events in life are as dramatic as telling off Mr. Boss and moving to the easy money of air conditioning maintenance and plumbing. Although necessary and often financially rewarding, these jobs take study, skill, and patience. And even making a lot of money as a TV repairman may not fetch a correspondence school graduate a gorgeous wife if he has acne.

The promise of job success through mail order is the siren call so many of us suddenly hear when we are frustrated by life's misfortunes and inequities. How many normally sane people find another Friday's typing duties unbearable or another blue Monday at the hamburger stand demeaning? And in the back section of *Redbook,* there is a chance to escape to the life of a cosmetologist; in the last pages of *Motor Trend* lies a

the rhetoric of cheap mail order

career in the retail automobile business. Each job ad promises escape from drudgery to a pleasant, even irresistible life style.

Medical Breakthroughs

An important category of *fantastic claims* is the use of proclaimed medical breakthroughs to convince readers that a mail order product is better than orthodox medical treatment. An extreme example is a company that claims their chemical throat pad is better than most plastic surgery. A person with a wrinkled, tired throat simply ties on the pad nightly, and a new, smooth throat appears in a matter of days. If the product does not work, remember the ad claimed the product was better than *most* plastic surgery. It is possible that your case is one of a small minority of resistant throats.

The ads claiming medical breakthroughs appeal to that peculiar American faith in progress and miracles. One can guess that the people *out there* still believe in exaggerated claims that "9 out of 10 doctors" prefer a mail order product that is "5 ways more effective" than surgery. However, this strategy has been so overworked that ad writers find it difficult to be convincing. The result is a heaping together of medical breakthrough claims—seemingly to catch everyone somehow. Reports are staggering if true that medical tests by a "leading NY doctor" prove that a teen-ager's "epidermis" (legitimation tactic for skin) will be scientifically rejuvenated in an "antiseptic, anti-bacterial" cream. If these claims are not enticing, many companies toss in the "completely hypo-allergenic" label, which means *safe* to medically alert readers. A piece of plastic is technically hypo-allergenic, because it contains no known allergents; but no one recommends that you rub your face with a comb. If the above breakthroughs are not enough, many ads claim their product is a "scientific" form of relief. The implication is that many researchers created this product under rigorous testing procedures, using the scientific method in clean, hygienic laboratories. That's a lot of work to discover a better truss or a bust expander consisting of a wood board with two round holes.

Make It Easy On Yourself

The final *fantastic claims* category promises relief or success without inconvenience. "Just Give Me 10 Minutes a Day"; "Simply go to sleep and when you wake up...," "Your pores drink in the hormones while you sleep"; "Just try for seven nights—lose 80 lbs. in 14 nights." The claims, in calling for little effort from the user, make the appeal attractive. To lose weight through exercise and a sensible diet requires effort and will power. How many instant dieters relish the tedious workouts, the starvation jitters, when a chronic gorger can eat all he wants and lose a pound a day? The secret of the diet ads is turning up your furnace and burning off the fat fast or swallowing a piece of candy and finding your appetite dramatically diminished. The *make it easy on yourself* strategy is seductive to all ages—from the scrawny little kid wishing for a massive chest to the older folks with cataracts who send for magnifying eyeglasses.

HARD SELL STRATEGIES

Many of the strategies of mail order are typical of other industries selling merchandise of questionable need. The difference is usually in the brashness of the appealer. These hard sell strategies are characterized by the emphasis on denigrating the potential user, attacking alternative methods and products, or promising unrealistic results.

Humiliation

The strategy of humiliation takes many forms in mail order. Not many young ladies cherish "ugly, unwanted, upper lip hair." Few readers will forget the advertisement for hair remover featuring a scantily clad, gorgeous woman, except for one apelike, hairy leg, prominently displayed to the reader. The body building ads ask if you are ashamed of your body and plead that you not be "skinny, thin, and shapeless." The fat people ads condemn "unsightly bulges," and the acne removers cite "ugly looking" eruptions and "disfigurement." What makes humiliation work as a strategy is that the ads publicly label our secret sins. They know that we eat frugally at lunch with friends, but stalk the refrigerator at night. The ads not only prominently display the resulting disfigurements but detail all the consequences we most fear.

"Is that why guys don't date me?"
"Another 60 pounds and I'll wrestle in the 125-pound class."
"No one marries a wrinkled widow."
"I'll get that bully with another 30 pounds."
"Do people really notice that I stoop?"

The decision to send a coupon is a positive enactment on the problem and temporarily resolves our guilt. "Wait until the package comes and I'll spring into action like a tiger." The relief we feel knowing help is on the way is comforting; and in the absence of any concrete help, it's a psychological sedative. An alternative would be to grab the sand kicking bully's ankle and twist hard. Unfortunately, as with exercise and starvation, the punishment may be much too painful compared to the easy hope coming in the mail.

Alternative Method Put-Downs

In many ads an attempt is made to attack the other methods of solving weight problems or acne. It has become an essential strategy of the advertisers to somewhere mention the "many faddish diets that almost starve you to death," or to remind the reader that our product is "not a paste-on that may fall off." The strategy to criticize the competition's product as inferior recognizes the constant searching and resulting hopelessness of the chronic dieter or seeker of a natural looking toupee. There are among us those citizens who race from cure to fad and back again, trying to correct a real or imagined malady. The *alternative method put-down* says this cure is the one that will miraculously transform you into a goddess or a weightlifter. The other methods failed because of obvious weaknesses that we scientific researchers have only recently conquered. "You understand me," weeps the sinner, "that diet was hell." In effect, the *alternative method put-down* strategy allows the consumer to thrust into his private history book of previous failures and heartbreaks—the earlier mail order flops.

Ratio Strategies

The final *hard sell* is the *ratio strategy,* a technique illustrating amazing results by citing people who made dramatic changes in weight or size. The ratio ads use exotic measurements as proof, and the 56-inch chest, 21-inch biceps, and 30-inch thighs become primary evidence. Many ratio ads feature testimonials from grateful people who benefited from a better ratio.

> "I have gained six beautiful inches and it is worth more to me than I could every say . . ." Ms. OD, *Chicago*

The letters rarely describe how the miracle happened, how much work transpired, or the full name of the sender. The magic is in the ratio of going from a 32AA to a 36C or in flattening your stomach from 44 inches to 32. The workability of the ratio strategy lies in the fact that readers recognize the desirability of attaining the numbers. A 32-inch waist for a male is enviable, and who disputes it? The promise of 32 inches may speed the money on to the company headquarters, where 48-inch waisted workers pack dynamic springs into mailers.

VISUAL STRATEGIES

The visual strategies begin with the readily indentifiable *before and after pictures.* In the mail order world, nothing is as convincing as living proof of fantastic results. The reader is confronted with an endless parade of former fatties—now thin as firewood kindling—and of flabby adolescents—now grown into muscular men. The pictures usually are dark and grainy, implying a candid, unretouched quality. Many *before and afters* are posed naturally fat and slouching as a *before,* and then the same model is reshot posing erectly for the dramatic 80 lb. weight loss. It is not hard to imagine most of the *afters* sucking in their stomachs to reveal their rippling muscles or copious bosoms. A photographer can always retouch whatever is inadequate.

A combination of the *medical breakthrough* and *before and after* visuals is the famous half-face acne test. In this dramatic visualization a teen-ager's face is split down the middle with the untreated half erupted by acne and the other half clear, after a short treatment of the acne remover. It's a nice gimmick, absurd enough so the user won't attempt to duplicate the miracle and yet persuasive for those believers in visual evidence.

the rhetoric of cheap mail order

What makes *before and after* visuals effective is a combination of trust in photographs and the accompanying plain folks' testimonies. In the world of attaining belief there is little written evidence as convincing as a camera accurately reproducing the event.
A picture may be worth a thousand words and perhaps two thousand when combined with the public testimony of private citizens. "I have nothing to hide," is the posture of the ads; and unless the reader is cynical, he will respond "Hey, he's like me."
The *after* picture of the now-slim housewife speaks visually to all fat housewives—hope, optimism, a chance for a way out.

The majority of visuals in cheap mail order surprisingly are not *before and afters*, but simply beautiful *afters*. Mail order advertisers feature voluptuous women with long, flowing tresses as happy users of their wigs and bust creme developers. Many of the women are clad in bikinis or negligees, openly enraptured with life and themselves, looking sexually devastating. The men, often wearing clinging bathing trunks, appear ruggedly handsome and are surrounded by adoring, sexually devastating females.
The models, though gorgeous, have a vague, undefined quality to their faces and bodies. They are not real people but visual caricatures who readily can be substituted for anyone in the country who cares to swap places. The ads invite the reader to *begin to live* by sending in the coupon. There is only one ugly person in the world, and that is *you*. The rest of the world is not only having a fantastic time but is virile, looks great, and is waiting for a new *you* to join it. The only way your world is going to change for *you* is to send money—now.

NAMING STRATEGIES

The final strategy is obvious and yet potentially the most persuasive. For many people the name becomes the object. For these people, the name "Elmer" is a curse and "Ethel" and "Shirley" lack glamour. So they frantically seek names that will bring us luck, please the ear, and somehow captivate our personal and public acquaintances. It is little wonder that mail order strategists call their muscle men "Charles Atlas" and "Mike Marvel," and not "Marvin Zink" or "Harry Knoshnect." "I'm sending away to 'Marvin Zink' for a karate hand-crusher." It simply does not wash, any more than would a take out food chain called "Chicken Feathers" or "Bloody's Beef Sandwiches."

The number of *naming strategies* seems endless. In the mail order business "Eileen Feather" is billed as the "nation's leading figure authority." The small-busted women of the world can send to Mark Eden for help. A weakling can drink "Super-Pro 101," which rushes to his muscles for super power. A "Sta-long" nail kit will go with a "new look" bra from "Countess X" or the no bra illusion from "Nude-bra." When overweight, try a "Fayd" diet, a quick shot of "Super-C," and get rid of those age spots with "Age-Wise" cosmetics. If there is a mail order product a name will be devised to suggest the product's power, use, or desired result.

The naming strategy is a natural outcome in a society so impersonal, so lacking in close relationships. When interpersonal contact is missing, consumers take outward symbols as evidence of integrity, quality, or reliability in lieu of their own personal verification. Howard Johnson is a middle-class name for a middle-class motel, and McDonald's is not an exclusive French restaurant.

THE WORLD'S GREATEST PERSPECTIVE

The original catalogues of the late nineteenth century were aptly labeled "wish books." A farm family in rural America could send for a vast array of products that small country stores could not stock and sell. The great catalogue mailers such as Sears and Wards are somewhat out of the wish book business, since their products now are available to most consumers through retail stores. These catalogue companies now primarily sell convenience and price. The cheap mail order advertisers are still in the wish book business. Their products are not readily available in retail stores, and they play directly on the fantasy of the consumers. Although the mail order product may not be as substantial as the Sears washer, it still represents release from drudgery into a world of pleasure.

Another important difference between the great catalogue houses and cheap mail order is that the latter plays on naiveté, hopelessness, and desperation. A cheap mail order advertisement speaks to the discontented people who grasp for easy solutions when all else appears to fail. For these consumers, knowledge of strategies and not legislation is the answer.

As for the remainder of the cheap mail order strategies, they exist more or less in the great catalogue houses. What is the Sears' Ted Williams label but a *naming strategy*? The catalogue houses offer their money back guarantees, fantastic claims, and visuals of attractive fashion models using their products. Convincing consumers to send money through the mail requires reassurance and encouragement, whether selling Neiman-Marcus matched airplanes or fashion-designed derrière shapers. The difference between a $329.95 triple-action, top-rated washing machine and a $2.00 bust creme developer featuring living fluids is not in how they are sold. Besides, by selecting the latter, the buyer skips service calls and saves $327.95.

Most consumer-oriented guides recommend that bilked mail order customers use the various legal lines of communication to receive satisfaction or their money back. A mail order customer can discover the holder of a Post Office box by writing the postmaster or by calling long distance information to discover specific names for communication purposes. In most large cities, local newspapers feature "action line" columns that track down difficult-to-reach companies. In addition, the Attorney General's office in most states has increasing power and jurisdiction to lasso companies that make false claims. But how much detective work is warranted for a $2.00 bust developer that fails to develop or a $1.00 booklet that does not correct bed wetting? And, how many citizens are willing to be identified as one of the local "bulgers" who bought a defective "Tummy Trimmer?" In the final analysis, the best protection against cheap mail order is not sending for the item in the first place.

The purpose of this chapter is to detail strategies that lure unsuspecting consumers through cheap prices and easy promises to solve their personal problems. For most people, a well-developed body comes from hard exercise and not "powerful" liquids and mysterious heat-producing sweat suits. When the public fully understands these realities, cheap mail order will no longer sell.

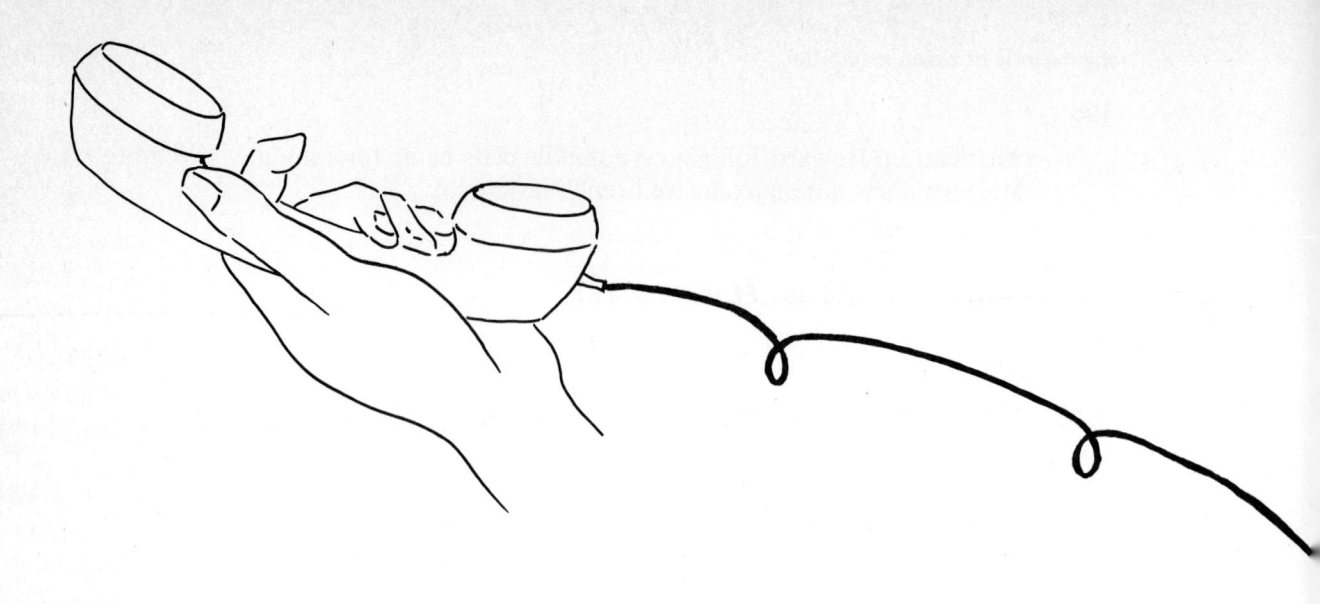

PHONE MAGIC: NEED A MAGAZINE?

RING...RING

"Hello!"

"Is this Mary Jean Good of 414 West Locust?"

"Yes...it is."

"Well, Mary Jean, I'm conducting a survey for a leading polling service to discover the reading habits of good Americans like you."

"I don't want any magazines."

"No, Mary Jean, we're not selling magazines...We're a polling service. If I ever try to sell you a magazine, you tell me to stop and you can hang up. Fair enough, Mary Jean?"

"I guess that's all right...but..."

"Now, Mary Jean, did you read the story about Jackie Kennedy Onassis in *Ladies' Home Journal* this month?"

"Yes!"

"What did you think of it?"

"I thought it was well written..."

"Call me Edith..."

"Oh, well, it was well written, Edith...I felt for her, do you know what I mean?...Well, I liked it."

"You're a good critic, Mary Jean, and my company would like to give you a gift for your participation."

"Gee, great!"

"How would you like six months free delivery of *Ladies' Home Journal*?"

"Thank you...I..."

"For participation in our survey we are gifting you six months free with no strings attached...and for only an additional $34.90, another two and a half years of *Ladies' Home Journal* and one year of *Cosmopolitan*...we'll send that right out, Mary Jean...congratulations...and thanks much for participating."

HANDY HOUSEHOLD TELEPHONE PUT-DOWNS

"Gee, I'm glad you called. I don't need magazines. . .but how would you like some long-life peony seeds I'm selling for our local church? They cost only. . . ."

"How long have you been working at this job, Edith?"

"Do you mind holding the line? My son is throwing up."

"Do you mind if the line is tapped? I'm doing a book on telephone hustling."

"I really enjoyed talking to you, Ma'am. . .but I'm only eight, and my mommy's at the store."

"Send me everything as fast as you can. I've declared bankruptcy and I take what I can get."

the greeting cards: super environments

9

A strategy calculated to improve your image in another environment is the greeting card. To think of someone else is a gesture that civilized society marks as generous, considerate, and thoughtful. The greeting card industry makes it easy by adapting their presentations to whatever occasions represent a major market in the world.

The card industry is a true presentational form standing for whatever is programmed into it. A card is selected at a rack that is specially designed to carry only notes of sentiment, hope, humor, or pity. The card selector either doesn't have the time to write a personal note or feels the commercial card industry—with its professional artists and engravers—can convey his sentiments better than he can himself. In a society passionately devoted to expertise, he feels that only a professional could capture the sender's own personal feelings.

The cards are arranged on the racks according to sentiment and occasion. A sentimental, gushy card can praise anniversaries in one little, frilly number; next to it may reside a vicious, counter-culture card attacking the same institution. The buyer does not find it strange that the same company can play both ends of the social spectrum. The card industry portrays any viable, commercial sentiment, and the buyer ferrets among them for suitability. Why should the buyer protest the manufacturer's inconsistency in card design? The buyer cooperates with the manufacturer by sending the commercially designed missile to a target deemed appropriate for the message. A nostalgic card for Aunt Fanny, something cynical for Cousin Lester, and for Herman, an out-of-focus love scene. Instant sentiment is not far removed from instant soup.

The greeting business begins with the frosted, traditional cards which—since their introduction in the late nineteenth century—mark anniversaries, weddings, and funerals.

the greeting cards: super environments

The cards often have flowery, glittery covers, heightened artistically through the judicious sprinkling of an outside layer of sparkling dust. The outside script usually is characterized by curlicues and says something prosaic like "To my dearest beloved," "In your time of need," "To Grandma and Grandpa." Inside the card is a long, rhythmic, sentimental verse of high praise for the person and the occasion.

My Only Love

A reminder of the Oak tree's rustle.
    You mean more to me than
Freshly crushed magnolias trodden.
    Oh, whither thou remain in
My cozened purview till March's
    Wind blows steady apace.
To the hustings for Love's passion
    Only can make your Confirmation a hit.

The greeting card industry has moved into the contemporary market for any number of occasions. The industry is quick to pick up on the slang of whatever generation is buying the cards. The strategy is to employ the slang to communicate with the buyer who uses the slang to communicate with his friends. If this relationship appears less than natural and spontaneous, go back to Chapter 1 and reread the section on *illusion* and the producer-consumer relationship.

THE SLANG PLAN

1. A number of fairly spontaneous slang terms emerge from the public psyche.
2. The card industry uses them to communicate. (So do the soda pop industry, the cosmetic industry, and other youth-marketed industries.)
3. The "together" public buys these sentiments to express commercially their feelings.

"It's your bag, baby."

SEXIST!

"Let's get it together."

I'M DOING MY OWN NUMBER!

"We're number one."

RIGHT ON, PIG!

the greeting cards: super environments

A popular variation of the contemporary youth card is capturing the social trends. In the late sixties, a with-it card featured a cute, long-haired hippie on the cover who encouraged the cardee to burn draft cards, wear long hair, or protest becoming a year older. The note on the inside was absurd—"Burn this card"—and hopefully set up a cardee howl. This approach manages to recognize the importance of the youth movement and yet, through satire and parody, it establishes the sender as being one who sees through the movement. The approach announces to the receiver that, "I am a together person because I did not send you a traditional card, but I'm aware that all of this protest stuff is trendy and uncool. Put on my head a large 'G' for Genius." The beauty of this strategy is that ecology, women's rights, abortion, or energy crisis simply is fitted into the scheme. The use of parody and satire allows the card company to stand for everything and for nothing.

A popular mainstay of the greeting card industry is the celebration of religious holidays. What Christian American can resist the red-suited Santa pulling his sleigh over the North Pole, the angels doing their lute number, or the cameo portraits of Christ with sparkling dust? For those of the Jewish faith, there are Torahs, gilded Mogan Davids, and "living color" interpretations of Israel. If you cannot afford the better quality religious cards, you can always buy large assortments of miscellaneous greeting cards from door-to-door salesmen—who represent the products of companies who advertise in the back sections of comic books.

"Morning, Ma'am! If I sell 1,500 more decorator-designed,
gift-boxed Christmas cards,
I get a three-day, all-expense paid tour of the Holy Land!"

Then to appeal to those playful cardees who think religious holidays are to observe, but not to take seriously, the card companies designed the fun religious card. These cards playfully spoof the tradition, without offending those people who sort of believe. So these cards are for people who like the holidays, believe faintly in religion, but who are sharp, contemporary iconoclasts.

On the first day of Hanukkah,
   My true love sent to me...
A chicken in a Hanukkah tree.

On the second day of Hanukkah,
   My true love sent to me...
Two chopped livers,
   And a chicken in a Hanukkah tree.

For those Americans who like to personalize their messages and see the greeting card as too rigid, the card companies have designed very soft, artistic looking cards that give the illusion of being old, tasteful prints. On the inside, the sender is given a variety of sentiments from which to select his special touch and then discard the inappropriate remainder.

the greeting cards: super environments

Outside—Your Love

Inside—*Makes my world go 'round!*

or

Outside—My Love

Inside—*Is like a squishy, ten-pound, fresh, whole liver.*

That the card sender can select from only a limited number of sentiments is restrictive, but not as restrictive as having only one choice. Again, the appearance of choice is not unlike a similar illusion in the supermarket—a can of Campbell's Golden Mushroom is not drastically different from a can of Heinz's Cream of Mushroom—but you are free to select either.

Finally, if the world of centralization, standardization, and waxy sentiment is upsetting, take consolation in the following. For this consumer, people in the card industry have designed messages that lament Institutional Rhetoric and offer relief... which in a real way is the ultimate consumer manipulation. The consumer spends seventy-five cents to purchase a standardized card lamenting standardization in a rip-off, mechanistic society.

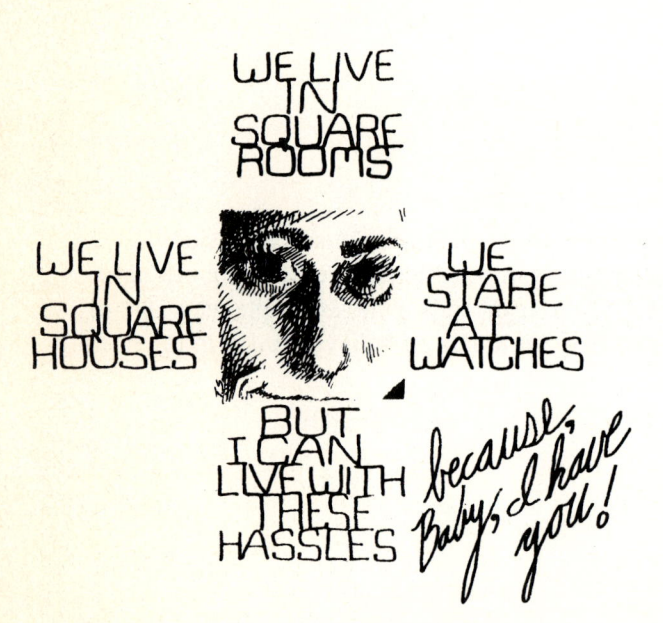

WE LIVE IN SQUARE ROOMS
WE LIVE IN SQUARE HOUSES
WE STARE AT WATCHES
BUT I CAN LIVE WITH THESE HASSLES *because, Baby, I have you!*

When a society finds that only an industry can properly select a note for an individual to send to an acquaintance the communication system is suspect. There is little reason a consumer cannot simply write a note expressing grief, happiness, or congratulations. But in a society of four-color presses and clever jingle writers, we give up our provincial habits and succumb to technology. We end up sending the best example of our *image* and not the best example of our *feelings*.

the media and the cereal bowl

10

Whenever America's children have that empty feeling in the morning, they reach for a great American bowl of cereal. I don't care whether the cereal is Rice Krispies fortified with EIGHT ESSENTIAL VITAMINS AND IRON or Jean LaFoote's Cinnamon Crunch with free cut-out planes on the back of the carton, there is little in life more patriotic than starting out the day with cereal. Eggs, bacon, and toast aren't American—the kids who eat these products are oily and foreign. In five years, these kids will be wolfing down chocolate bars, knocking out street lights, and playing with rhinestone-encrusted yo-yos. The youngsters who eat cereal have good teeth, red hair, and wear polo shirts. They are the future student council leaders and cheerleaders who gave up play for occupational placement goals at ten years of age.

There are three media areas in which cereals primarily are sold: on television, through strategic supermarket placement, and through related appeals of the carton and giveaways. And this troika is as natural to cereal as Snap, Crackle, and Pop!

Since the earliest days of radio cereal advertising, the hero of the adventure made personal testimonials for the product.

Hey, kids! This is your little friend Hoppity. Have you had your Stingley Flakes this morning? No? **Well,** I bet you're tired and run down. . .no energy to play ball and nag Mommy! **Hellfire,** the answer is a bowl of SF with milk, because even dumb kids know milk and cereal equals energy. **Into the tummy** goes SF, milk, and out comes muscles. . .muscles to beat up Daddy when he comes home drunk. **Super cartilages** to bind those muscles so you can tear apart Christmas presents! **And kids,** remember, BHT is added to packaged material to preserve freshness and it will not soften your mind!

the media and the cereal bowl

How many kids ate Wheaties because radio hero Jack Armstrong, the All-American boy, recommended the product for power and energy? How many kids bought the Dragon Eye ring that Jack used in his escapades? How many kids developed wheat rashes after ten years and 3,650 bowls of milk, fruit, and Wheaties? How many bowls of Wheaties before the body says "Enough," and erstwhile rippling muscles become unpopped kernels? Well, cereals still are being sold to kids by using the same strategies of identification, but the heroes are now replaced by assorted cartoon figures.

TELEVISION

The children's hour is Saturday morning when the kiddie cereals and toy manufacturers vie for the mind of the Great Little American Consumer. Now no one is saying that cereal is bad for kids...at least when a cup of milk is added the nutrition shoots up. The Saturday morning cereal race features children's cereals advertised by commercials that stress animated characters, novelty prizes, special mail-in offers, a particular flavor, and the appeal that essentially, cereals are for kids. The cast of cereal stars includes such favorites as Fred Flintstone, the Crunchberry Beast, Quangeroo, and assorted other monsters, pirates, and animals.

The important strategy on Saturday morning is to make the characters of the sponsoring commercials seem interesting, fun, and involving to children. A child can spend Saturday morning with many of his favorite cartoon friends including the Pink Panther, the Brady Bunch, Scooby Doo and his Gang, Tony the Tiger, and Count Chocula. Some of the friends are cartooned series characters, and others are cartooned commercial cereal advertisers. For most young children who enjoy cartoon programs, there is little apparent difference between programs and commercials. What real difference to a child is there between the cartoon program, *The Pink Panther*, and the cereal commercials that Tony the Tiger advertises? Both the characters are clever cats, presented in bright color, and seem fun and loving to a child.[1] This strategy of blurring program and advertising distinctions is borne out by an NBC study[2] which found that not only do children watch commercials as intently as they watch the regular programs but also that they enjoy commercials; they memorize them, repeat them, look for the advertised product in stores, and if the parents are buying another brand children will ask them to switch to the commercial's product. Little hard sell of the product is needed or even desirable with this fun strategy. If the kids like Cap'n Crunch they will ask Mommy or Daddy to buy the bright red carton with the smiling blue-and-yellow-suited Cap'n on the front. There is no need for logic or limited time offers. For parents who find this strategy particularly manipulative of children, they can be assured that similar strategies are used on adults. When Mom buys a hot comb because she admires Billie Jean King or Dad buys a shaving cream because of Joe Namath, they are responding to a similar strategy; it is just that children seem more vulnerable.

---

[1] I owe this observation to an unpublished study by Julie Heller and Martha Koch, "The Rhetoric of Children's Cereals," Northwestern University, March 1974.

[2] Girard Chester, Garnet R. Garrison, and Edgar Wills, *Television and Radio*, 4th edition (Englewood Cliffs: Prentice-Hall, Inc., 1971), p. 8.

THE SHELF

The moment of cereal truth arrives when the parents glide down the aisle with little Tracey sitting in the cart, eye level with the high-profit, high-impulse children's cereals. The established family cereals such as Corn Flakes, Puffed Wheat, and Cheerios are normally bottom shelved. These cereals are placed furthest from eye level, because they are purchased by shoppers who usually know what they want in morning nutrition. A shopper will reach "down low" for a product in demand by household members. In contrast, the less popular, adult cereals such as Total and Alpen are placed on the top shelves, where the taller adult easily can see them. But the seated child sees only brightly colored cereal boxes featuring the Saturday morning television lineup. She calls out, "Freddie Flintstone," remembering the cartoon of that name and a character with great appeal for children. Or, she cries, "Jean LaFoote," recalling her favorite cartoon commercial featuring the New Quaker pirate. And if the name is not a bell-ringer, she may shout, "Plastic Spy Kit," "Coloring Book," or "Snowmobile." At this point, a classic confrontation ensues, not unlike the teacher-student encounter of an earlier chapter. The confrontation is between a child and his parents, and it is appropriate to ponder the following questions:

1. Why do parents take the kiddies to the store?
2. Why do parents give in to their demands?

The answer to number one is that the parents didn't hire a baby sitter but opted instead to remove the children for a Saturday morning constitutional away from Count Chocula and the rest of the Saturday morning cereal crowd. It is ironic that whisking the children away from the media cereal barrage only results in a direct confrontation with the product in the store. The answer to number two is blackmail. The agony of watching your child throwing a temper tantrum over a 79¢ carton of presweetened, fortified cereal often is not worth it. The child's cries echo throughout the store, banging against the rear meat case and reverberating to the front reaches of the checkout counter. In our culture, the crying child often symbolizes neglect and adult coercion; normally, parents are not eager for that stigma. The suffering child has the parents on her own turf—the cereal aisle—and now pays back Mommy and Daddy for allergy shots and asparagus.

"I want it, Mommy." (Sweet time)

"No." (Damn you)

"Give it to me...you promised." (I'll get her)

"Keep quiet, *please!*" (Shut your damn mouth)

"Wahhh" (I'll put pressure)

"All right! **Here—take it!**" (Damn that kid)

Into the cart goes the cereal, and the child shuts up until the cooky aisle is reached. There is little question, however, that the big moment for kids in a supermarket is the cereal aisle, and for most parents, it is a Consumer Dunkirk.

GIMMICK PREMIUMS

The last line of attack by cereal manufacturers is the large variety of added inducements to buy the cereal. In 1901 the folks from Quaker Oats advertised that a label from a box of their cereal accompanied by five cents sent in the mail would deliver a fortune-telling calendar in fourteen colors.[3] The gimmick business really took off in the thirties and forties when cereal makers were devising irresistible lures for young consumers. All over the dial excited announcers promised thrills, intrigue, and secrecy if listeners would send in coins and boxtops.

> **Listen boys and girls. . .**be the only kid on the block with a **genuine** Dragon Eye ring that **glows in the dark. Yes. . .the same ring** that has a secret decoder that lets you receive confidential messages from **Jack Armstrong, the All-American boy. SO RUSH RIGHT DOWN** to your local grocery store and ask the grocer for a package of your favorite cereal. . .When we last left Jack, he was tied to the rudder of a submerging German U-boat. . . .

And kids did rush right down to buy the cereal manufacturer's products when they offered sports instruction books that made champions, a square-inch deed to the Yukon, or a set of Tom Mix cowboy spurs. The cereal people discovered early that cereal and gimmicks were integral to sales because of one simple fact—the product may taste unpalatable to kids. The reality is that a kid may like the premium and hate the product—resulting in a mediocre-tasting, weirdly packaged box of presweetened mush selling like hotcakes if the premium is right. So if Kermit wants that plastic flip game Mommy or Daddy must buy the product, let Kermit reach in and retrieve that flip game, beg Kermit to eat the cereal, suffer the agony of refusal, and then place the gameless box into the garbage—representing a record consumption rate for any product!

In any given period of Cereal Time, the premium strategies can vary.[4] The first type is the "in-pack," which means a premium stowed inside the box is free, except that you paid for the cereal. Kids prefer the in-pack strategy, because it allows them instant gratification, something they rarely are denied. A variation of the in-pack strategy could be called a "back-pack," which often is a game or puzzle on the back of the cereal carton. The strategies vary for each cereal; Kaboom features U.S. road signs on the panel, and Lucky Charms uses a Leprechaun game in honor of its dimwitted mascot. The folks from Booberry advertised a free coloring book that had to be sent away for and is known as a "free-in-the-mail." If you want Tony the Tiger's new "Put the Tail on the Tony" game,

---

[3] Arthur Marquette, *Brands, Trademarks, and Goodwill* (New York: McGraw-Hill, 1967), p. 129. Marquette discusses the premium business as the Quaker Oats Company developed it.

[4] An excellent source for details on premium offers is Maurice I. Mandell, *Advertising* (Englewood Cliffs, N.J.: Prentice-Hall, Inc., 1974), pp. 598-603. I also found useful an unpublished paper on cereals by Jim Corradino, Steve Gorshow, George Lisle, Robyn McGill, Janice Molnar, Nancy Morris, and Reggie Panarese, "The Rhetoric of Breakfast Cereals," Northwestern University, December 1973.

the media and the cereal bowl

you must send two boxtops of Sugar Frosted Flakes and a buck. The latter combination is termed a "self-liquidator," a premium priced to retrieve a producer's costs. A kid can spend the best of his childhood in an endless cycle of mushing, marking, mailing, and "self-liquidating." At the age of twelve, he graduates with a CA (Cereal Addiction) and moves into rock radio promotions.

The point for parents is that Kermit may hate cereals and prefer coffee cake, but bakers do not give free ecology stickers inside their products the way Puffa Puffa Rice does. And if little Kermit does not like any cereal, his parents are not going to buy any of the cereals and their premiums. So little Kermit is going to go uncoded, seriously retarded in back panel games; and he may be the only little kid on the block without a plastic Dot 'n' Flasher from the Honeycomb folks. "I want" is seriously repressed in Kermit, and the condominium developers begin wondering if chateau models featuring free lounge chairs will move in the next generation.

If this information is not sufficiently depressing to parents they can always ponder the "premium/no premium gambit"[5] as outlined by children's cereal researcher Ron Goulart. In this version, the child buys a newly introduced cereal and receives a nice premium for his selection and loyalty. The next box purchased contains no nice premium, and the child can't understand it. The cereal manufacturer made no attempt to convince this immature consumer that subsequent boxes contained premiums; yet a child can be deceived readily, a notion that seems integral to cereal strategy.

So we have here a Great American cereal game played by Mommy, Daddy, Tracey, Kermit, cereal manufacturers, and the media. We begin the game with a presweetened, non-nutritional product, add a cute cartoon character, put the whole mess on Saturday morning television, hope the kid will sit in the parent's cart in the supermarket and either grab the cereal or raise a fuss, and throw in the premium in case the kids cannot stomach the product. Now mix, stir, and shake with your Sonny Shaker with which, through the aid of one Cocoa Puffs seal and $1.75, you are now self-liquidated—and you have the media and the cereal bowl.

THE CEREAL COUNTER

A parent has a number of choices to counter the media and the cereal bowl.
The first strategy would be to educate Tracey and Kermit on the manipulation of the cereal manufacturers. A good lesson is to buy the cereal, and while eating the product discuss the value of the cereal's nutrition and the worth of the premium offer.
Even a kid will soon discover that a plastic disc lasts for only one spin and that perhaps a sounder idea is to buy cereal for taste and nutrition and go to a toy store for spinners. A presweetened cereal ought to be honestly discussed with the child as an expensive item, and the price and quality should be debated frankly. Maybe the children will

---

[5] Ron Goulart, *The Assault on Childhood* (Los Angeles, Calif.: Shelbourne Press, 1969), p. 248.

the media and the cereal bowl

begin understanding cost differences and manipulation. The cereal bowl is certainly a logical place for most parents to begin and an opportunity to start training an effective consumer.

If logic fails a parent can forbid television viewing on Saturday mornings and be steeled against extortion in the supermarket. The world may be a better place for it.

The Great American Adult Cereal Recipe

...By the folks who brought you milled corn, sugar, salt, and malt flavoring with vitamin A, sodium ascorbate, ascorbic acid, thiamine (B_1), riboflavin (B_2), niacinamide, vitamin D, pyridoxine (B_6), folic acid, and a few harmless softeners.

When you whip up a batch of SALMON COOKIES using Oozo's Kron-ites—you'll be in seventh heaven.

EASY SALMON COOKIES

1/3 cup margarine (Kron-marg) or butter (Kron-butt).

1 can No. 300 red sockeye salmon (Kron-swim).

18 cups Oozo's Kron-ites.

1. Measure margarine into a child's sled saucer; melt over a number 3 can of Sterno and add a fifth of vodka. Add salmon until they melt gently. Remove from heat.
2. Add Kron-ites cereal; stir until vodka begins to turn crimson.
3. Spread warm mixture in larded 22 x 14¼ x 6 1/3-inch pan. Using waxed paper (Kron-wax), press firmly into even layer. Write your name and each family member's name on each square. Note: "John" for "Johnnie," since squares will be small.

Yield: 62 worthless 2 5/8-inch squares. Now throw away the squares and drink the vodka.

four quick money-making media specials

11

MAKING MONEY CHATTING ON THE TELEPHONE: CONFESSIONS OF A CALL-IN HOST

One of the Great American Institutions is the listener call-in to a radio or television talk host. The caller picks up the phone and dials the program's number to ask a question, make a comment, or to chat with a guest expert. The format allows people out there in Radio or TV Land a chance to strike a telling blow for a new highway, against minority housing, for a new downtown stadium, or about whatever news event is swirling in the public's consciousness.

The media strategies of the call-in combine the immediacy of the phone and the distance of radio and television. The phone is personal, because you make the call and you are in one-to-one contact with another person. A radio call-in show is a two-way telephone conversation between two faceless people upon whom many faceless listeners eavesdrop. In the television version, you at least can see the talk show host and guest, but of course the caller remains faceless and so does the audience. The methods of controlling such a diverse situation are not always easy or successful:

Service

Caller: Hello, Jim!

Host: Yes, speaking.

Caller: Say, I bought a new car ninety days ago, and the **DAMN THING'S** been in the service shop for thirty days. Every time I ask the service manager, he says they need another couple of days. What do you think I should do?

four quick money-making media specials

Host: Well, Ed, as a car dealer, what do you recommend this guy should do about his car?

Ed: Well, I hope he doesn't burn it in front of my showroom. Ha! Ha! Actually, he should do business with a community-oriented dealer.

Host: What's that, Ed? A dealer who sponsors softball and bowling teams?

Ed: No, not just that. We donate cars to driver's education classes, too.

Host: Well, how about the car? If it was my car, I'd tell you to **TAKE IT AND STICK IT.**

Ed: Well, I guess if it were my car I'd sell it.

Host: Thank you for calling, sir, and I hope you have more luck with the next car!

The host of a call-in show has a number of strategic gambits to unleash on the public. Most advantageously he controls the buttons that connect and disconnect all incoming calls. Most callers are on a seven-second delay that screens obscene or particularly obnoxious phone callers. When the host wishes to terminate a call he simply hits the button.
If the caller is nasty, the host can say, "Thank you very much and have a good day," all the while talking into a dead phone, already having clicked off the caller. In this fashion, the listening audience thinks that the host handled the caller with acumen; in reality, however, he tapped him off and then chatted with absolutely no one on the line.
The caller who complained of his disabled car was treated to a two-way discussion between the host and the guest that never provided an answer to his question. An answer to the caller might have been a suggestion to contact the automobile manufacturer's regional representative for prompt resolution of the problem. However, the listeners heard the host terminate the conversation with an airy, "Thank you for calling, sir, and I hope you have more luck with the next car." The caller never had an opportunity to press for more information since by then, he was holding a dead line.

GREAT AMERICAN CLICK-OFF LINES

"You have every right to your opinion, sir...why don't you have a hole drilled in your head and pass as a bowling ball?"

"729-1200 is our number, and we are talking with America's answer to Adolf Hitler."

"It takes all kinds, folks. And now a word from America's Number One Fortified Donut Mix. Oh, are you still on the line?"

"Please call again, ma'am. Preferably after you have had brain surgery."

"Got to run, friend...keep up the good political work and maybe Millard Fillmore will come back and you'll have a presidential candidate that matches your philosophy."

The call-in host can control a show through a number of other strategies as well. A caller has little knowledge of the advertising and time schedule of the program for that particular day. Most hosts can limit both the callers' and the guests' speaking time by claiming some media event is going to occur, ranging from an advertisement to that old clock forcing a change of subjects. By hanging on, the caller is retarding the wheels of technological progress. In postponing a station break, he perhaps is causing thousands of listeners hardship—although it is difficult to tell how. If the caller persists in chatting an effective device is to remind him of Federal Communication Commission regulations, and let him fantasize the spectre of one hundred government agents surrounding his house for chatting too long on a call-in show.

A similar advantage is the simple fact that the host is host, and he knows the director, producer, and everyone else concerned with the operation. A guest or caller immediately recognizes that he is functioning in someone else's territory, and an effective host will reinforce this position in a number of ways. A Johnny Carson will tell an "in" audience joke that only regulars will understand. Other hosts look away while the guest speaks or force the guest and caller into areas of nonspecialty and subsequent stupidity. Nothing is so deadly as for an author-guest to realize that the host is focusing on a minor point in Chapter 2 while ignoring the theme of the Great American Novel. An obvious counter-strategy for the guest is a direct affront such as, "I don't want to talk about that." Yet, with book buyers out there among the listeners, a surly demeanor could mean fewer sales for the author. And if the guest author is not willing to take the Great American Risk, he remains boxed and disastrously manipulated by the host.

Birds

Host: The flight of starlings is Octoberish. . .am I right?

Guest: Well, I'm not sure. . .my book is on the Civil War.

Host: Yes, but isn't it true that starlings were released only twenty-five years after the termination of hostilities?

Guest: I'm afraid I don't know. . .my book ends with Andrew Johnson.

Although the host can control the caller through click-outs, by knowing the schedule, and by forcing irrelevant questions, he faces a number of communication problems. There is scant live feedback in media presentations on radio or television. The callers may seem tedious and the guests verbose; yet the host has no immediate public response to which he may adjust. In a sense, like most electronic media and despite caller responses, call-in shows exist in a sealed time capsule. For the period on the air, hardly any information leaks in from the real world, ironic since call-ins are supposed to represent a keep-in-touch-with-the-world format for the public. Most programs and callers are topic centered, and nothing short of an on-site earthquake can stop the flow of conversation about burglar-proof locks, inflation, or income tax reform. The host and guest labor in the studio fundamentally cordoned off from reality, and only after the program ceases does the real world intrude.

four quick money-making media specials

Another communication problem for a host is the demands on his content selections by station ownership and sponsors. While the host attempts to create an interesting format, program directors, sponsors, and often public interest groups fight to prevent him from attacking their position or product. A sponsor calls the station and speaks of fair play and libel. The station management has a choice: accede to the demands, thereby saving advertising revenue; move into safer topic areas; or assert the station's right to free expression. A few stations can afford to fight, but the majority easily acquiesce to demands. It is no wonder that consumer problems often are sadly neglected, while consumer products and services are emphasized. The airwaves abound with invitations to buy products, but there is little advice available for the consumer if some of the advertisers' promises fall short. And a cynic might ask, why not? Private radio and television stations exist primarily for profit, and the host is the public image member of the profit team.

The strongest weapon for the consumer who feels manipulated by the host or station policies is to tune out. If enough listeners make the fundamental decision to ignore that particular program, the rating services will reveal a decline in audience. If media advertising is effective, the listener drop-off will cause a subsequent effect on sales and a change in station attitudes toward call-in abuses. A disgruntled listener can also call or write the station manager and sponsor, citing specific grievances. This strategy is particularly potent when combined with the tune-out.

Finally, zealous consumers can take on the host over the airwaves. However, the seven-second delay and the topic-switching power of the host make this gesture a form of communication suicide. But if you must, remember the following media behavior suggestions:

1. Ask the host for specific definitions.

2. Never allow the host's *ad hominem* arguments (attacks on you personally and not on the issue) to obscure the issue and place you on the defensive.

3. Ask the host questions instead of continually answering questions the host asks you.

4. Keep a careful record of the host's positions on your topic, and cite contradictions.

5. Stay cool—never lose your temper.

To make money chatting on the telephone is not an easy task for a call-in host or the station. Despite the seven-second delay, the broadcast is live, potentially explosive; and it demands a firm control, a quick mind, and a cool temper. If you have these characteristics, perhaps you can replace the following washout:

***

Gentlemen:

Having just watched your Friday night call-in, I am at a loss to explain why a public service station allows Irv Rein to appear on the air. He displayed the following negative qualities:

1. Clumsy, inaccurate, and generally inadequate use of language.
2. Lack of information on the topic of consumer credit—the lawyer had to correct him on his misapprehension.
3. Annoying repetition of the mindless ejaculation, "You know."
4. Rudeness to callers, from, "You're on the air"—which callers obviously did not understand as a signal to talk—to interrupting callers, to abruptly concluding the call before the caller could possibly have felt any satisfaction with the answer.

If your station cannot afford properly qualified people for its programs, it should not attempt the kind of program that requires skill, judgment, eloquence, objectivity, and good manners.

Yours sincerely,
O.D.

***

THE GREAT AMERICAN COOKBOOK: FAST PRINT DOUGH

If you would like to enter the media world and you earned at least a *C* in Creative Writing, try writing a cookbook. A cookbook is fun to write, and your prestige in the neighborhood will bound to the top of the cocktail party circuit. In addition, the local newspapers will run a picture of you signing autographs for book buyers; and since cookbooks sell steadily for a number of years, you can afford buying more food for practice.

```
╔══════════════════════════════════════╗
║                                      ║
║         Wilbus                       ║
║         Hermes                       ║
║                                      ║
║      NOTED Author                    ║
║       WILL BE AT THE                 ║
║     Chestnut Book Shoppe             ║
║    TO AUTOGRAPH HIS NEWEST BOOK      ║
║      Four Minutes to Eggs            ║
║                                      ║
╚══════════════════════════════════════╝
```

The first thing a prospective cookbook writer needs is an angle. No one is going to publish your book if you write a simple, straightforward explanation of how to cook food. This kind of book really is a cooking encyclopedia, and it already has been written, and very well. *The Fannie Farmer Boston Cooking School Cookbook* will tell the cook how to blanch, braise, barbecue, saute, deep fat fry, poach, steam, and stew. But out there in the Great American Food World are millions of people who want either to be the center of attention in the kitchen, to lose weight, or to seduce someone through the magic of mallard eggs in tarragon flavored aspic.

A cookbook can be written for people who:
- hate to cook
- are too busy
- are too lazy
- want to be a gourmet on a cheapskate's budget
- want to lose weight while enjoying meals
- see themselves as relaxing with their guests while dinner cooks
- love artichokes, cheese, or raisins

The important strategy is for the author to appear to be specific in point of view, yet broad enough in appeal to reach significant audiences. The majority of Americans

four quick money-making media specials

view themselves at one time or another as busy, lazy, poor, reducing, relaxing, or hung up on a single food. A cookbook easily could be dedicated to one of these types. A clever cookbook writer will not write a book for left-footed soccer kickers with tennis elbows, but will instead create an illusion of specialness.

> *This book is dedicated to*
> *folks who rise before 8:45 A.M.*

The majority of cookbooks reveal their special point of view in pithy revelations of how the author came to write the book. It is important to note that the cook is whimsical about his or her unusual qualifications. A cookbook writer ought not to be depressing about motives, since cooking is fun, joyous, and adventuresome. Betty Wason of *Dinners That Wait*[1] learned many of her exotic recipes while wandering around Europe as a foreign correspondent. Arlene Cardozo, who wrote *The Liberated Cookbook*,[2] was inspired as a youngster by her mother's example of calmly serving delicious hors d' oeuvres to twenty legislators and the governor who unexpectedly dropped by in the midst of her mother's bathing Ms. Cardozo's chicken-poxed sister, and shortly after a mental patient had painted their grand piano white with gold spots. In the meantime, Richard Gehman, who wrote *The Haphazard Gourmet*[3] was so inspired by Alexandre Dumas's celebrated *Le Grand Dictionnaire de Cuisine* that he decided to publish the cookbook that stewed around inside of him. And Ellen Ross embarked on the road to writing the *Reduce and Enjoy It Cookbook*,[4] because her husband promised her a return trip to Europe if she lost fifteen pounds. If some of these rationales seem less than earth shaking, recall that cookbooks compete on the bookseller's shelf like so much canned fruit; if the special view is not cute, urgent, or quaintly slapdash, it will not move.

The second crucial strategy in preparing a cookbook is to present recipes in a unique fashion. A recipe calling simply for ¼ teaspoon thyme, ½ bay leaf, 3 pints water, and a 5-pint saucepan with a few other accouterments does not make interesting reading. The recipe has to include some kind of story. Ms. Wason's book combines advice as to what quality guest should be served the dish with a running commentary on when to prepare and serve each item. For example, Step 5 of a recipe for late supper eggs includes such instructions as setting the table, filling the coffee pot with water, and the approximate time for the cook/hostess to dress and apply her makeup. The appeal is similar to that of an Army manual for raw recruits and is reassuring to a fledgling cook who worries about etiquette.

The appeal of *The Liberated Cookbook* is in its homey, personal asides from the author, who includes warm childhood memories, quotable adages from great aunts, and friendly gossip about her husband's colorful guests. Ms. Cardozo also supplies an "Idea Model" basic recipe, resembling a cook's adaptation of a business school's marketing model based on a steel plant. The appeal here is for business school graduates who want to learn to cook.

[1] Betty Wason, *Dinners That Wait* (Garden City, N.Y.: Doubleday, 1962).
[2] Arlene Cardozo, *The Liberated Cookbook* (New York: David McKay, 1972).
[3] Richard Gehman, *The Haphazard Gourmet* (New York: Scribners, 1966).
[4] Ellen L. Ross, *Reduce and Enjoy It Cookbook* (New York: Collier, 1963).

four quick money-making media specials

Mr. Gehman presents his recipes in an anti-cookbook style, claiming that fried chicken is boring, spending pages on irrelevancies such as his feelings about de Gaulle, and lambasting the fork as an unnecessary utensil.

Ellen Ross uses the well-worn "so many days" recipes for weight loss combined with calorie portions similar to this *GACC's* version:

Dinner: 530 calories

Orange a la Stewed Chicken—trimmed nicely to balance your gram
intake times 44 which is the combined height of 8½ women. . .325 calories
½ cup broccoli ala Green Hornet . . . . 35 calories
one new potato. . . . . 45 calories
angel food cake, one 2-inch slice. .110 calories
coffee with skimmed milk and saccharine. . . . . 5 calories

---

Fatty dieters like planning recipe menus for every meal and can count to their hearts' content in this version. If none of these recipe versions is appetizing, the variations are endless:

Allergy-Free Meals
Plumber's Hot Food Specials
Retired Officer's Exotic Memoirs
Quarterback's Favorite Barbecues

Fixing Food on the Expressway
Eating Like the Animals
Food for Lovers

BEYOND COOKBOOKS

If the cookbook world seems narrow, you can write "how to do it" books on fixing gutters, flying kites, or tuning an engine. The style is similar to that used in cookbooks, but adapted so that the author writes about years of awkwardness ending with the mastery of crocheting through patient practice. If that appeal fades, medical recovery books are a good possibility if you survived—*My Nine Lives as a Cardiac Case* or *Psoriasis: Affliction or Salvation*?
If all else fails, try writing a children's story with this handy, all-purpose recipe:

One mouse (friendly)
Two kiddies (half-baked)
One mommy (harried)
One daddy (big)

One postman (friendly)
Three bullies (half-baked)
Two sheep (harried)
One house (big)

A Perfect Soap Opera Script

Scene: lawyer's office, mental institution, bedroom

Fade In:

Dr. John: Liz, is William coming to discuss your divorce?

Liz: I should hope so, dear. . .he decided last night that little Joey is old enough to be told the truth about us.

Dr. John: Hmmm. Who told him about Ina Jane's affair with Dr. Steve?

Liz: Charlotte told him at the club after breaking the news that she's heading for Aruba to have her baby.

William: Hello, all. Oh, don't be startled. I know everything and I now understand.

Liz: William. . .I didn't mean it to happen this way. After John cut out my mole, I felt differently toward you.

Dr. John: You see. . .

William: No, no. . .I understand. I now have my architecture practice going well. . .I just received that Holstein contract.

Liz: Why, William—that's marvelous! You've wanted that award for two years. Congratulations, darling. . . .Goodbye, John.

Fade Out.

JEFFERSON CARPET TV AD

Fade In:

Hi, Folks, Alistair Jones here for JEFFERSON CARPET. . .914 South Newport. . .your friendly carpet center.

TONIGHT AND TONIGHT ONLY we will carpet your entire home for the incredibly low price of 129 dollars and 50 cents. That's right, for a limited time only, the folks at Jefferson Carpet will carpet any size home for just $129.50 in a dazzling array of carpet colors. . . the latest, newest bright reds, soothing greens, earthy rusts, yellows as bright as Sunkist's finest. . .

AND FRIENDS, you need no money down at Jefferson Carpet. . .the folks at Jefferson Carpet are offering special financing for this one big offer of the year. BUY IN NOVEMBER and you will not pay a red cent until Groundhog's Day in February. The number to call is 215-4600 for a visit from one of our carpet specialists. That's Jefferson's call center—215-4600. Operators will be on duty for the next 24 hours to take your call, and remember, if we sound cheap, think of what the other guy is making! Now back to our feature movie, Burt Lancaster in that swashbuckler, *The Crimson Pirate*.

Fade Out.

SECTION FOUR
STYLISTIC STRATEGIES

In a society so image oriented, it is natural that style
becomes a principle strategy. If the producer's style
is effective it ought to encourage consumers to interact
with the producer in a manner advantageous to the latter.
This section discusses several communication styles
that some producers have successfully cultivated to force
unlucky consumers to relate to them with unfortunate outcomes.
The styles range from the delicately nurtured Princesses
to the "Queen-for-a-Day" bridal shop atmosphere
to a carefully designed Coke bottle, and it includes a set
of occupational styles - those of doctors and taxicab drivers.
The reader will find that regardless of how a style is acquired,
it can become a major undertaking for a consumer to penetrate
the style of a great practitioner.

the great american princess: a stylistic myth

12

FOR THE BUDDING ROYALTY IN YOUR HOUSE...

THE GREAT AMERICAN Princess game
ALL AGES

© BARKER MOTHERS

THE PRINCESS GAME
WAS DESIGNED BY AMERICA'S TOP PRINCESSES! DO YOU WANT THE CHINA-DOLL SECRETS OF **SANDRA DEE?** THE DARK, SMOKEY MYSTIQUE OF **JACKIE KENNEDY ONASSIS?** THE COOL CHARM OF **MARISA BERENSON?**
LEARN THESE GREAT STRATEGIES!

THE MOTHER PUT-DOWN!
THE FATHER RIP-OFF!
THE BOYFRIEND EXTORTION!
THE STORE RETURN SMILE!
THE RICH UNCLE INGRATIATOR!

In our primarily sexist society, the chief acquirer of goods is the woman. Through role designation, she is entrusted with family purchasing. Besides being responsible for the cleaning and baby sitting, the woman has been reared to purchase, while the male is groomed to produce and provide the income for the woman's consuming. The natural extension of this role bifurcation is the production of a super consumer—the Great American Princess (GAP)—who by her upbringing and development becomes the ultimate purchaser of advanced technology and premium brands—*the best* money can buy.

In a society so relentlessly materialistic, it is only logical that we have produced a mythological Goddess of Consumption—the GAP. Though in every section of the country there are both men and women who dress and acquire in sensational fashion, we have created a female figure as the archetype for our admiration and scorn. We envy the GAP because she is the possessor of fine adornments that we covet. Yet, we also have contempt for her because we realize that unending acquisition is part of a twisted value system. The lure of advertising, the peer group pressure of upward-striving neighbors, the superb technology of our age—all these combine to make us super wishers, if not super consumers. The GAP serves as a symbol for the transference of our own apprehension and guilt feelings. The GAP is our mythical symbol of the post-industrial consuming machine— reared, raised, freed, and functioning to fill a role dictated by a sexist society. We are all part GAP. Although few people reach the pure GAP state in attitude and performance, most of us share at least some of her most obnoxious characteristics.

This chapter considers the characteristics that make up the GAP stereotype. The male's treatment of the GAP also will be analyzed, because ultimately he is the producer who comes into greatest conflict with this super consumer. His behavior, often so irrational toward her, is a demonstration of what occurs in communication when a culture produces a package so slick and so threatening that many people respond to it emotionally and violently.

HER STEREOTYPE

The stereotype of the Princess begins with the notion of her origins. She is not the type of princess born into the role, such as Princess Anne of England, nor even the princess who marries into the role, such as Princess Grace of Monaco. These princesses are old-fashioned products of another era and sensibility. The Great American Princess I am discussing is made, not born, to royalty. She is the Princess of Consumerism, and her domain is Elizabeth Arden's Beauty Salon; her staff is an Alexandra de Markoff blusher; and her power is reflected in her charge card.[1] She began her reign in the aisles of the supermarket, crying for Fruit Loops; she developed in the local department store returning ill-fitting party dresses; and she blossomed the day she was issued her own charge card. Sound familiar? It should; we all are touched by this myth.

Another distinction to clarify about the Princess is what she does *not* look like. She isn't your pale, sexless, suburban housewife running around in a buff-colored Volkswagen Squareback, clothed in a rumpled wool sweater, tweed skirt, and a pair of Red Cross oxfords. Nor would you find the Great American Princess milking cows, garbed in a Princess Peggy $8.95 Sunday supplement special, touring the West in a Winnebago motor home, devouring hog jowls and grits, or scrubbing floors in anticipation of her husband's Friday night poker party. The Princess rarely touches farm animals; she orders her clothes from Saks, tours in a jet, lunches sparingly, and the only scrubbing she does is of her face.

In a sense, the Princess is a strategy of presentation. She can be Black, Greek, Italian, Jewish, Norwegian, or Arabic, and still be a Princess.[2] As long as she understands the rules, any young lady can play the Princess game.

[1] The Elizabeth Arden charge card advertises that "Pink Power is the effect of the Elizabeth Arden Charge Card in Salons around the world. Carry yours always for maximum shopping ease, convenience, and correct billing—and for a wow welcome when you travel."

[2] Julie Baumgold, "The Persistence of the Jewish American Princess," *New York Magazine,* March 22, 1971, p. 25. Though many people regard the Princess as a Jewish phenomenon, Baumgold makes the point that neither economic class nor religion is crucial to the development of a Princess and cites Bette Davis, Yoko Ono, and Wendy Vanderbilt as examples of Princesses whose backgrounds differ widely.

the great american princess: a stylistic myth

What is the game? The game is developing a style in which people are forced to relate to you in a certain manner. You receive, they give. You expect, they provide. Yet throughout this procedure, there never is a suspicion of charity but rather a feeling that plying the Princess with gifts is only natural, and is at one with the Universe.

GREAT BEGINNINGS

Typically, the Princess myth begins at an early age. Even though she is not royalty, one cannot expect her style to be shaped and become effective in a short period of time. The training begins when the Princess-to-be is still in the crib. The family hovers above the baby, gesticulating wildly, cooing and clucking, and—most importantly—rarely leaving her side. When Baby screams from colic the household freezes in a paroxysm of anxiety.

> "Does Baby feel okay?"
>
> "Harry, bring Cute'ums a rattle."
>
> "Come to Mommy, Sweetie."
>
> "Turn down that TV, Billy. Baby is trying to sleep."
>
> "Doctor, I know this is silly, but..."

Future training of the Princess, according to observer Julie Baumgold,[3] continues at the dinner table. Harry gets the tail of the T-bone, while Baby gets the center of the steak, and, God forbid, if Baby uncovers a bit of gristle amidst the juicy center, the offending cartilage is spat into Mommy's waiting palm. A Princess spits into the hand;

The GAP Test

		Yes	No
1.	Did you compete cutely with Mommy for Daddy's attention?	___	___
2.	Did you ever wash the dishes? (Note—except for holidays when showing off for relatives.)	___	___
3.	Did you buy items of clothing in multiples?	___	___
4.	Did you read *Marjorie Morningstar* and weep?	___	___
5.	Did you pet on first dates?	___	___

Key: 1. yes 2. no 3. yes 4. no 5. no

If you scored correctly in all five categories, you are a true Great American Princess. If you scored four out of five, you are an 80% Princess. If you scored less than 80%, order the Princess Kit and at least consider buying multiple copies of this book.

---

[3] Baumgold, p. 27.

the great american princess: a stylistic myth

the rest of us know that if we are lucky enough to get steak, we are more than happy to swallow any impurities the cow harbors. The true Princess eats only the protein-rich yolk of the egg, the unbored, lightly matured ear of corn, the sole whole cherry on the Danish, the small end of the sparerib, and the cheesiest slice of the pizza. If a pimple should arise from all this nourishment, the child's servants—Mommy and Daddy—will rush forth with dermatological remedies from alcohol to Stri-Dex.

The result of all this work and training is the image of a carefully coiffed consumer who knows her way around beauty salons, Bonwit's, and PTA boards. She is the girl comedian Mel Brooks immortalized on David Susskind's television show as a real dating problem because of her high expectations. If you shake her hand, said Brooks, *she expects a date.* Kiss her a peck and *you owe a diamond ring.* If you get a little dirty, *it's marriage.* And if you don't marry her—*you pay alimony anyway.*

PRINCESS PUTDOWNS

The whole idea of marrying a GAP may by now turn off many red-blooded American males, but the scenerio implies some rather interesting fringe benefits. In fact, many of those men may be underselling their own potential for a great life by overlooking the Princess as a marriage partner. An important part of the myth glamorizes the Princess's adeptness at handling and putting down protagonists in face-to-face interactions.
The Princess is alleged to be great at cocktail parties and unlikely to burden a mate as a "clinging vine." A true Princess is superb at discussing a thousand different subjects without truly understanding any of them. She has mastered a number of responses that are difficult for the questioner to pursue.

"Getting Abstracted"

In this example, the fundamental question of attendance never is answered. Instead, the Princess leaps ahead to a more sophisticated level of discussion, the sleazy quality of the third act. Her use of the term "tacky" implies a condescending attitude toward the ensemble that, at the same time, does not invite his response. To ask a Princess why the third act was tacky is potentially suicidal. First, his question implies viewing a dance without any critical appreciation of what he saw. Second, his inquiry sets him up for a discussion of dance esthetics that, unless he has read *Newsweek's* latest piece on modern dance, will leave him duly impressed and out of the game. The Princess's move from the specified dance performance to the general subject of dance is of course strategic and if executed with any kind of sophistication, will leave the innocent questioner—who originally held all the cards—bewildered. After all, he did see the performance from the third row. Label him *gulled*.

"Can I Help You?"

In this example, the male is initiating what appears to be a promising line of exchange. He has money and infected sinuses, and for these reasons, he's off to a prestigious, ennobling vacation. The Princess counters with immediate recognition of his exotic paradise and then advises the unasking foil on an excellent eating spot. The use of nautical terms, of "cafe" instead of restaurant, of the name of an alleged manager or waiter is bait that sets him up for the kill.

MANIPULATOR ARUBA 2

"WHO'S JOSE?"

"DID I SAY JOSE? (HESITATION TO REVEAL A FAMILY/RICH PERSON'S SECRET) JOSE IS THE BEST BARTENDER IN ARUBA. TELL HIM YOU WANT A PRINCESS SPECIAL OVER ICE WITH A TRACE OF LEMON."

WHEN USED WITH ARUBA 1, THIS CARD IS GOOD FOR FIVE SPACES TOWARDS "TOTAL CONTROL"

"A Favorite Haunt"

The game continues with the "he" being led into one maddening position after another. If the Princess is particularly adept, her foil ends up asking about hotel accommodations, airplane tickets, and sightseeing tours. If the Princess is single, she may be invited along—but not for anything dirty.

"Man's Bestiality"

MANIPULATOR

THIS CARD MAY BE KEPT UNTIL NEEDED OR SOLD

"DID YOU SEE THE REDSKINS PLAY LAST SUNDAY?"

"(INDIGNANT BUT STILL FRIENDLY) FOOTBALL IS A REENACTMENT OF MAN'S MOST SAVAGE BESTIAL TENDENCIES."

"I'M NOT A BEAST!"

"OH, I WASN'T TALKING ABOUT YOU, HONEY. I MEANT THE MALE SPECIES IN GENERAL."

ACTUAL SIZE

This particular game is effective, because it combines some of the most characteristic Princess themes in one short exchange. The big, mean male who struts his machismo around a 100-yard football field, yelping such inanities as "47 Power Left," is a beast—but the cool Princess sees football for its most obvious trait as a little pathetic. She didn't say it was pathetic, but most sensitive males would understand the thrust. Her last sally is the type of cut reserved only for worst enemies. He's not a beast, not even a regular male, but probably some kind of harmless neuter.

The two main themes of the Great American Princess at parties often distressingly combine ambiguity and dominance. But in the institution of both themes, the victim rarely perceives genuine hostility. And why should he? The point of the Princess's strategy is to *look good*—to walk away from each encounter with a magnificent smile and a toss of her well-coiffed hair—in *control*. And if you deplore the absence of real communication in these examples, reflect on the purpose of the cocktail party, an institution constructed to facilitate a number of people to get to know each other *fast*. Such necessarily speedy transactions rarely promote deep understanding with a discussion partner.

THE PRINCESS AND SEX

Another peculiarity of the Princess is her alleged attitude toward premarital sex. The Princess is introduced to flirting when she plays courtship games with Daddy. "How about a date?" "Where do we go?" The Mommy knows that she is competing with her five-year-old for Daddy's attention; but she usually doesn't mind, because the care and breeding of a true Great American Princess demands this training. If a Princess is properly developed, she begins her sexual life at summer camps during her early teens. A camp is perfect for these innocent trysts, because nature is sweet, fresh, and beautiful. At home, the parents can conjure images of Salem cigarette advertisements with camper lovers racing across open fields to embrace briefly, then to take a nice, healthy walk. This kind of introduction to kissing is far better than grabbing and clutching in a tacky garage. . .a little kissing, a few brushes, but nothing really dirty.

This careful nurturing of the Princess's sex life produces a submyth—the Great American Tease. A tease is someone who through a series of verbal and nonverbal signals, promises sexual activity that will never be delivered. The intense stare, the melting crush while dancing, the snug bodysuit—all promises of a great future. These moves, like political slogans, are lead-ons to an empty future—moments not just right, a dress that must never show a wrinkle, a mother watching from the front window, all spelling *zero*. When he tries to move over in the front seat of a car she clings to the door like a mop to a wet floor; offer her a motel room, she offers him a non-Princess friend; buy her a lobster, he gets the empty claw. But he shouldn't despair, for she is saving herself for marriage when all that care and breeding will pay off in unleashed passion—a suitable reward for waiting so long. All the suitor needs is to buy a $1,500 engagement ring, to tolerate a $17,500 wedding, to finance a honeymoon on the leeward side of Aruba, and to hold a CPA's position for $35,000 and up—and she's landed.

ORDER NOW! NEW, 2ND EDITION PUT-DOWN CARDS!

A SERIES OF 143 LINES GATHERED BY PRINCESSES FROM NEW YORK TO LOS ANGELES! HERE'S JUST A SAMPLE!

SALE **SALE**

PUT-DOWN

"WHAT'S A GREAT LOOKING CHICK LIKE YOU DOING IN A PLACE LIKE THIS?"

"WAITING FOR A FRUITCAKE LIKE YOU TO SWEEP ME OFF MY FEET."

THIS CARD MAY BE KEPT UNTIL NEEDED OR SOLD

ACTUAL SIZE

SIZZLERS! FIRECRACKERS

DAZZLING REJOINERS TO END:
- TAXI DRIVER HASSLES —
- BARBECUE TIDBITTERS —
- LEERING BELLBOYS —

SEND $3.98 TODAY!

TO: GREAT LINES, INC.
ZINC, NEBRASKA

IF YOU DESIRE A PLAIN WRAPPER, WRITE P.W. ON ORDER
IF YOU WANT TO PSYCH MAILMAN, ASK FOR CLEAR WRAPPER

HOW DO MALES REALLY LAND PRINCESSES?

The strategy for courting a Princess begins with the understanding that her Mommy and Daddy are the suitor's opponents. Why should an unkempt, unworthy bum make off with such a sweet, delicate prize? He doesn't deserve her! In fact, no one deserves her, so let's get on with piercing the first line of defense.

The Princess, like any member of royalty, is not picked up off the street like many non-Princesses. This means that great hustling lines shouted from inside a car window are empty fire power.

Useless...useless...useless. Great American Princesses must be courted strategically. They can be found at such high-class places as museums, churches, synagogues, or art classes. But a pursuer must be selective: a Norman Rockwell show or an antique place setting exhibit is unlikely to produce a Princess of the age he wants—so he looks for the French Impressionists and macramé workshops.

the great american princess: a stylistic myth

If the pursuer can't manage an introduction, there are some lines that might interest a Princess:

HUMOR LINE

"I'm a war bond salesman for the UJA."

COUNTER LINE

"What's a nice girl like you doing in a lousy place like this?"

"I know you! You're a prostitute I saw entertaining at a fraternity rush!"

The advantage of humor and counter lines is that they afford the Princess an opportunity to demonstrate her subtle sense of irony. The suitor *must* respect her, since he uses only the lines that a person of some intelligence would understand as parodies. In addition, the counter-lines enable her to look good by countering counter-lines with bright retorts: "What's a nice girl like you doing in a lousy place like this?" "Oh, I thought this was the waiting room at the Penn Central Station." Or, "You're a prostitute I saw entertaining a fraternity rush!" "That's right, did your Mommy give you the ten bucks yet?" A further advantage of the counter-exchange is that it allows the Princess to role-play sexually without making any deep, personal commitments. (Remember Romeo and Juliet on the telephone.) If a relationship begins on a light-hearted level of parody, one can't be too disappointed when it ends with her father flashing lights into his parked car and insisting that Marilyn come in from what might have been debauchery.

Another excellent place to court Princesses is the suburban shopping center that serves as a magnet on Saturdays. Hanging around the center will yield an endless cornucopia of beautifully dressed, mascara-smeared, unmarried Princesses sailing through the more expensive shops, buying a belt there, a shirt here, and a one-pound box of Mint Meltaways for later.

GREAT AMERICAN "STOP" LINES

1. Dress as a hippie and stand in front of Bonwit Teller. Not a dirty hippie, but a clean-cut, long-haired hippie. Princesses love to take home clean hippies. And if you are bright, clean up slowly, and show earning potential, you could become a Prince.

2. Get a part-time position as a salesman in a specialty shoe store. The image of placing the shoe on the Princess's foot is irrevocably tied to the Cinderella myth; and though the job is back-breaking—tugging and pulling—it offers chances of meeting Princesses as great as those of a lumberjack meeting trees in western Washington.

the great american princess: a stylistic myth

Now that the pursuer has met and hopefully arranged a date with the Princess, he has to get by the sentry system—the mother. When the doorbell rings, the mother leaps to greet the prospective husband with the swiftness of a lynx. The alacrity is necessary only for the mother's questioning, since the Princess needs at least an additional thirty minutes to prepare for the date. So he stands in the doorway waiting to exchange blows with a master inquisitor.

Now that's a bad exchange with a Princess's mother, because unless he is the right Farr, there is little chance of his controlling the conversation. A far better strategy is to know her husband's occupation and tailor answers to it.

Then the suitor follows with a quick attack on surgeons who leave sponges in patients' abdomens, finishing off with some observations on the kinds of people who enjoy cutting and watching blood spurt.

The reason for such an all-out attack on the mother is that it will force her to warn her daughter against future dates with a common butcher's son. Any Princess worth her blusher is not going to listen to orders and will insist on further dates. And since the suitor was losing because of his father's lowly occupation anyway, why should he play it straight? Well, now he has met the Princess and befuddled her mother. That leaves only the conquest of the Princess.

CONQUEST STRATEGIES

A woman lumped into the stereotype of the GAP is likely to be treated to a bizarre array of conquest tactics. The GAP, an exquisite package of elegant clothes, exotic smells, and great put-down lines, is not dated like most normal human beings. She must be landed like a prized, fighting, killer shark. The stalking male sees himself going off to battle as he combines some of the gamesmanship strategies with an intensity of maliciousness rarely seen in producer-consumer relations. He sees himself as the ultimate benefactor in this duet, and he demands the consumer be properly tamed before he starts paying off. So he sets off to corral the myth as a soldier, armed with an impressive arsenal of nasty probes and rejoinders. In this producer-consumer game, by his very actions he unknowingly lowers himself into another myth—*the male as supreme being.*

The myth of the male as the all-conquering hero leads him into both comical and ruthless gamesmanship strategies. A popular version revolves around the Princess's clothing consciousness. In this tactic, he attempts to unnerve the Princess's sense of social aristocracy by embarrassing her publicly. Before the date, he runs out to a cheap discount store and buys a light blue, rayon sports jacket that originally was $35.95 in 1964 but has plummeted to a tempting price of $9.95 or three for $16.50. On his first date with the Princess he wears the price-tagged jacket. She asks with more than a hint of discomfort, "Are you going to remove that tag?" The suitor, feigning puzzlement, dumbfoundedly gropes for the tag with a free hand while offering profuse, if off-handed, apologies. The act of removing the tag is such a mammoth favor for the clothes-conscious Princess that the suitor now thinks he is beginning to assert control. "What if he decides to replace the tag?" broods the Princess. He imagines that the specter of his boorishly revealing the price of the jacket to her friends places the Princess in a one-down position that is frightening for her to contemplate. It might be...and yet, when one shadowboxes with a myth, a number of surprises should be expected.

"I'm glad you're wearing the price tag, Harvey...my friends love bargains."

"A price tag? Oh, I didn't notice, Harvey."

"If you insist on taking it off, Harvey, but I really don't care."

the great american princess: a stylistic myth
....
147

There are variations of the above conquest strategy. In order to capitalize on the Princess's image of herself as a person of class and quality, the tactician may try to rattle her with the threat of lower class vehicle transportation. When they reach the curb in front of her home, he lets her ask about the evening's transportation. He simply replies that he has lost his license, and either she drives or they take a bus or hitchhike. The suitor hopes that the Princess will lose her carefully preened poise, imagining herself alighting at Alice's party from a semitruck hauling Rhode Island roosters.

If that tactic involves too much self-sacrifice, he might escalate to developing a strange gagging sound every ten minutes.

YOU DEVELOP AN ODD GAGGING SOUND EVERY TEN MINUTES

WHAT'S THAT? THAT NOISE!

WHAT? WHAT NOISE? =GRUK=

ADVANCE 1 SQUARE

STRATEGY SQUARES SHOW YOU THE WAY TO "TOTAL CONTROL"

the great american princess: a stylistic myth

148

He hopes that after a number of strange grunts that she will begin imagining that the noise is in her head. And when a person thinks she is going crazy, reasons our hustler, she rarely can control someone else's behavior.

Once the Princess is apprehensive about her date's embarrassing her with a price tag, a bus ride, or a croak, he quite dramatically moves to the next level of control—disdain and sarcasm. A straightforward question is met with mockery.

Princess mythology equates these traits of aggressive hostility with money-making potential. This kind of rudeness should then work, because the Princess—though perceiving herself as dainty and prim—needs men who make money. What better demonstration of those traits than the ability to be hostile toward a person of refinement who could do you favors?—A Princess.

A further opportunity to reinforce the control and increase the communication violence comes when the Princess begins to apologize for looking so good, for buying so much, and for consuming far more than her share. At this point, her date begins relentlessly agreeing with her about her duty to accept such gifts that obviously give her parents so much pleasure. This agreement, he thinks, will startle her, since he has already been so nasty in earlier treatment. But this agreement is used only for strategic contrast and has little to do with friendship. When she is thoroughly confused and her sterling silver squash blossom necklace is undulating in anticipation of launching her counterattack, he abruptly stops agreeing. The hook, he hopes, is sunk, and he moves to the ultimate weapon.

the great american princess: a stylistic myth

Now is the time for the silent treatment, which is a strategy based on the most deep-seated of all Princess stereotypes—the indulged child. She yells; he looks ahead without any trace of regret, pity, or understanding. The Princess should hate silence. Remember the mommy and daddy waving and cooing to amuse the Princess infant? Remember the mommy accepting the gristles of meat? All attention. Now absolute silence. And if the skeptic thinks the Princess will reject him because of his inconsiderate treatment of her, he is fond of recalling the following:

PRINCESS MARGARET MARRIED TONY

MARTHA MARRIED JOHN

EDITH MARRIED ARCHIE

Our hustler has now demonstrated counter-tactics for Princess conquests born out of desperation and mythology. He has endured the effective Princess put-downs and now feels that only by striking quickly and at vulnerable psychological soft spots can he conquer. Maybe it isn't so strange; how many of us have used similar tactics when trying to counter-control a manipulator?

THE REWARDS

The script for marrying a Great American Princess calls for considerable rewards for those who harpoon a Princess. At restaurants when the children act up, the Princess will crush them with violent orders—"Shut up, Mark"; "Eat with your fork, Stewart"; "Jenny, get off the floor"—and with the appearance of the waiter, she will move quickly from anger to smiling grace— "Would you mind bringing my son another fork?" When the husband needs a decorator's estimate, the Princess will move to the phone and consult the yellow pages list of possibilities. Most male readers will note that this activity is one he will be spared. And, if there exists a decorator who works cheaply and decorates magnificently, the Princess will find him. The decorator will paint, paper, and plaster to warm the cockles of a husband's cheap little heart.

If these rewards appear modest for putting up with such grief, remember the principle of regeneration. The Princess of today will become the Queen of tomorrow and the producer of our next generation of Princesses. The opportunity to eat at the breakfast table with a Queen and her court is not shared by Americans who dated simply normal human beings.

If the opportunity to eat regally is not enough, a suitor might consider the fact that he will have to become enormously wealthy. The Princess *demands* large hordes of money to enable her to garb her courtly body in furs, jewels, and I. Miller shoes. And the suitor must not forget that great amounts of costly, back-up maid services will be essential for the Princess.

LEDGER

One cleaning lady	$40 a day
Or live-in	$250 a month plus expenses
22 hours of baby sitting	$33 a week
Transactional Analysis Session	$12.50 apiece (group rate)
Yoga	$5 a session
Gardening Labor	$35 a week
Indoor Tennis	$300 a year (excluding apparel)

In addition, if the Princess has a mother, the husband is expected to pick up the expenses for her lodging, whether it's with the family, at the Green Meadows Rest Home, or the Deauville Hotel in Miami Beach. So he works! If he fancied himself as a teacher, he had better open a business college; if he thought a government job would be restful, he had better start selling to the government; if he thought running a gas station would be swell, he had better get into the transmission rebuilding business. He needs money to finance this operation. Remember, a true GAP does not ask a husband for something like a normal human being might—"Do you think...?" Instead, she announces—"Which of these two suits do you like better, Herman?" If you find the launching of a Princess frightening, you probably could not make a lot of money anyway.

If the reward of being driven to earn large amounts of money fails to thrill a suitor, consider this little speculation. It is rumored—*rumored*, mind you—that Princesses do not mind if their husbands dally on the side, as long as they pay off the Princess in worldly goods. What is a worldly good?

Worldly Goods Ledger

A lunchtime flirtation with a waitress	=	a little bauble (opal, sapphire)
A night with your secretary	=	A fur coat (sable, mink)
A weekend in Aruba with a model	=	A three-week summer vacation in Greece and a little sexual deprivation.
A move out of the house for three weeks	=	Major sexual deprivation and an Oldsmobile Cutlass Supreme with stereo and a new house.

the great american princess: a stylistic myth

But notice that the ledger rarely, if ever, equals divorce. As long as the sinner pays off and the extortion continues, the Princess really is quite happy. After all, the amount of gifts multiplies amidst the circumstances of guilt. Real human beings demand divorces, confiscate the silverware, make terrible scenes, and run to the nearest lawyer. A Princess may make trouble, but it is noise and not action. The move to the lawyer is probably a fake, and the lawyer knows that as well as the Princess does.

THE LAST GREAT AMERICAN PRINCESS

The Princess is a style created by the post-industrial revolution. That she expects to be treated to the spoils of its latest technology is a product of a land and culture thoroughly indoctrinated in producing and absorbing. That we may resent her is evidence that most of us recognize greed in our fellows and in ourselves; that we may fail to join in her quest may be more by accident than by design. Who can resist Lucien Piccard watches with gold inlaid diamonds? Who would prefer a ten-year-old car to a new one? Who enjoys suffering in the summer when the weather is 100 degrees? And for a couple thousand, cool air will blow you to sleep.

In addition, Princesses are as much victims of society as are other groups forced by circumstances into an unflattering style. In preliberation days, an intelligent woman had few opportunities to practice her cleverness in corporate or institutional societies. She was forced into a role of existing only for her husband and family. If he was a successful lawyer, doctor, or contractor, she could live well by accepting his offerings. And, instead of expending her energies toward worthwhile enterprises, she was left to squeeze and connive her largess from a gift-giving husband. She may have lived well, but her husband determined her fate since he defined the terms of their relationship.

That so many parents raised their baby daughters to serve in the Princess capacity was simply a granting of reality. In a male-oriented society the daughter must learn how to expect, to be clever and not threatening, to be demanding financially and not emotionally, to be a Princess and not a scrubwoman. If the child is suitably trained and then preserved through her teens she will be directed toward a deserving, high-earning male. The male must be a good provider or all the efforts of the parents go to waste. Therefore, the Princess's parents carefully select summer camps and qualify dates at the door.

The future of the Great American Princess syndrome may well go the way of such other archaic institutions as waves of immigrants and Great American Princes. The Prince, noticeable on slow Sundays in a Saint Laurent, color-coordinated shirt and sweater, with lightly tossed, hot-combed hair and a mincing walk, is primarily tedious. The Prince is boring, since he has little time to execute Prince practices; he pursues a business career for 12 hours a day. A similar fate may strike the Princess as new opportunities allow her greater emotional and vocational freedom. Parents discovering that Lauren can become a doctor may stop priming her to *marry* one. The liberated woman may be too busy to spend Herbert's money, or she may discover that she makes more than Herbert does.

AND OF COURSE,

THE PRINCESS GAME.©
GAME BOARD

ACTUAL SIZE 20" X 20"

WHERE YOUR MOVES MAKE THE DIFFERENCE BETWEEN PRINCESS AND PEON.

the rhetoric of the bridal salon

13

Even if she is not a GAP, any American girl can become transformed into a fairy princess when she goes to buy her wedding dress. Most brides think that this opportunity will be their only one to get married and therefore feel compelled to go all the way.

Going all the way in the bridal business means to celebrate the ritual all the way. A wedding expert, Marcia Seligson, claims that a formal bridal gown is worn by 84.5 percent of all first-time brides. The wedding industry, consisting of all products and services associated with the first marriage, contributes a mammoth $7 billion a year to our economy.[1] This business is large and pushy and plays on the illusion that marriage in America is forever, forever, and forever. So spend it all—it's your only chance.

Despite the cultural shock of the late sixties, with its frankness and emphasis on natural life styles, the American Wedding remains a stronghold of tradition. The wedding includes the standard practices, beginning with the selection of a large house of worship or hotel for the ceremony (catered by drones in black and white uniforms). The remainder of the rituals are observed scrupulously from "Do you promise" to the elegant, catered repast, Uncle Ben's official tossing rice, imported champagne, an unobtrusive obtrusive photographer, perishable cut flowers, and the inevitable, coy exit of the bride and groom. This four- to six-hour blowout costs in the thousands, money that could have been a down payment on a home. If you still are not dissuaded, the game formally begins with purchase of the key prop of the ritual—a real, store-bought, white lace, veil-attached Bridal Gown.

A girl who wants to play the Great American Bride must play the Go-to-the-Bridal-Salon Game to acquire her gown. In most cases, the prospective bride never again will

---

[1] Marcia Seligson, *The Eternal Bliss Machine* (New York: William Morrow & Co., 1973), p. 2.

the rhetoric of the bridal salon

enjoy the experience of owning a custom-fitted dress. Nor will she again have the delightful experience of being pampered, relentlessly fawned over ("Oh, I love short necklines on you, honey"), and sold a couple of yards of lace, net, and train for between $300 and $400.

THE SALE 1

Bride: "I'd like to try this on."
Saleslady: "What is the date of the wedding?"
Bride: "August Fourth."
Saleslady (in stunned disbelief): Of *this* year?"
Bride: "Why, of course."
Saleslady: "Do you wear a size 10?"
Bride: "Yes, I do."
Saleslady (in relief): "You're very fortunate. We have a few size 10's in stock."

THE BEGINNING

The object of the bridal shop strategy is to make the bride feel like the GAP feels every day. A GAP lives the Rhetoric of Expecting, and the bridal shop creates an environment where any girl can expect, if only on a temporary basis. Many of the shops use timeworn clichés to reinforce the opulence and specialness of the purchase. Some shops use the Grecian Goddess, the image of virginity, to create the right mood. One chain transforms its lobbies into Greek Temples with the ceiling wafting to a high point in the center, and a forest of Greek, not-for-spitting urns. One could argue that the atmosphere of a French bordello hardly would be appropriate for such an occasion, and yet the number of virgin brides is not on the increase.

In most shops, the first live acquaintance for the bride is with the lady at the desk, where appointments are made, names recorded, and salesladies assigned. This ritual was altered in one chain shop, where the bride's tap of an ornate brass knocker bolted onto the massive, carved wooden door is greeted with courtliness by a young male charmer. This virile looking deskman in his mid-twenties records the vital information and escorts the bride down the aisle to a waiting room. Some brides confess that the young charmer has a flirtatious manner, as if he had just been smitten by the girl of his dreams. The charmer who in other enterprises would be known as the front man,[2] through his personal approach to the bride, hopefully can produce a certain loyalty toward his employer's shop. If the charmer can inspire an affection similar to what the young lady later will hold for her obstetrician, the shop's sale will be effortless.

---

[2] In the automobile business, a front man often is a young, nice guy who shows the customer a car and is relieved by a veteran salesman when the discussion turns to price and trade-in. I am here indebted for the concept of the charmer to an unpublished paper by Jean Jarman, "For Richer... and for Poorer," Northwestern University, 1973.

the rhetoric of the bridal salon

The bride then is seated amidst grandeur and luxury to which she is not often accustomed unless she is a GAP by trade. Is marriage to Leonard going to be like this? In one shop the bride is seated in a French cafe to nibble croissants and read *Bride's Magazine*. In another shop, the main attraction is the ornate bathroom, draped with flocked wallpaper, lavishly painted in garden green, and plumbed with a paisley wash basin and gold-handled water faucets. Will Leonard provide in this style? Or she can look at the carpet in the various shops, which probably will be regal (red, gold) or softly feminine (lavender, powder blue), or she can merely think about life with Leonard. In any event, the atmosphere is posh and intended to soften sales resistance.

THE SALE II

Sales Lady (condescendingly): Can I help you dear?
Bride (helpfully): I'm looking for something with simple lines—high-necked, and no frills.
Saleslady: Hmph, are you a professional designer? We carry only quality. I assume the wedding is next season.
Bride: It's on August Fourth.
Saleslady: In three weeks! I'm sorry it's impossible.
Bride: But I wear a size 10!
Sales Lady (exiting): There's nothing we can do for you!
Bride (still seated in the private room): Bitch.

Or, it can go like this:

I am led past the open door of the stockroom, huge and filled to the ceiling with hundreds of dresses. She starts out with three dresses, which she helps me in and out of in four minutes flat, at all times reminding me to put on my chic wedding hat (two ounces of net and wire for $56). Two dresses are eliminated, and she returns with two more while I am undressing. While I try on the fourth dress, another girl enters and removes the rejected dresses. By the time I've tried on the sixth dress, the salesgirl is really moving—now she switches models and convinces me to try on a blue, ruffled halter dress—not traditional but fun. All the dresses that I try on are "sweet" or "fun." By the time I've tried on the fifteenth dress I'm dizzy, and I ask to see the first dress again. The girl is looking a bit worried. "Well, I don't know if I can find it. Someone else could have bought it." And the way they are moving bodies in and out, someone *could* have bought it. She brings it back—beaming—and declares: "That's you!" It certainly is more "me" than some of the more flamboyant desecrations I have been shown. I hesitate. She says they accept personal checks. I put a deposit down, and walk out of the store and collapse.[3]

---

[3] Kris Plummer, "The Marriage Mill," unpublished paper, Northwestern University, August, 1973. Ms. Plummer also recorded the dialogue for Sale I and Sale II which appear here as adaptations.

the rhetoric of the bridal salon

This bride unfortunately was a "loner" who—without an entourage of 12 bridesmaids, the promise of 800 guests, and plenty of out-of-towners attending—got swirled through the bridal shop. The real money is made on multiple attendants' garb, mothers-in-law frocked in low-scooped cocktail dresses, and accessories from watch bands to garters. So if you are a hatcheck girl who is returning to a small town in Wyoming for the wedding, where the attendants are making their own dresses and will slip into white smocks to serve the ice cream and cake at the reception, the bridal shop service will be of lightning speed.

If you are having a big wedding, the closer will enter the room and warbling effusively, roll her eyes heavenward, and bless the dress and the happy mating of the bride and it. A good closer will circle the bride several times, alternately touching the sleeves and kneeling to run fingers lovingly over the hem. The encircling movement of the closer is not unlike a pagan worshipper paying homage to the Sun Goddess. At the conclusion of the ceremony, the bride can expect a request for a $25 deposit to start construction on the gown. For this fee, the bride also can expect to be ushered from the premises in style.

THE CHARMER AND THE EXIT

Charmer (escorting princess by the arm): **How definite** are your wedding plans? ...I'd like to have your phone number.

Bride (blushing becomingly): Oh, I'm **really** getting married!

And a perfect day ends for the bride-to-be.

GREAT AMERICAN BRIDAL SHOP COUNTERS

The counters for this kind of selling strategy are complicated, because there are readers no doubt who choke up when the word "bride" is mentioned. An image is conjured of a sweet, beatific, freshly scrubbed young lady moving languidly toward a tousle-haired, six-foot-tall young man—former camper—with a pack of Salems in his coat pocket. An additional complication is that many of the really nasty strategies probably will be avoided by readers since marriage is sacred and why not enjoy the bridal myth?

Handling the Charmer

Obviously, the charmer is selected by the bridal proprietress to flatter the bride-to-be into feeling that she still is desirable to other men. Perhaps his proposition gives her the illusion of having one more fling. The counter for such charming tactics is straightforward. When the charmer turns suddenly and asks for a date, the bride should grab his frail body boldly and give him a vigorous kiss—bending him cleanly at the waist. Then she shouts "RAPE" to everyone in the shop. They, of course, will believe her claim because she is a bride and not, we suppose, a prostitute. The charmer will go back to the car wash whence he came.

Handling the Saleslady

If the saleslady is throwing dresses at the bride like wet spitters, there is another strategy. Each time she moves the customer from one dress to another, the bride accidently rips the dress as she steps out of it. After $1000 worth of lace and taffeta, the saleslady will slow down.

If the saleslady is as haughty as the Size 10 "Hmpher," another possibility is the Promise of Millions strategy. Suggest that Daddy is the largest importer of wasps in the continental United States and that 5,000 personages ranging from the late Duke of Windsor to the inventor of Skittle Ball will be attending the gala wedding. You want a charming, inexpensive dress to demonstrate frugal intentions to Daddy, while setting him up for the financial kill, a wildly extravagant wedding with 150 attendants. If you have been reading this book carefully, you might even hint faintly that a wedding invitation might await the shopgirl who dresses this wedding.

When the closer asks for the $25 deposit, turn to your saleslady in surprise and with a hint of disappointment. The saleslady, nonverbally picking up the expression of horror, will implore the closer to use a little common sense. At this point, if you have incredible gall, you might suggest to the ladies that the initial dress ought to be on the house.

WHY BOTHER

Well, you passed bride gamesmanship and now you face only the caterer, the florist, the photographer, the clergy, Holiday Inn, relatives, and two sets of quarreling parents.

General Strategies of Weddingship

1. Find exactly what the caterer means by "house roast beef."
2. Call the Better Business Bureau to see if the photographer is a blackmailer.
3. Do not buy from florists who steal from graves. The price is cheap, but you may get married only once.
4. Give the clergyman ten minutes for his speech, and make sure he doesn't talk about apples and oranges if the marriage is mixed.
5. Call each parent the night before the wedding and tell them the affair is off. Then start all over again.

THE GREATEST AMERICAN STYLE: THE COKE BOTTLE

In the mundane world of glass bottled beverages, the Coca-Cola soda pop container stands alone as the mark of excellence. Competitors place their sweetened soda in a variety of containers ranging from smoothly curved to grainy, but the Coke bottle alone has a style that by its presence in your cupped hand gives you stature. What is a bottle of Orange Crush, Dad's Root Beer, or Seven-Up next to the Coke bottle? A mere imitation. The Coke bottle has satisfying ridges serving as grips for drinkers as they hoist the liquid to their parched lips. Even if a pop drinker was blindfolded, the ridges would assure the drinker that the liquid is Coca-Cola and not Pepsi or Royal Crown. To complete the image of the Coke bottle is a nicely tapered bulging middle which not only identifies the product but implies ampleness combined with full-bodied richness. Undoubtedly, Coke has style.

The Coke brand sits on the supermarket shelf as distinct from the other sodas as Michelob is from sarsaparilla. Should I buy it? Remember the thousands of Coke signs in restaurants, hot dog stands, and drug stores proclaiming, "Enjoy Coke?" How can you resist? In some neighborhoods, the red and white Coke sign is the brightest item on the block.

When drinking from a Coke bottle, a consumer is handling the bottle of his ancestors. America turned from wire ice cream chairs, soda jerks, and open pickle barrels to molded plastic swivel seats, automation, and impersonalization; but there is still Coke. The advertisements for Coke moved from turn-of-the-century country estates, to World War I doughboys, to the twenties and gay flappers, to the thirties and families clustered about their front room radios, to the forties' soldiers and sailors, to the fifties' recreation rooms, the sixties' "real thing" generation, and the seventies' image of unbigoted and cool. For the Coke bottle, that's a lot of image and part of its accumulated style.

The Coke bottle represents traditional American values and ethics of an earlier age. That any soda pop is of questionable nutritional value seems to mean little in the selling of Coke and its identification with solid America. Eight-year-olds may be ruining their teeth, but the gesture of drinking Coke is somehow patriotic.

When Seven-Up launched its Un-Cola attack on Coke, they used the forces of the counter-culture: psychedelic posters, television ads featuring offbeat characters, and revolutionary Un-Cola decals. Seven-Up's anticampaign is their tacit admission that Coke identifies with the solid, middle-class virtues of America and that the only inroad into that market is to use an underdog motif.

Even if the Model A is gone along with clean air and Herman's Groceries, the Pause that Refreshes remains with us—The Greatest American Style.

two stylistic strategies: doctors and taxicab drivers

14

TOYS

Hey, kids! **THIS** is the section of the Great American Communication Catalogue you've been waiting for! And, boy! Do I have some surprises for you!

NEW!

DOLLS FOR BOYS AND GIRLS

DOCTOR DOCTOR

Learn how to save humanity, ease suffering, and make money!

AND CAPTAIN CABBY!

cigars not included

Learn how to swear and chew cigars!

CAB SOLD SEPARATELY

When urban dwellers look at occupational styles that interest many of them, the doctor and the cabbie pose an engaging stylistic similarity. They both meet the public, offer fundamentally service activities, and in doing so, adopt occupational roles that frequently dominate their relationship with the consumer. That the doctor makes a lot more money than the cabbie is not so much a communication difference as it is one of supply and demand. If all the cars and trains and buses were banned except for a specially delegated cadre of cabbies, their income might be comparable to doctors'. But even given the disparity in their economic gain, both are forced to communicate with consumers, and their styles of communication are not always dissimilar.

COMMUNICATION CONTACT

The cabbie and the doctor must both meet their consumers. In the case of doctors, the contact is varied, since a consumer can talk to the doctor on the phone, can see her in the office, or can meet her at the hospital. The cabbie is limited in communication to contact with a switchboard operator directing him to the customer, his own on-the-street hustling, or to a peculiar communication arrangement marked by his speaking into a rearview mirror. There are advantages and disadvantages to each approach. Since doctors make more money and have so little time, they will be treated first.

THE DOCTOR AND THE PHONE

The patient often calls during the day, and the call is returned when the doctor has a spare moment or is specifically returning calls. The patient, when receiving the doctor's call, answers under any circumstances including eating dinner, taking a bath, or closing a multimillion-dollar real estate deal. If the patient is sick, he cannot afford to put off the doctor for an evening while he burns up, coughs up, or throws up. The phone call is traditionally a one-way discussion in which the doctor identifies himself—solicits symptoms—and, in turn, the patient hastily recites the day's accumulation of medical misfortunes.

RING...RING...

"Dr. Burns."

"Yes, Doctor, I'm glad you returned my call."

"What's the problem?"

"Itstartedlastnight—asorethroatwithaheadacheandpainintheear."

"Any fever?"

"Alittle..."

two stylistic strategies: doctors and taxicab drivers

RING...RING

"Dr. Stearns."

"Jimmyfellandhurthisheadwhileplayingontheswingandheisbleedingfromthehead."

"Well, take it easy...I'll call the hospital and you drive him there carefully."

In most instances, the doctor not only controls the circumstances under which the phone call will be interacted but how much time will be allocated for the discussion. The doctor not only calls when she pleases but terminates the call when the patient's immediate medical future is diagnosed. The patient feels compelled to recite ailments as fast as possible and may even forget a few items such as hemorrhaging or dizziness.

It is clear that a doctor is a well-paid, treasured commodity in a sickly nation. Why should a mere housewife, who has responsibility only for the pre-five development of a couple of kids, the preparation of meals for an overweight CPA, and the cleaning of a three-bedroom, two-bath, two-car garage, brick ranch, control a conversation with a doctor? All she can do is to recite the litany of the ailments, call the pharmacist, and stay awake all night.

But the doctor is able to define the problem as flu, chicken pox, measles, or bronchitis; and with this ability to diagnose and heal, she controls a decidedly one-sided communication.

THE WAITING ROOM

The waiting room often is an extension of a doctor's intended personal relationship with his patients. The doctor's central waiting room strategy seems to be to abate tension in the patient. In most waiting rooms, the physical objects line the walls and feature a sofa, a few armchairs, coffee tables, and a magazine rack. The intended effect is openness; and with the many chairs, the room provides an illusion of giving a choice of seating. The colors of the furniture are most frequently autumnal browns or subdued blues and greens. The impression of the colors on patients should be restful and quiet—hopefully diminishing anxiety toward the impending examination.

The other physical objects in a doctor's waiting room also are selected to enhance tranquility. In most offices, a bland music trickles from a programmed speaker system soothingly featuring Mantovani or Percy Faith playing "Greensleeves" and other semiclassics.

two stylistic strategies: doctors and taxicab drivers

While listening, the patient can select from a covey of magazines enclosed in antiseptic plastic covers that advertise a local drugstore. A survey[1] of doctor's waiting rooms revealed that the usual subscriptions include *House Beautiful, National Geographic, Travel, Today's Health, The New Yorker* (for its humorous cartoons), *Sports Illustrated,* and *Holiday.* Noticeably absent are sexually provocative magazines such as *Penthouse, Playboy,* and *Playgirl,* or even cheaper pulps such as *Photoplay* or *Teen Screen.* Also absent are clocks. In a total of seventeen offices surveyed, there was only one small clock, and that was an hour slow. Time should not move in a doctor's office, since clock-watching produces tension and may remind the patient of how long he has waited.

A disconcerting note in the doctor's strategy of tranquility is the need for a receptionist. Most doctors' offices have a sliding glass peephole for introductions, leave-taking, and bill-paying. Too frequently a new patient arrives at the office, breaking the waiting patient's reverie with an abrupt introduction of reality. "I have a urine specimen here," waves an anxious patient clutching a brown bag. "I'm a welfare patient, where do I fill out the forms?" pleads a young mother. "I'm in pain, and either I see the doctor now or I leave," rasps an anguished elder. The receptionist often responds to these incursions with a whispered response to maintain the prescribed decorum, hopeful that the patient will imitate her. But still the mood is broken, and even in the most clever of doctors' waiting rooms, the control of subdued colors, harbor paintings, and Muzak can be shattered.

Another problem in a doctor's waiting room is that the open area in the middle of the room facilitates a certain amount of patients' staring at each other from the border seats. How many communication situations feature fifteen sick people lining the walls, hacking, wheezing, burning up, and occasionally crying out in agony? The magazines finally are perused, and little is left but to stare at broken noses, autumnal paintings, and and to overhear a line or two of personal conversation:

> "If she doesn't operate this time, I'm going downtown."
>
> *"She'll operate. She almost killed my sister."*
>
> "Then why do you still come here?"
>
> *"I'm not driving downtown; the parking is murder."*

The result of all this communication is a patient not particularly buoyant when the nurse calls his name. He lays down his magazine, stands rather awkwardly—reluctantly acknowledging the luck of the call—and moves from the waiting room through the doorway into the privileged sanctum.

An alternative to the tranquil blandness of a doctor's waiting room would be to convert its atmosphere to that of a home improvement showroom. For example, instead of showing a film entitled, "How to Panel a Wall," a surgeon could premiere a filmstrip featuring "Dr. Roll's Great Cuts." In the film strip, Dr. Roll could demonstrate his best surgical moments and narrate them for a patient's edification. The patient would gain confidence as Dr. Roll skillfully skewers a diseased gall bladder from a well-known real estate salesman. When his mask comes off, six dancing, masked nurses swirl about him

---

[1] Joan Diamond, Karen Kline, Ken Markowitz, Bruce Nemirow, Leah Rosch, Jim Schorfheide, Julie Simon, "The Waiting Room," unpublished paper, Northwestern University, March, 1974.

two stylistic strategies: doctors and taxicab drivers

chanting his name in ten different languages. Dr. Roll could end the demonstration by raising the diseased gall bladder high on his knife, smiling, and saying simply:

> "My record is 99 and 44/100% pure.
> Give me your diseased organ and I'll give you a fair trade-in and have you home safe for only a couple of bucks more than the three lower-priced surgeons."

THE DELIVERY OF THE SERVICE

Once the patient is called into the doctor's office, the manipulation environment changes dramatically. The nurse often probes the patient about his ailment and then sticks a thermometer in his mouth. The patient is placed in a small, off-white cubicle, usually adorned with the doctor's certificate of graduation and specialty work. On a metal table is a plastic container of tongue depressors and a sterilization container for old bandages. The rest of the room includes two chairs, a cattle scale, a wash basin, and an examining table with a disposable, white paper cover. This is the environment where the patient waits for the unpredictable entry of the doctor. Little noise intrudes into the cubicle, except for a random hurried shuffle, an occasional "Ouch"; and as the minutes tick by, the eternal question recurs, "Why didn't I bring that magazine in here with me?"

Bang! The doctor enters with a quick movement and the patient's life chart in hand. The doctor is stable, reassuring, and seems positive about the road to medical recovery for the patient.

> **"What's the problem."** (Extracts the thermometer.)
> **"Temperature?"** (None if the doctor shows up early.)
> **"Sore throat?"** (Going around.)
> **"Mmmmmm..."** (glancing down throat).

Advice to Pre-Meds: What Should You Look Like?

The female doctor ought to be mature and efficient, her sensible brown hair in a flat twist, and her resonant, positive voice in a European accent. The male doctor should be tall and strong with a full head of blonde, straight hair. After all, if you are ill, you do not want the doctor to look weak, scrawny, and anemic. If the doctor is so good, why doesn't he do something about his limp?

If you are weak looking and want to be a doctor, my advice is to find a specialty that would not be affected by your particular malady. For example, if you are crippled with arthritis but have clear skin, try dermatology. If you have shaky hands, rather than becoming a surgeon, use your flaring nostrils to become an allergist. The patient will see your nostrils efficiently ingesting and exhaling air and know you are qualified for giving shots at $10 each. If you are a pervert, gynecology could end only in misery, but who cares if an ophthalmologist has a foot fetish during his off hours? If you are a physical wreck, there is always psychiatry. All you need is an M.D. degree, a dark suit, and the ability to keep your head moving up and down.

Experienced M.D.

two stylistic strategies: doctors and taxicab drivers

At this point, obviously the patient is in a one-down position. After waiting for an hour in an autumnal shaded somnambulist factory and being transported into an isolation chamber of antiseptic white, that suddenly is invaded by a white-coated medical personage, the now docile patient is fully prepared to be told what peculiar happenstance of Dame Fortune has invaded the body.

A PROBLEM OF IDENTITY

In the ancient days of medical care, a doctor looked at the entire body.
In this age of specialization, many a doctor now looks only at parts.
To these medical specialists, the patient is a urinary tract, a deviated septum, or a detached retin
The problem with the specialist is that the parts do not always equal the whole.

> A PROBLEM OF IDENTITY
>
> I started going to a gynecologist when most girls were being fitted for braces. Because, you see, I had dysmenorrhea (severe cramps). I felt terribly important.
>
> The word "stirrups" to me did not conjure up Trigger, Roy Rogers, roundups or shootouts at Dry Gulch. No, I immediately thought of cold metal against bare feet, paper blankets, "slide all the way down, please," and rubber gloves.
>
> Since I was an Army brat and moved every year, I had a different gynecologist every year.
>
> I was eighteen when I had my first D. and C. I also had a new gynecologist. He was a devastatingly handsome Yalie who was serving his time in the medical corps.
>
> The day after he performed the operation he came to the women's ward to visit me.
>
> "Which one of you is Sally Quinn?", he asked in a loud voice.
>
> "I am," I whispered, dying.
>
> "Oh," he said. "I didn't recognize your face."
>
> —Sally Quinn[2]
> (Reporter, *The Washington Post*)

[2] Barbara Seaman, "How Gynecologists Exploit Their Patients," *New York Magazine,* August 14, 1972, p. 53.

THE GREAT AMERICAN DOCTOR COUNTER

The answer to the doctor's opening request for your ailment is a list. A self-controlled patient merely hands the doctor a list and says nothing until it is totally read and digested.

> Dear Doctor Jones:
>
> I have the following information to report on the condition of my health.
>
> 8 P.M.—headache
>
> 9:30 P.M.—Continued headache, mild sore throat.
>
> 11 P.M.—Added backache and after taking 2 plain aspirins, slept.
>
> 7 A.M.—Awoke to bad cough, sore throat, mild temperature of 99.6°
>
> 8:30 A.M.—Called your office and made appointment for 1 P.M.
>
> 11 A.M.—Vomited, temperature now 101.°
>
> 1 P.M.—Began waiting in your waiting room.
>
> 1:30 P.M.—Finished magazines and had chills.
>
> 1:53 P.M.—Was sprayed by probable TB victim seated next to me.
>
> 2:10 P.M.—Transferred to the examining room.
>
> 2:35 P.M.—Doctor entered.
>
> Sincerely,
>
> *Janice Smith*
>
> Janice Smith

Will this little gambit provoke your doctor to uncontrolled rage and end in a refusal to heal your feverish body? It might. On the other hand, the doctor is a healer, and he now has the full, clear data upon which to judge your case. And after all, a consumer would not think of going to a supermarket without a list of intended articles for purchase.

The exam is an interesting communication experience because it synthesizes the entire event. The mood is often serious and unnatural, since the patient does not feel like clowning and the doctor is expected to be solemn as a reinforcement of his occupational duty. A joking doctor may not evoke much confidence in a patient who seeks to be healed. An effective doctor will touch a patient somewhere to establish contact simply because people like to be handled. Down the throat goes the tongue depressor.

"Say 'Ah'...hmm, a little red. Throat sore?"

"You got my note."

"Oh, yes...ears okay. Spread out. Hmmmm, hemorrhoids."

"Hemorrhoids, I've got a cold."

"Well, you also have hemorrhoids."

Now the doctor moves into a prescription rhetoric:

"Take this four times a day and call me in a couple of days if it doesn't get better."

"How about the hemorrhoids?"

"Oh, just exercise and drink eight glasses of water a day."

two stylistic strategies: doctors and taxicab drivers

The key strategy in most doctor-patient relationships is control. The doctor asks questions and the patient responds. A patient who tries to reverse the relationship may just be asking for trouble. After all, the doctor knows medicine and the patient can generalize only from his own specific case. The patient is last seen holding a prescription, maybe an order for tests, or—God forbid—a hospital date. As he leaves, a new group of 15 hackers and wheezers sit in the waiting room earning their entry into the healing world.

Great Doctors' Bedside Manners

A collection of doctors' mannerisms developed by some of the richest doctors practicing in the continental US.

*Says Mrs. Eunice Gaberdine of Brooklyn, N.Y., "My doctor was a real bitch. One time my mother was dying of an incurable disease, and she asked me if I preferred to pay now or later. I switched to a doctor who uses GDBM and I've never been happier. My father was sinking fast with kidney failure, AND I WAS NEVER MORE DELIGHTED."

*Says Aram Ovaroff of Red Cloud, Nebraska, "My doctor has a postnasal drip which he dries on his patients' clothes. I felt that for $15 a visit, that was a bit degrading. Now I switched to a GDBM user, and my new doctor not only stifles his nose, BUT TURNS HIS BACK IF HE HAS TO SNEEZE."

Well, Doctor, it's up to you! Bound in kidskin $15.95
Other books of interest:

STRETCH YOURSELF TO PATIENTS by *Willis Germ, M.D.*
A guide to height attainment through exercises. $3.95.

BEING A SPECIALIST WITHOUT INTERNING by *Ernest Laser, M.D.*
Don't lose heart transplants to surgeons again.
All you need is confidence and common sense. $12.95.

THE NAGGING PATIENT by *Anonymous, M.D.*
A terse, "how-to-do-it" discussion of getting rid of hypochondriacs.
Includes 15 full-color pages of nonverbal disgust. <u>Very expensive.</u>

THE DOCTOR'S WIFE by *Gwendolyn Hochsnyder*
A snappy primer on landing the girl who can serve as a doctor's wife.
Includes voice tests to determine if she can master "The doctor is not home," and "I'll have him call you." $6.95.

Other volumes available include **THE DOCTOR'S HUSBAND** and **FAMOUS DOCTORS' BEDSIDE JOKES**. Send check or money order to "Doctor's Pal" (DP), Box 1295, Surgical Lane, Texas.
(Calls returned after 5:00 p.m.)

THE TAXICAB DRIVER AND THE HUSTLE

In the first section it was clear that a doctor controls his patients by carefully structuring their communication experience. It is equally clear that cabbies have little going for them, since in the public's view, hacking is one of our less desirable occupations. The thrill of fighting traffic twelve hours a day for a top wage of $40 is not particularly attractive. Still, to have meaningful communication with a customer, to enjoy a day's work and a good day's tips, are all worth working for, from a cab driver's point of view.
The problem for the cabbie is that unlike the doctor he has to hustle to dominate.

The cab driver is in a situation in which the consumer can control the communication if the cabbie is not clever. The patient needs to talk to the doctor; but in the cab, conversation is the customer's option. If a customer orders a cab, the cabbie's only challenge may be to work up the fare and increase the tip, but making communication contact with an uninterested customer or one with transportation options is a more sophisticated problem. An adventurous cabbie might alight from his vehicle to entice a gaggle of airport bus passengers into his relatively private conveyance. The driver moves under the hotel's canopy and in the style of an evangelist smites the sinful bus as "an overpriced, crowded, reeking, stench bomb." Turning to a likely trio he informs them civilly that three can ride his cab for the same fare as a bus trip. . .then dramatically opens the cab door and shouts "Who's escaping?" A less direct sidewalk hustle involves milling among the passengers muttering about "the guy who last night was asphyxiated by an airport bus muffler leak," or lamenting "the bald tires those people leave on their buses." What is effective about sidewalk hustles is that the cab driver has a wide audience from which to seek a fare, and the scattergun flood of appeals can strike a customer who hates reek, stench, accidents, or who just loves a bargain.

Some people may even ride because they like the old-world style of courtliness; a driver is supposed to be a servant, and coming out of the cab to greet the public may stir memories of times past, when taxi driving suggested Eastern European immigrants who called everyone "Ma'am," were studying medicine to save crippled children, and drove black Pierce Arrows with red velvet seats. The beauty of the art of the cab hustle is that if it fails, at least the cabbie gets some fresh air.

Another common communication contact for the cab driver is being hailed on the street for a ride. Often this type of on-street communication is brief, nonsustained, and to the point. The passenger says, "1503 Oliver North, Driver," and the cabbie is supposed to nod agreement and drive to the destination.

A problem that arises in many large cities is that some drivers prefer to skip tough neighborhoods or suspicious fares. The cab business is unique in that it is conceivable that a stranger may get into the cab and ask to ride a distance to an uncertain area of the city. The driver, unlike the doctor, has little opportunity to qualify the passenger as trustworthy. The next fare may be a mass murderer or a Supreme Court Justice. As a result, cab drivers have developed a number of defensive strategies calculated to quickly discourage undesirable fares.

two stylistic strategies: doctors and taxicab drivers

"Where are you going, Miss?"
"29th and Foster."

Rationale 1: "This is my lunch hour sister."
Rationale 2: "Tank's empty kid."
Rationale 3: "That's foreign territory chum."

The cabbie can now only swish away from the curb, leaving the rideless customer frustrated and sometimes angry enough to report the offense to the cab board or the local newspaper's action column:

> **Dear Action Line:**
> I was leaving my mother's house on East 73rd and a cabbie refused to take me to my apartment at 29th and Foster, insisting she had to drive back to the garage. I don't believe her. What can be done for the average citizen?
>
> Walking Sal
>
> ***
>
> **Dear WS:**
> We investigated your meandering cab driver and found that she never returned to the garage at that hour of the day. She is now serving a seven-day suspension meted out by the Cab Board.
>
> Action Line

[Cartoon: "HI, BUD. WHERE YA HEADED?" "OVER BEHIND THE TOY BOX." "UH, SORRY, KIDDO. I GOT FOUR FLATS."]

If a doctor refuses to see a patient, there are no suspensions. But a taxi driver who fears for his life is easily suspended because he is truly expendable. And what of the fare, Walking Sal, who certainly deserves a ride to her home if she can afford it? They are both victims of a producer-consumer relationship that, because of urban neglect, becomes a violent communication experience. When Walking Sal mentions that address, the cabbie suddenly becomes fearful, and Sal, reading that fear, becomes aware of her inability to go where she wants. There are no options for the consumer. A suspension follows, but no one really believes that Walking Sal will get her next ride.

two stylistic strategies: doctors and taxicab drivers

Well, let's assume for illustrative purposes that a consumer decided airport buses were inconvenient or the cab driver was eager to accept fares that day, and a passenger ducked into the back seat of that cab.

> **WHAT SHOULD A CAB DRIVER LOOK LIKE?**
> A taxicab driver ideally should be short and squat, wear a cap, and chew cheap cigars which she spits out the window. An effective driver should also have a gravelly, gruff voice that sounds like a combination of phlegm and tobacco juice coupled with years of breathing bus and truck exhaust fumes. In addition, a cabbie should have a large enough mouth to automatically tell customers "Good morning" or "Good afternoon" when they enter her cab, and "Take care" when they leave.
>
> What if you have a thin, tall body, you don't chew, and you can't stand caps? Then you become an elementary school teacher.
>
> Signed,
> Too Tall

TAXICABS AS WAITING ROOMS

Most cabbies do not have the opportunity to select their vehicles. Usually, the cab driver is handed the keys to a company-owned cab, equipped with whatever amenities were offered by Detroit. Though the doctor can select his waiting room environment, the cab driver is at the mercy of designers who mass produce motorized gentility.

The fare steps into the back seat and sits on a cushion covered with vinyl. Perhaps it is the same quality vinyl as in the doctor's office, but the vinyl and car colors are company-ordered for durability and ease of cleaning. The doctor decides what will surround his patients, but the cabbie merely accepts whatever his employer tenders. This difference is crucial, since one communicator can shape an environment while the other can merely adjust his environment after the important decisions have been made.

two stylistic strategies: doctors and taxicab drivers

When the fare sits back in the seat, he can stare at the cabbie's license or he can gaze through windows at passing scenery. The consumer sees a fleeting array of stores, traffic lights, blinking signs, and pedestrians, a scene often not too restful. The cab driver can structure the viewing environment only to a certain degree, since few patrons will pay for a pastoral detour. The doctor has little trouble controlling his patient's scenery, since a waiting room is essentially a sealed environment with only occasional incursions from the outside.

Many cab drivers try to divert their depressing waiting room scenery through small talk. In the cab business, "old ladies"—whether male or female—are people who demand extra service. Many old ladies enjoy chatting with the driver about life's little bumps and heartaches. Some people like to talk about their cheap brother-in-law or the high cost of tuna fish, or the weather, or sports. A nice, friendly, running commentary from a cabbie keeps the old ladies happy and diverted and may earn the cab driver a substantial tip.

An effective cab driver tries to alter his waiting room environment by carefully structuring his remaining rhetorical choices. He personalizes his cab by deciding if a customer wants to read a newspaper, be left alone, or chat about the day's events. If the customer is from out of town, here's a cabbie's sage advice.

> The first thing to remember is to always ask where they are from and what kind of business they are in. Whatever it is they are selling or buying remember you have a relative in the business. Ask them how long the convention is going to run and how they like the show. Pretend knowledge of their product even if you never heard of it. In extreme cases claim to come from the same state they come from and talk about its outstanding features. Give them a guided tour if asked. Yes, that's the Sears building. The Standard Oil building is in the middle and the Hancock is to the left. Throw in some history; if you don't know any, make it up. Always tell them where to find a good time. Laugh at their dirty jokes. Pretend to know where they can get a little free action or where they can go to get some action for hire. Tell them of a little place you know where they can have a nice evening without getting ripped off (besides McDonald's). Answer all questions no matter how absurd they sound. Most conventioneers are good for a dollar tip if so handled. On long trips always have a copy of the daily paper and offer it to them to read to catch up on what's happening. If coming in from the airport try to make arrangements to pick them up and take them back out after their stay. When they get out, hesitate with the change; they usually let you keep it.[3]

An additional communication problem for a cab driver is the lack of face-to-face communication with the fare. The doctor not only faces a patient but is allowed to touch,

---

[3] Lawrence Garcia, "The Art of the Short Con," unpublished paper, Northwestern University, July 1973. The research for this section was based in part on Garcia's field study on taxicab driving.

poke, and feel. It is difficult for a patient to ignore this kind of pummeling and not pay attention. A cab driver is looking forward at traffic and has to shout his comments while occasionally glancing at his passenger through the rear view mirror. A noncommunicative fare can simply ignore what is being said. This reality leads cab drivers to develop a peculiar in-cab rhetoric that only plays off a fare's comments. The driver who is tip-minded fills in requests for ball scores without quarreling about a team's manager, or points out famous landmarks without worrying about appreciative acknowledgements from the fare. If a fare likes to observe political trends, criticize smog, or predict the weather, an effective driver will always concur. The fare is talking to the back of a head, and the voice from the front seat is that of a personally selected reinforcing automaton. An abrasive cab driver will receive only minimal tips, and unlike an abrasive doctor, the cabbie will end up poor.

THE GREAT AMERICAN CAB DRIVER HUSTLES

Indicate that cabbing is only a sidelight to pay bills while studying for a Ph.D.

NOTE: It still doesn't warrant appearing smarter than a fare.

Offer the fare a free guided tour of the city.

NOTE: Meter continues to run.

Always ask fares if you can smoke.
Not many people ask any more, and your
courtesy will be appreciated.

NOTE: Cancer warning.

Develop a peculiar hesitation in your speech to indicate even speaking to the fare is presumptous.

NOTE: "Aaaahhh."

DOCTORS AND TAXI DRIVERS

A stylistic strategy can take many shapes and forms. It can be acquired through cultural consumerism as with the Princess, developed by a Coke Syrup manufacturer, or occupationally assumed as in this chapter. Doctors and cab drivers do communicate with the public but obviously under radically different circumstances. When a person makes a decision to assume an occupation, certain stylistic conventions of the position naturally follow. A doctor finds that because of a patient's expectations, time commitments, and a shortage of skilled medical personnel, certain communication practices are more effective than others. It is not because of a personality deficiency that a doctor is abrupt on the phone but rather because the profession has adopted an institutional rhetoric that is efficient and is designed to serve the greatest number of people. This institutional rhetoric allows the doctor to control a patient's communication through his ability to structure expectations from the original phone call, to the waiting room, to the examination cubicle.

two stylistic strategies: doctors and taxicab drivers

The style of the cab driver is marked by subservience to the consumer that he conveys. A person may be a Ph.D, a lawyer, or a millionaire, but when occupationally driving a cab he is defined as a noncontroller of communication. The cabbie adopts communication that tries to appeal to different facets of a passenger's character, since being too friendly, aggressive, or hostile discourages tips. Unlike the doctor a cabbie operates in a company-selected environment from a limited number of automobile interiors—Chevrolet, Plymouth, Ford, Checker. And to complicate the communication, a driver cannot even face his fare for most of the conversation. It is little wonder that cab drivers are short and doctors are tall.

In the two examples in this chapter it is clear that occupation often determines the quality and level of communication. Though both doctors and taxi cab drivers meet the public, only one is able to dominate through position. Even a reticent doctor is unlikely to allow patients to control their relationship, but a dynamic cab driver rarely is able to manipulate the conversations in a cab. The styles of interaction often are determined by evolving occupational norms that become institutional rhetorics, consistently transcending our personal communication styles.

THE SUDDEN COMMUNICATOR

This is the actual, true story of William Arnold, who drove cab until he met a mooch who caused him to drive 650 miles and blow his transmission. William was disillusioned when he heard of me—Kinkla Stevens—the world's richest service station owner. When folks drift into my service station, out comes my squeegee—swish, swish—and under the hood I lurk. Gold, riches beyond dreams, harbor under a motorist's car hood. "Check the oil filter?...Air filter's dirty...Fan belt needs replacing." Read how I taught William Arnold to get out from behind his Checker cab and move into the lucrative service station business...

"Why," you ask, "does Kinkla call this ad 'THE SUDDEN COMMUNICATOR?'" Because, my friends, a service station attendant leaps upon a motorist with the swiftness of a panther. "How many batteries need replacing?" "When was the last time your car's windshield washer fluid was checked?"

WEALTH—IMMENSE WEALTH FOR THOSE WHO KNOW HOW TO COPE.

Send for my book TSC *today* and learn how to be the thief under the hood. If not entirely satisfied, receive not only your full money back, but a worn fan belt. (We reserve the right to substitute premiums of equal value.)

Red Binding $3.95
Cream Binding. $4.95
Oil-Smeared $6.95

Send TODAY to:

THE SUDDEN COMMUNICATOR

Kinkla Stevens
Rebuilt Lane
Delco, MO. 021470
No COD's, please...

SECTION FIVE

PROGRAM STRATEGIES

A program strategy is an institutional rhetoric designed for complete control of the consumer through step-by-step planning. In our society, a number of communication programs have been scripted that the producer is conditioned merely to recite. The most common example of this type of manipulation is door-to-door encyclopedia salesmen, with their carefully planned and rehearsed presentations that seldom vary from customer to customer. In this section, we discuss million-dollar clinics and new car deliveries and present briefer examples of a number of specific programs. In each instance, a program is being used by a producer to influence and control the responses of a consumer.

how to make one million bucks in a free society

....

15

YOU CAN TURN FIFTY BUCKS INTO ONE MILLION DOLLARS

JUST LIKE T. OSWALD REINWANGER

BOO BOO HISS HISS BOO HISS BOO

BEFORE

YEA! CHEAR CHEAR YEA RAH

AFTER!

How many of you really want to make a million?

Okay, okay, those of you who sincerely want to make a million, repeat after me—"I want to make a million, Irv!" Louder! "I Want To Make A Million, IRV!!"
That's better! This is gonna be a great session.

Now, I know some of you are cynics about my plan for making a million, right? Of course you are. We have a society that is nourished on pessimism and despair...
You know, my friends, this country wasn't started by boo-birds and nay-sayers.
It was started by can-do Americans who said, "I can do it, I can do it."
And *You* can do it if *You* believe.

How many believe in ME? Beautiful...really beautiful. Now my friends, I'm going to test your belief...see if you really believe in me. Take out a five-dollar bill. COME ON, TAKE IT OUT. Thank you...Now close your eyes. Do you believe in me?...
Good! Now wave that five-dollar bill over your head... keep on waving...
do you still believe in me?...KEEP ON WAVING....

Hey, you're shocked!...That man went and took my five dollars!...
Well, friends, that's lesson Number 1—never trust anyone, not even your football coach, your mother, or your chiropractor, because, friends, the only one who counts is Y-O-U and that spells YOU.

To teach you that lesson, I'm not going to give you back that five-dollar bill...
because where MONEY is concerned, people remember better. But I'm going to give you something for your five dollars. A way of life. I repeat, a goldplated, silver-threaded, platinum-laced opportunity to make a million. One, I said O-N-E MILLION B-U-C-K-S...
each of them shiny, sparkling new and yours if you want it.

Do you want to hear how to make a million? Okay, okay, I'm going to tell you how.

how to make one million bucks in a free society

How many of you have heard of T. Oswald Reinwanger of Cincinnati, Ohio? Not a soul. Well, let me tell you how I first met old T. Oswald. He was working at a riding stable as a collector of manure. That's right, friends, old T. Oswald shoveled manure for nine years before that fateful day I happened on him. He was a sallow, thin, unappetizing creature with large pockmarks covering his face like small craters on the moon. His breathing was heavy and forced and reminded me of an asthmatic in deepest ragweed season. He stank not only from his lowly occupation, but from the stench of a failing and degenerate life.

He was a failure, friends. As sure as I stand here before you, he wasn't worth the postage the government spends on mailing welfare checks.

But I saw something in old T. Oswald. I decided he could be the vehicle to prove my theory. I hesitated for only a few seconds, and then I yelled exuberantly, "I'm going to save you, T. Oswald!" And he said, "No." And I shouted repeatedly and jubilantly, "Yes, Yes, Yes." And let God be my witness, I converted him on the spot.

I said, "T. Oswald, what do you want to do for a living?" He said, "I want to sell cars, Irv." I said to T. Oswald, "There are twenty-two magic words that will transform you into the best salesman in the world if you say them every day. . .every day. Pop out of bed, look in the mirror, suck in your gut, and say, "I am the best salesman in the city of Cincinnati and I will sell more cars today than I have ever sold." TWENTY-TWO MAGIC WORDS that can change your life, too.

Well, old T. Oswald walked into an automobile showroom and got a job on the spot. The first day he cleared the showroom of cars. . .and my friends, he has never stopped. TOP SALESMAN. . .SALES MANAGER. . .OWNER. . .MAGNATE. . .ONE MILLION DOLLARS! T. Oswald is now a strapping six-footer with a body like iron and eyes that glint like the Hope diamond. He walks down the street and people stare at this well-dressed Adonis with admiration and envy. My God, what a build!

T. Oswald's story is no more miraculous than Rachas Oszmansky's. Who is Rachas Oszmansky? No one in this room knows of this simple, humble immigrant who could barely speak the English language when he arrived in the United States on a cloudy day in 1946. He stumbled around, confused, and finally ended up waiting on tables at a Greek restaurant in San Francisco. He thought a fifty-cent tip was a lot of money.

I was chewing my gyros when I felt those eyes piercing at me through the cigarette gloom of the Corinthian Restaurant.

"What are you, sir?" I queried.

"A lonely waiter," he answered simply.

"Not any more," I rejoined, curtly. I gave Rachas my eighteen-word uplift and he repeated it every day for over twenty years.

           1   2   3   4   5   6   7   8   9

"The only thing stopping me from my million is

     10 11 12   13   14   15 16 17   18

that I'm not working harder than the other fellow."

He is now *Mr.* Oszmansky, and every day before 9 A.M. he makes ten calls to prospective clients for his life insurance agency. Every day like a clock, he rises early and makes those calls. Rachas is a rich man today. When he enters a restaurant, the owner calls him by name and shows him the best table. His wife, a former Hollywood star, adores him, and winters they vacation in Aruba. He says of his association with me, "Irv taught me the meaning of life, work, and happiness. I owe him everything."

Would you like to be a magnate like T. Oswald? A great success like Rachas? Well, I've told you only a portion of what I told those fortunate men. The rest is coming, if you really want it...

WILL YOU SETTLE FOR 39¢?

The million-dollar clinic is an offspring of a normal desire to savor the fruits of a freewheeling capitalist system. How many schoolchildren haven't heard of Andrew Carnegie, Henry Ford, and Seymour Chaff? Seymour Chaff? Well, you see, it's the Seymour Chaffs of the world who keep the million-dollar clinic system working.

The audience for a success clinic often consists of salesmen who work on commission and down-and-almost-out businessmen. Most salesmen have periods in their careers when everything seems to go sour. The product may be cyclical or in a price squeeze. The salemen may be pressing so hard that the clients are frightened by their aggression. A million-dollar sales clinic tries to restore incentive and drive in the salesmen—"I can do it." He leaves the clinic buoyed and enthusiastic over his next sales prospect. If he scores quickly with a sale, the clinic may be just the medicine he needed for a lift. If he goes for a period without success, the confidence instilled by the clinic wears off, and he is back in need of help. The failed businessman comes to the clinic with another motive. He is looking for the key to the magic kingdom of capitalism. For this person the clinic is a morality play of *the good life*. The clinic leaders have failed like him but now enjoy incredible affluence. Their successful conclusion is what the loser sees as his third act.

A success clinic combines a natural desire to make a million dollars with a mystical package of self-motivation and ritual. The clinic is centered on a successful business figure who has made large quantities of money in a short period of time. Ideally, the leader is a living embodiment of the success creed—coming from a poor origin, suffering many defeats, refusing to give up, and ultimately making a fortune.

It is also essential that the success figure has a flashy style—he writes phone numbers on the margins of $100 bills, pays for a New York operation for a Peruvian waif, owns a fleet of personal Learjets to pick up friends and acquaintances; a successful clinic figure might marry a beautiful blonde, drive a Ferrari, smoke five-dollar cigars, and captain a 700-foot yacht. Inevitably, it is his style and what it buys that attracts the disgruntled salesmen, hairdressers, and mailmen. Interestingly, women are included in the clinics' operation only as collectors' items for the money-makers.

For most people, their first contact with the success clinic idea is through the millionaire's best-selling book. The book is the capsule philosophy of the leader, written in a prose style that often can be described as a combination of the ranting yells of the University of Texas cheerleading section and the claims of the Sunday ads for Zayre Discount Department Stores. Another category of success talk eschewed ranting and instead promised in seductive language "Castles in Spain."

YOU CAN TURN FIFTY BUCKS INTO ONE MILLION DOLLARS

WITH THE MAGIC WORDS THAT CAN CHANGE YOUR LIFE!

"YOU GUYS FEEL LIKE A MILLION, YET?"

FOREWORD

Sizzling Your Way through Life

EVERYBODY, AS A CHILD, has sat back and dreamed, built Castles in Spain.

Everybody has dreamed of being a doctor, a lawyer, a merchant chief, dreamed of being a nurse, a wife, a career woman in *real life*.

What has happened to our dreams?

We end up by being an accountant, a housewife or engaging in some everyday occupation.

We still have our dreams—we still make them come true, and the purpose of this book is to help you translate dreams into fact.

It will give you practical, not theoretical ways, to get along better in life—and sell yourself.

It will help you to attain the daydreams that may have blown up, or become nightmares.

There are 101 daily situations in our lives where the right word at the right time will spell success for us. Situations, where the proper technique in getting along with others will help us to attain our Castles in Spain—help us get along better, help us to be richer in life.

Elmer Wheeler

The emphasis in the success books is upon formula phrases:

Eight Magic Words	"One single, bold act may change my life."
Nine Magic Words	"The anticipation of selling is the curse of selling."
"Get" Mottos	"Ten phone calls before 9 A.M."
Maxims	"The thing that keeps men big is thinking big."

Layered over the phraseology are large numbers of rules for conquering cowardliness. Some of the books feature daily uplift strategies to handle the common stresses of mankind's afflictions. Get out of bed—Face the mirror—Shout into your image, "Be Enthusiastic!"; "I'm Number One!"; or "Today I Get Mr. Big!"

The important considerations in all the rules and mottos are discipline and believing. Underlying all success talk is the notion that in a country this ripe for exploitation all that is needed is desire...desire...desire. You out-desire the other guy, and like Vince Lombardi's famous Green Bay Packers of the sixties—you win.

A small dog with guts beats a gutless big dog any day!

And if you fail, you neglected to "say and do" every day, and you deserve to lose.

[1] From the book, *How to Sell Yourself to Others* by Elmer Wheeler.
© 1947 by Elmer Wheeler. Published by Prentice-Hall, Inc., Englewood Cliffs, New Jersey.

YOU CAN TURN FIFTY BUCKS INTO ONE MILLION DOLLARS

BY READING IRV REIN'S MILLION SELLER:

HOW I TOLD ONE MILLION PEOPLE HOW TO MAKE ONE MILLION DOLLARS AND MADE ONE MILLION DOLLARS BY DOING SO.

*BUT WAS AFRAID TO ASK

BY IRVING J. REIN

The actual clinic often is a big-money spin-off from a best-selling book. Excellent examples of books with clinic potential are such best-selling success works as E. Joseph Cossman's *How I Made One Million Dollars in Mail Order*,[2] Napoleon Hill's *Think and Grow Rich*,[3] and W. Clement Stone's *The Success System That Never Fails*.[4] The book is necessary because its popularity draws curious crowds to the clinic, and its author provides a key success figure with whom the audience can identify.

HOW TO RUN YOUR CLINIC

The first move is to rent a hotel ballroom or a civic auditorium. The rental ought to be plush—reeking with class. A meeting in a rundown part of town in a fleabag hotel would attract only indigents. Next, flood the town with "private" invitations to the clinic at, say—$50 a day. People like to receive "private" correspondence congratulating them on being "nominated" to your clinic.

QUICK MATH

300 people x $50 a day = $15,000.
$15,000 x 20 working days a month = $300,000.
$300,000 x 10 months = $3 million.
Subtract $600,000 for expenses...*Total Profit* = $2,400,000, not including add-ons such as sale of cassettes and books.

The actual presentation is a combination of revivals and sales meetings. A warm-up personality is employed to ask and answer questions, introduce guests, build up expectation for the big man. If the audience is lucky enough to get number one, he comes on looking razor sharp—Glenn Turner, formerly of "Dare to Be Great" success clinic fame, wore yellow-striped three-piece suits and shoes of unborn calves' leather, hair side out. The delivery style is acrobatic, with lots of running, jumping, leaping, and throwing.

---

[2] E. Joseph Cossman, *How I Made One Million Dollars in Mail Order* (Englewood Cliffs, N.J.: Prentice-Hall, Inc., 1963).

[3] Napoleon Hill, *Think and Grow Rich* (Greenwich, Conn.: Fawcett Publications, 1960).

[4] W. Clement Stone, *The Success System That Never Fails* (Englewood Cliffs, N.J.: Prentice-Hall, 1962). Hill and Stone collaborated to produce one of the best-selling of all positive-thinking books, *Success Through a Positive Mental Attitude*, (Englewood Cliffs, N.J.: Prentice-Hall, Inc., 1960).

how to make one million bucks in a free society

A great opener is to throw money into the audience, and while the hopeful, manic millionaires scramble for the dough, shout—

**Vermin! grovelers!—
fighting for a few hundred bucks!
It's chicken feed!**

It is important for the million-dollar clinic to create an atmosphere of nonconcern for money. Who cares about a couple of bucks? Think big! Then follows a series of confessionals—real and imagined—of amazing success stories. T. Oswald Reinwanger's and Rachas Oszmansky's stories are told with all the appropriate verve and distortion necessary to entice converts. Then it is only a quick step to your plan for success, which includes anything from three to twenty-five magic ingredients. Then some group participation is encouraged to practice the "together" magic. Some homilies follow about the silliness of succumbing to defeat. After all, didn't the leader fail seventy-seven times in a number of schemes? But you *will* hit—if you believe. Then sell some books, cassettes, autographed pictures, and send them home to conquer the Real World.

PYRAMID SALES

A variation of this pitch is the clinic featuring a pyramid sales product. Some of the million-dollar clinics have been promoted around secret motor additives, cosmetics, or any other product that can be merchandised by direct or door-to-door sales. The object of a pyramid is threefold.

1. Sell a citizen a distributorship. He in turn can—
2. Hire a sales force to peddle the product door-to-door, or—
3. Sign up other citizens to distributorships and receive a nice commission.

In fact, most citizens sell distributorships instead of peddling door-to-door; thus—the theory of the pyramid. Those who begin at the bottom of the pyramid (the organizers) make money; those buyers who follow the initial organizers into the pyramid sell to a diminishing market—so diminishing, in fact, that theoretically, the latecomers are selling in a zero population situation. If everyone who previously bought a distributorship has sold his product to expectations, there is no one left in the world to whom to sell. This product is a beautiful one for a million-dollar clinic. A salesman must be extraordinarily motivated to sell a product to such a dwindling market.

IF YOU DON'T GET CAUGHT LAST!

"Excuse me, sir. Would you care to purchase some snake oil?"

"Are you kidding? I'm a DISTRIBUTOR!"

The people attending the clinic are ideal victims for the pyramid. Here is a concrete product on which to put those magic seven words to use. And the advantage of buying a distributorship here and now is reinforced by the simple dictate, "Get it done today."

HOW ABOUT $1.39?

Is it really possible to make a million? Is the million-dollar clinic really such a rip-off? After all, there are large numbers of poor people who have moved up to Fleetwoods. Then how do *you* do it?

One obvious method to make a million is to start your own millionaires' clinic. There is plenty of room in the "self-help" tradition in America for a newcomer like you. Ever since the great American Ben Franklin began his Almanac, telling Americans how to live a fruitful life, the market has been right for "think yourself to success" philosophies.

In a period when consumers are befuddled by the depersonalization of relations and are burdened with ever-increasing bureaucratization of life, the notion of individual success certainly is appealing. In every nook and cranny of America there are people who harbor a faint hope that a magic combination of hard work and faith will produce for the individual a triumph over the corporate mentality. In every million-dollar clinic there is idealism—not cynicism, hope—not despair, freedom—not restraint. A fundamental belief in the "self-help" tradition is that each person is individually endowed by the Creator— regardless of race, creed, color, or circumstances—with the basic equipment to succeed. This fundamental dogma, drawn from many American examples of success, is appealing to most of us.

The negative side of the philosophy is that many clinics are spawned to hawk the success idea *and* the accompanying merchandise. The "faith talks," "daily reaffirmations," and phony success stories all lend an air of fraud to the program. It is one thing to believe in yourself, to renew your faith daily, and to feel that America is a land of opportunity. It is a totally different proposition to be sold a package of inspirational books and cassettes by a group of cynical program designers.

If the million-dollar clinic idea does not appeal to you for making your million, turn the page for a mailing program that is equally lucrative.

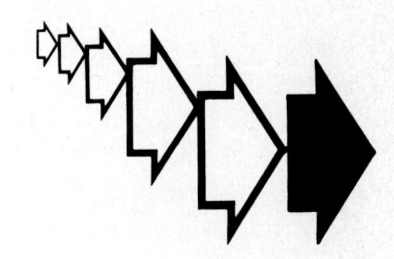

WIN $100,000 CASH
OR
TWO NEW HOMES
OR
A LIFETIME INCOME

FIRST ANNIVERSARY FALL COMMUNICATION GIVEAWAY
If one of the six numbers in the attached Entry-Order card is the lucky number of the day your entry reaches us, you are that day's winner. One of the winners in our Anniversary Giveaway is...YOU, Mrs. T. Oswald Reinwanger.

A telephone call to the Reinwanger family in Cincinnati could bring news of a GRAND PRIZE...INCOME FOR LIFE! And if you order our new GREAT AMERICAN COMMUNICATION CATALOGUE you will receive a 50% discount on an autographed, two-part record collection of the author singing thirty-five, best-loved Bible songs. With every bonus order, Mrs. T. Oswald Reinwanger, you will receive—absolutely free—a piece of the returned tire used in "The Rhetoric of Complaining." So—MAIL YOUR ENTRY CARD TODAY!

Detach Bonus Numbers Along Perforation

Six Bonus Chances Assigned to:
Mrs. T. Oswald Reinwanger

Z28	acne	hair cream
Lunch	tuna fish	Bjorn Borg

VIGNETTES OF PROGRAMMED INSTRUCTION

~getting oiled~

"Yes sir."
    "Fill 'er up."
"Oil's down a quart."
    "What kind of oil do you have?"
"Regular grade 65¢, super grade 85¢, premium grade $1.05."
    "What's the difference between the grades?"
"Are you going to keep this car for more than a year?"
    "Yes."
"Get the super grade."

ELEMENTARY PROGRAM

"In what year did Columbus discover America?...Billy?"
    "1492, Miss Jackson."
"Very good, Billy.
Now what was the name of the first pilgrim ship
to land in America?...Sally?"
    "Sea Lion."
"Wrong Sally. Did you read the assignment?"
    "Yes...I mean, no."
"Bill?"
    "Mayflower."
"Very good, Billy."

Communication in a Mattress

Communication in a Mattress

"Hi, I'd like a mattress."

"You've come to the right place."

"That's great. What do you have?"

"Well, have you ever bought a mattress?"

"No, but I heard that it should feel hard."

"Right...what's your name?"

"Steve, Steve Arnemeyer...I mean Aurnameyer."

"Right, Steve...now lie down on this Sealy."

"Gee, a Sealy...How much?"

"Don't worry about it...now lie down on this Englander. How does it feel?"

"Great, gee, an Englander...my parents had a..."

"Right, Steve, now lie down on this Serta. How does it feel?"

"Swell, how?..."

"Sure, they're all great, Steve, and they're expensive. Did you ever hear of the Gribbles Mira-Hard Mattress Company of Red Cloud, Nebraska? Of course not...but for $35 more than these name brands, you can get a Gribbles with anti-dive, torsion lift, hydraulic springs...and if you buy today, we throw in an astronaut-tested, lino-hard, mattress cover with washable action, astro-soak, and Columbia bicycle gears. And if you buy before 3:30 P.M., we throw in three dozen safety-tested prophylactics."

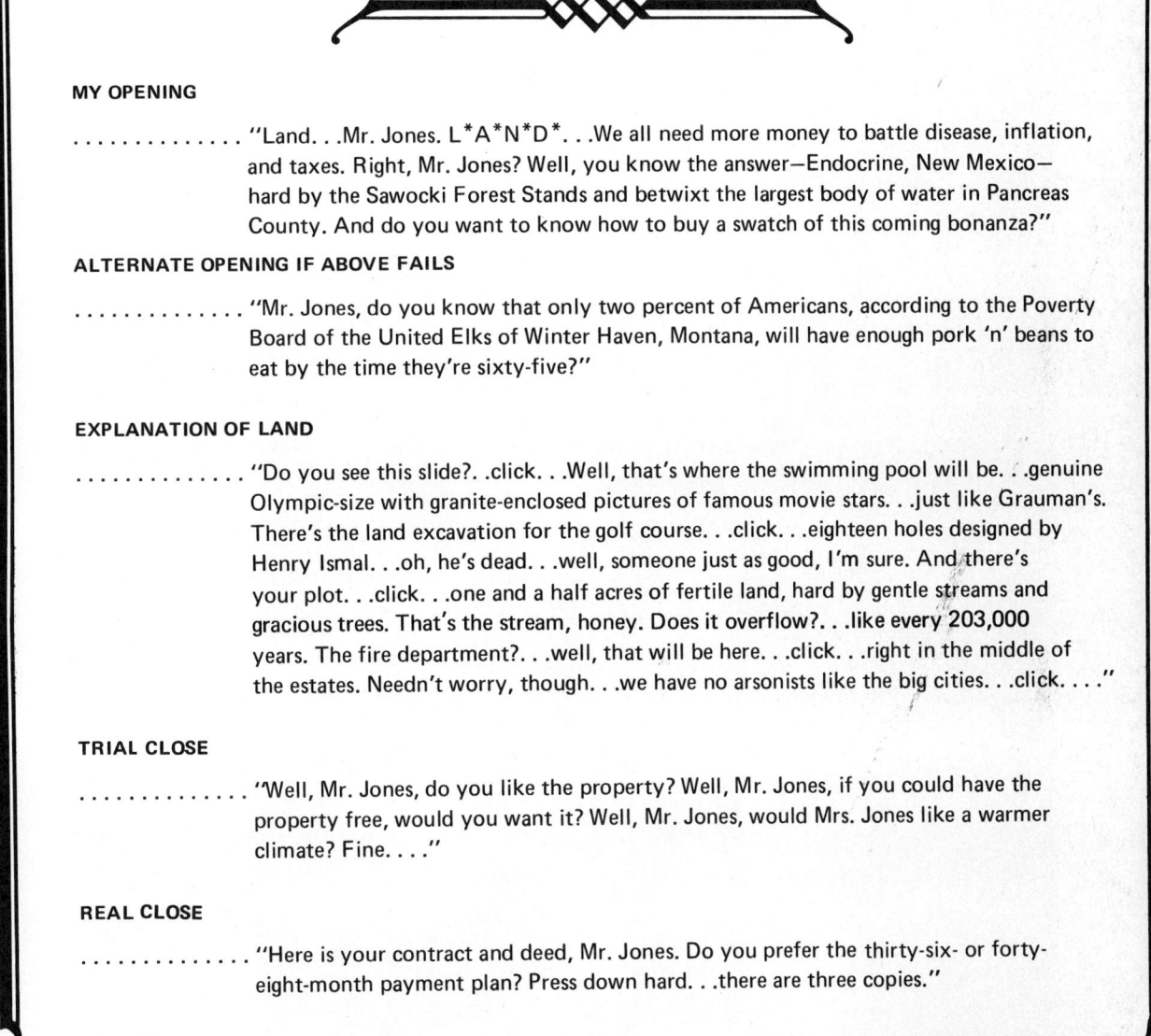

The Great Land Hustle

MY OPENING

..............."Land...Mr. Jones. L*A*N*D*...We all need more money to battle disease, inflation, and taxes. Right, Mr. Jones? Well, you know the answer—Endocrine, New Mexico—hard by the Sawocki Forest Stands and betwixt the largest body of water in Pancreas County. And do you want to know how to buy a swatch of this coming bonanza?"

ALTERNATE OPENING IF ABOVE FAILS

..............."Mr. Jones, do you know that only two percent of Americans, according to the Poverty Board of the United Elks of Winter Haven, Montana, will have enough pork 'n' beans to eat by the time they're sixty-five?"

EXPLANATION OF LAND

..............."Do you see this slide?..click...Well, that's where the swimming pool will be...genuine Olympic-size with granite-enclosed pictures of famous movie stars...just like Grauman's. There's the land excavation for the golf course...click...eighteen holes designed by Henry Ismal...oh, he's dead...well, someone just as good, I'm sure. And there's your plot...click...one and a half acres of fertile land, hard by gentle streams and gracious trees. That's the stream, honey. Does it overflow?...like every 203,000 years. The fire department?...well, that will be here...click...right in the middle of the estates. Needn't worry, though...we have no arsonists like the big cities...click...."

TRIAL CLOSE

..............."Well, Mr. Jones, do you like the property? Well, Mr. Jones, if you could have the property free, would you want it? Well, Mr. Jones, would Mrs. Jones like a warmer climate? Fine...."

REAL CLOSE

..............."Here is your contract and deed, Mr. Jones. Do you prefer the thirty-six- or forty-eight-month payment plan? Press down hard...there are three copies."

nobody's perfect: strategies in delivering new cars

16

THE INSULT THAT MADE A MAN OUT OF "RALPH"
YES, SIR. YOUR NEW CAR WILL GIVE YOU THE BEST GAS MILEAGE POSSIBLE.
HA HA HA HA
AS LONG AS YOU CAN PEDDLE!
CAUTION CARS EXITING
HA HA HA HA
THE BIG BULLY! I'LL GET EVEN SOMEDAY!
DON'T LET IT BOTHER YOU, LITTLE BOY!
AWARDED THE TITLE "THE WORLD'S MOST PERFECTLY SUSPICIOUS MAN"
Irv Rein
DARN IT! I'M SICK AND TIRED OF NOT GETTING THE CAR I ORDERED! IRV REIN SAYS HE CAN GET ME A REAL CAR!
BOY, IT DIDN'T TAKE REIN LONG TO DO THIS FOR ME! WHAT A MANIPULATOR! THAT BULLY WON'T SHOVE ME AROUND AGAIN!
LATER
... NOT ONLY DO I WANT THE CAR I PAID FOR, I AM ALSO SUING YOU 'TILL YOU BLEED!
YES, MR. NADER!
OH, RALPH! YOU ARE A REAL MAN AFTER ALL!
HERO OF THE SHOWROOM
GOSH! WHAT AN EGO!
HE'S ALREADY FAMOUS FOR IT.
IRV REIN ON TV
5 FREE GIFTS IF YOU BELIEVE THAT, BOY, YOU SHOULD ORDER TODAY!
WIN THIS VALUABLE TROPHY
Dear Irv: Here's the sort of car I want:
(CHECK AS MANY AS YOU LIKE. IT WON'T HELP)
☐ BIG ☐ COLOR ☐ NEW ☐ WORKING
☐ LITTLE ☐ B&W ☐ USED ☐ UNEMPLOYED
PRINT NAME .... AGE .....
ADDRESS ....
CITY & STATE .... ZIP CODE .....
LET ME PROVE I CAN MAKE YOU A NEW MAN!

In few activities do human beings find themselves so emotionally charged for communication combat as in the purchase of a new automobile—that magic moment in Americana when Dad, Mom, and the kids chug down to the car dealer to buy the latest in American technology. A couple of bucks here, a few extras there, a promise of a guarantee, and the deed is done. For $3,650 and your dilapidated 1969 Plymouth Fury III, you now have a new Buick Century with air conditioning and anti-dive control. A few minutes of signing documents—then out to the car for an inspection, a smile, and the world now has another happy, smug, new car owner...for at least a couple of miles!

Unfortunately, the car-buying acts described in these few sentences are not really that simple or rewarding for the consumer.[1] Buying a car can be a headache, a heartburner, a nerve-gnawer, and a skin-erupter. It can be that time in life when all reality is suspended as you and that salesman face each other across an aluminum desk with a green ink pad to shoot out a deal:

> "Okay, I'll try $1,300 with the boss!"
>
> "$1,300! Are you kidding? I'll give you $1,225 for that tub."
>
> "Listen, $1,250 is the best we can do."
>
> "We might be talking at $1,237 plus a radio."

---

[1] See Irving J. Rein, "The Rhetoric of the Car Lot," in *Rudy's Red Wagon: Communication Strategies in Contemporary Society,* (Glenview, Ill.: Scott, Foresman & Co., 1972), pp. 118-27; *Edmunds New Car Prices,* (New York, 1976), publishes ten editions a year, all containing information on buying a car.

nobody's perfect: strategies in delivering new cars

Strangely, however, in conducting research on strategies in automobile selling, it became apparent that the buying-selling shoot-out is secondary in manipulation to the actual delivery of the car. *Consumer Reports*[2] claims that of the new cars they recently tested delivery defects ranged from nineteen to forty per car—from broken windshield wipers to deadly exhaust leaks and serious motor failures. The situation presents a practical communication problem. How does a salesman convince a customer to take home a car that may be in worse shape than the one traded?

I was in a position to observe the salesman-customer interaction while employed by a large automobile dealership for an entire summer.[3] This automobile dealer hired me as a new car salesman to join a sales force of twenty.[4] My motivation for applying for a car salesman's position was, in part, scholarly. Primarily, I was interested in the dealership as a case study in manipulation, though admittedly there was also a fascination with the opportunity to assume an occupation far removed from my usual profession. Since I had left a Harvard Instructorship to accept a Northwestern University Assistant Professorship, my shabby clothes and quiet, financial desperation may have reinforced my persona as a hard-driving, fast-order-writing salesman. It was sufficiently persuasive to warrant my immediate elevation to the showroom and live encounters with customers.

The showroom floor is recognized by most customers as a place where extraordinary manipulative feats are engineered by sales personnel. The attempt to control the customer is part of the ongoing life style and reality of the showroom. It was not uncommon for a salesman to order Sunday-suited customers under a car to answer their own question about muffler quality.

> **"Tap that muffler—coated ceramic."**
>
> *"Yeah, really solid."*
>
> *"Good, come on out."*

In other cases, salesmen would instruct customers to jump up and down in trunks to test durability—"Jump higher, higher,"—or to climb on roofs to examine roll potential—"Hit it harder." It was only a short step from these bizarre occurrences to convincing a customer to sign a "buy" order without a notation of a specific car.

The automobile showroom is a rhetorical circus, with total dominance by the salesman over the customer as an anticipated-and-sought goal. A customer is cajoled, flattered, deceived, or coerced to buy a four-wheeled, motor driven, steel body that is useful for an increasingly limited duration. The consumer's potential protection in this highly manipulative situation is public knowledge of showroom sales strategies, which would encourage the buyer to exercise freedom of choice. The supreme weapon of the

---

[2] "Dealing with the Dealer," *Consumer Reports* (April 1972), p. 200.

[3] The dealership is one of Chicago's largest new and used car operations, moving about 500 cars a month. I was employed at the dealership during June, July, and August of 1969.

[4] The sales force ranged from fifteen to thirty, depending upon the time of year and the need to create competition among the salesmen.

consumer is his freedom to leave and shop elsewhere if the salesman is abusive or terribly dishonest. The car delivery interaction, however, is not usually considered a strategical situation that should be countered, since once the customer has purchased the car the delivery is taken for granted. This difference makes the delivery more difficult for the consumer both to counter and to win. The ultimate power of any consumer is the freedom to reject the dealer or to return his merchandise—even at the point of delivery.

THE DELIVERY

What makes the car delivery so verbally stressful is the salesman's realization that he does not get paid his commission until the car is successfully delivered and the customer rolls the car over the curb. At this point the salesman finally receives credit for the sale, and no matter what the customer complaint, a commission is paid. The salesman's task is to convince the customer to take the car and leave the dealership. In many cases the car is in such bad condition that his strategies must be extraordinary. Why would anyone want a car that barely runs or is falling apart?

At most dealers, there is a standard program designed for delivering the customer's car. The customer is greeted warmly by the salesman and confronted with a number of documents. His signature goes on licenses, sales agreements, and tax affidavits. Usually the customer is not allowed to see the car before the final sales agreement is signed and the purchase price paid. A number of excuses are used to cover the unavailability of a car before signing such as, "It's in the 77th Street lot," "It's being undercoated," or "It's being washed." Obviously the strategy is to keep the customer from seeing a car he might not wish to drive and own. Once the customer has signed and paid the salesman feels that having taken a final step, the customer is less likely to complain.

The thrust of the big dealer approach is to insure customer compliance by systematically following a number of business conventions. The development of an atmosphere of normalcy is begun with a handshake, pleasantries to the children, offering of Coke or coffee; finally the process is sanctified by a multitude of business expressions such as "warranty," "tax advantages," "equity," and "minimum maintenance." For the customer who earlier bought his car amidst a series of epithets, suspicions, and threatened walkouts, the opening gambit of the delivery is disarming. The communication posture of the delivery is unlike the hustle of the sales encounter and is structured to imply stability and professionalism on the part of the dealer.

The stage now is prepared for the next scenario. The customer, having been treated regally in Act One, is now set to be ushered into the presence of his new car. The contrast between the settings of closing the sale and of the actual acceptance of the car is dramatic. While the sales room is brightly illuminated, freshly painted, and sprinkled with modern furniture, most new car deliveries are made in a dark, oil-spattered corner of the service garage. The customer is generally prevented from seeing the car in natural or even good, artificial light. Nevertheless, the customer, having been reassured of the dealer's honesty, now expects a clean, sharp car—exactly what he paid for.

What You May Get—Case 1

Customer number one was sold a light blue compact for which he searched twenty-five dealers. The salesman, not having light blue, sold the customer black. "What's the difference, who remembers a color after a day, anyway?" The problem is to convince a crushed customer to take the black car after he left the showroom thinking he had bought light blue.

The customer is signed, then ushered into the presence of a hearse-colored compact. In this case, the service area was shaken by a low wail squeezed from the customer's innermost entrails, "Screwed again. God, screwed again."

The strategy taken by the salesman was to attack management. The salesman burst into the general manager's office and raged against the "error" and the manager's insensitivity to the customer. The encounter naturally caught every ear in the large showroom, and immediately a large crowd gathered about the group. The customer, cringing and stepping on the heels of the salesman—fearing the outburst would cost the salesman his job—took the car. Even the salesman's "request" to paint the car was brushed aside by the customer.

What appeared to happen in this transaction was threefold. (1) After a long search, the customer found the color of his dreams. His expectations were very high and he planned to drive the car home that day. He probably also had told his friends and neighbors about his successful purchase. (2) The sales transaction was normal: he paid the bill, received the license plates, and pocketed 2,000 S&H green stamps. (3) He was confronted with a difficult choice—to begin his search again with the risk of disappointment or to take the car. The display of the salesman provided the customer a graceful excuse with which to save face in front of his family and his friends. He bought the car—it had been an "honest" mistake.

What You May Get—Case 2

Another customer, after a fierce sales interaction with the salesman, finally bought a green sports car for a bargain $125 over dealer's cost. He traded in a competitive brand sports car. After the sales agreement was sealed, the customer confided to the salesman that the trade-in was a dog and needed a new transmission. That the customer had acted in bad faith only affirmed the irony of the delivery itself.

The new, green sports car, faintly glowing in the musty service shop, looked in sharp condition upon arrival. But when the customer started driving from the service shop, a loud banging arose. "What's that noise?" he shouted. "It's the boys in the service shop," the salesman shouted back. In fact, the banging was the left front wheel, hopelessly out-of-round.

The delivery of the sports car was pure con. All preceding interactions on the salesman's part had been courteous and routine. The only abrasive note had been the customer's relentless attempts to grind down the sales price. The car delivery program had been staged so beautifully and courteously from the point at which the customer had been put into the receiving situation that even this customer could not break the decorous mood. An effective new car delivery has a flow and momentum not unlike that of a well-staged play. The new car grinder could have changed the delivery's conclusion, but his interruption would have been unnatural, ruining the flow of events and causing stress. It takes guts to heckle a great performance. He drove out.

What You May Get—Case 3

The third example involved a young man of twenty-two who by his swaggering, self-confident manner, was buying not only a car, but his independence and manhood. This occasion was obviously the first time he had ventured forth to make a big purchase on his own. The car he was presented had a defect—the entire right side was bent. Apparently the factory personnel had assembled the car with creased doors and fenders. After examining the damaged vehicle, the customer asked the salesman for an evaluation. "That's factory design." "Oh, okay!" To confirm the diagnosis, the sales manager was called over to check the situation. "That's factory design." "Oh, okay!" The customer drove out to a straight world.

A crucial factor in this encounter was the young man's not bringing a friend for support and perspective. The salesman and sales manager defined the situation as "factory design," and not having any support, the customer capitulated and drove out with a lopsided car.

What They Got—Case 4

Two of the three delivery victims returned to the dealer to complain. The customer who received the lopsided car returned in two weeks with his father who threatened to sue the manufacturer, the dealer, and the salesman. The lower right side of the car was replaced eventually. The customer with the bad wheel returned a number of times, trying to have the situation corrected. He probably still is banging around out there. In each case, the return visits were accompanied by shouting, oaths, unpleasantness, and invective. In each case, the salesman received a full commission on the sale since the car had been delivered.

The three examples cited of car deliveries at this dealership are merely representative. A customer found his new car with spots all over the trunk. He accepted the explanation that they were water spots from a recent washing. He returned two days later to have an acid-spotted trunk repainted. Another customer was told his car was undercoated. He crawled under the car to study the spray job, wiped his hands, nodded, and said he was satisfied. Two months later, when greasing the car, a gasoline station attendant remarked that the car had never been sprayed underneath with rust inhibitor. Another customer unknowingly accepted a car with a leaking gasoline tank. When the customer returned that same afternoon to complain, he was told not to light any matches around the car—the service department was closed. In each case, we have a study in persuasion—persuasion that resulted in someone accepting a car in dubious and sometimes dangerous condition.

THE DELIVERY CON

The delivery situation is an illustration of institutional rhetoric used against customers. An automobile dealer frames the scenario from which the delivery is enacted. The use of professional conventions rarely is challenged, because the consumer is conditioned to respond in certain ways. A handshake, a large desk, cashiers, loan officers, business and government documents—they all suggest financial might and respectability. It is almost unconscionable for a consumer to destroy the symmetry and balance of such a program.

In the car delivery there seem to be four main strategies that are representative of the dealer's institutional rhetoric. In most cases, the strategies act to prevent a customer from making an intelligent choice about accepting or rejecting his new car.

First, there is general *ignorance of strategies*. Many customers have no idea of how manipulative the car lot is. The automobile dealers live on persuasion, and they have developed a fine art. There is, for example, a simple strategy as common as switching the model after purchase of a specific car. One customer bought a four-door hardtop to be delivered the following day. Within the next twenty-four hours, the management sold and delivered the customer's car to someone else for a higher profit. To the salesman, the problem was immense—how to deliver a two-door hardtop to a couple who had brought a four-door hardtop.

The choice of strategies is surprisingly large when fellow salesmen are questioned for solutions. The four-door is unsafe, poor handling, damaged, or flooded. There never was any time during the plotting period when telling the truth was considered. Instead, the couple was woven an incredible story beginning with an innocent question.

"Do you have any kids?". . . .
"Oh, my god! I can't sell you this car. . . ."
"Why? It's unsafe.". . . .
"It's a coffin—a coffin!. . ."
"Listen, I've got kids, too. How can I sell you this bomb?". . . .
"One hit—the rear doors fly open and—SPLAT!"

The customer is delivered an in-stock, two-door hardtop for an additional $100—which is the final indignity, since the four-door hardtop list price is $60 more than the two-door. This conning strategy is a play on the old theme of protection of family, coupled with the immediacy of being in someone else's territory. One reason the strategy works is the "Sacredness-of-the-Children" theme in American culture and the unwillingness of customers to entertain the notion that someone would be capable of lying on this particular subject.

The car lot is jam-packed with devices and ploys that comprise an arsenal of stock strategies. Few big-city operations fail to use bugging instruments in the showroom, fake price lists, and turnover artists who take over deals and close reticent customers. The customer who wishes to buy a vehicle without stress ought to familiarize himself with the institutional strategies of the car lot.

nobody's perfect: strategies in delivering new cars

Another strategy for delivering cars is the *salesman's willingness to take extraordinary risks.* Much of the salesman's conning is couched in an atmosphere of machismo that leads to doubling of the dealt hand. Many customers accustomed to normal interactions are not willing to call bluffs of communication strategies that go beyond the normal comprehension of reasonable behavior.

Many of the deliveries are outrageous risks taken by an individual acting on behalf of the institution. These cons are often two-part interactions with an initial con upon delivery and then a conning rejoinder when the customer returns to complain. Upon delivery, the customer queries:

"What are those spots?"

"Oh, we just washed it."

"Okay, just checking."

The customer returns later and confronts the salesman with the charge—"This goddamn car is covered with acid!"

The salesman employs the return rejoinder con—with the intention of placing the customer on the defensive:

"It is? Gee, it is."

"What kind of outfit is this, anyway?"

"Go screw yourself."

"WHAT!"

"I said go screw yourself."

"You can't treat me like this. I want to see the manager."

"Then let's go see the manager, BUDDY."

"What's the problem?"

"He insulted me and sold me an acid-spotted car."

"He's the best salesman I've ever had. We'll paint the car for you."

Or there is the straightforward response that is really more incredible than the former:

"THIS GODDAMN CAR IS COVERED WITH ACID."

"Gee, I'm sorry. I'll paint it," ingenuously answers the perpetrator.

The customer is grateful. The people at the dealership are fine people. They painted the car.

The interactions typically are abrupt, argumentative, and generally laced with obscenities. For example, the salesman sometimes will take a risk with "Go screw yourself" or "Let's go see the manager." Most customers are not used to the high-risk con and often back down under the stress. In the case described, the customer ought to be thankful. The people at this dealership could be persuaded. They *did* paint the car.

The risks taken at dealerships are considerable for a major corporation. One vehicle, totaled by a youthful driver a few minutes after delivery, was reassembled—then returned to the lot for sale as a new car. The loan paper was carried by the dealer and he decided not to take a loss. As earlier illustrated, many cars that never were undercoated were palmed off to customers as having $25 to $150 spray jobs. Even though the risks often constituted fraud, customers rarely called the bluff. The dealership was a wild kind of institution in which the cars served only as foils for the inmates.

A third dealer strategy plays on the *customer's fear of authority*. It is the kind of fear people often exhibit when confronted with an institution. An institution has money, lots of people, lawyers, and relationships with police. The old bromide, "You can't fight City Hall," is apt. The customer feels that if he makes one false move someone will arrive in the middle of the night—flash a badge—and take his car, furniture, wife, and kids. He thus can be conned.

The customer who accepted the two-door hardtop in lieu of an unsafe four-door is a typical example of this strategy. The institution defined the four-door as a death trap; and as an individual, the customer felt unqualified to challenge the decision. He could envision his family strung out on Highway 101 in a catastrophic, four-door hardtop-Greyhound bus collision. If he refused to accept the two-door, he would worry about the choice until the next time he traded. An institutional curse had been placed on his original choice. He was conned.

The final strategy most prevalent in delivering cars is using *the customer's own ability to fantasize,* thereby discounting the true condition of his car. The strategy is a variation of the old land boom con of wishing the situation were as painted. The land salesman sells you a piece of Florida or New Mexico that may be swampy or isolated and commits this larceny through grandiose word pictures—you, wearing whites and commanding a yacht; you, playing golf in mid-January; you, surrounded by young, attractive swingers at a swimming pool. The car delivery con also is based on visualization. The darkened delivery room is suggestive. The customer's willingness to wish away evidence that would destroy his expectations partially can account for the salesman's ability to convince him that the car's defects are water—not acid, styling—not creases, and shopworkers—not banging wheels. The support offered by the salesman is sufficient to propel the customer and his turkey over the curb.

BREAKING THE PROGRAM

As nearly unconscionable as it is for a consumer to destroy the symmetry and balance of such a galaxy of manipulative ploys, still the consumer *can* counter. A number of strategies can be employed to foil the institutional persuasion. *First, the customer can demand to see the car before he pays for it.* If he may not see the car, he should not complete the deal. *Second, upon seeing the car, the customer should insist on driving it around the block in daylight, noting any problems affecting tuning, braking, or wheel alignment. Third, the customer should then instruct the salesman to list each defect on his acceptance sheet.* The notations should include existence of even minor scratches and their exact locations on the car's body. This act insures prompt repair when the car is returned for service. If the customer fails to note a defect at delivery, there may be a dispute over responsibility when the car is returned for a remedy. *Finally, the customer should not be afraid to refuse the car if the condition is intolerable.* Most car dealers will arrange a replacement rather than lose a sale.

If all this plotting and nitpicking does not appeal to a prospective car buyer, he does have alternatives. He can live with imperfection, learn to jog, or buy his own car agency.

THE CLOSE

The car delivery is an example of an individual interacting with a large corporation on a large-scale purchase. What makes the situation even more threatening for the customer is that he has already negotiated strenuously with the company on the price of the car. He now returns to take possession, already feeling relieved but somehow uneasy.

In many cases, the salesman was forced to use high-pressure adjustment strategies to deliver the car. Most of the salesman's interactions were portions of the stock program used by large car dealers. In most cases, the cars were delivered in a fumy, semidark service area. The customer quickly was shown the car and hustled onto the street. The specific strategies used were designed hastily to meet the emergency. When customers begin to insist on seeing cars in daylight and reject obviously disabled merchandise the deception will change—but not cease. The car dealers merely will order the sun to darken.

The advantage of working for a dealer and observing strategies from the inside were obvious in the car delivery. A crucial factor in understanding the strategies of the car delivery interaction is the desperation of the salesman. There is an atmosphere of competition and anxiety that forces salesmen into conning. There are only so many live customers. There are only so many light blue compacts. The salesman is paid by commission; no customers, no merchandise—and he doesn't eat. I felt this pressure keenly by the end of the summer and was ready to do almost anything to deliver a car. The position was debilitating, degrading, and stressful; and only through direct participation could these observations be appreciated fully.

The same advantage of involvement also is a severe limitation of working within the company. It is not very hard to imagine becoming so immersed in the role that objectivity becomes a problem. There were times when I seriously could not resolve my own ambiguities about my ethics. I wanted to move a car. I had to conform to the management's expectations of proper conning methods. The management clearly fired salesmen for failing to conduct the program with élan. To stay at any cost to personal ethics is a choice someone in this position often has to make. But I was affected by my commitment to participate, and the analysis inevitably reflects this limitation.
I liked conning and yet was repelled at the same time. "Jump higher...higher..."

the great american finale

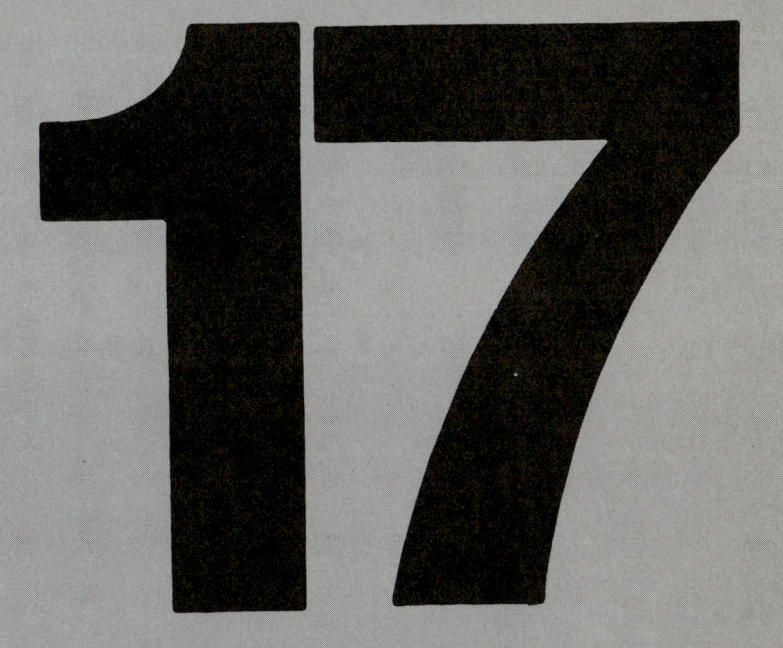

17

The Great American Communication Catalogue featured a large number of strategies in which a series of communicators exercised extraordinary control over the consumer. We observed students acquiescing to teachers, kiddies intimidating Mommy and Daddy for a sugar-sweetened cereal, patients hustled into small, white cubicles, and salesmen believing in a myriad of faith talks and get-rich schemes. In each example, the crucial element was an institution controlling a consumer through a communication program. Though sometimes they were effective, most of the efforts of the consumer to counter the program had severe limitations.

The obvious problem is that consumers really have no unifying bank of strategies upon which to rely. Unlike such sophisticated producers as IBM or McDonald's no organization coaches and trains consumers in communication strategies. The consumer movement has failed to develop a strategy training program that approaches the efficiency of corporations who enjoy the advantages of training funds and a central purpose. In fact, most consumers lack a communication profile—a set of central tendencies—other than such negative characteristics as gullibility, frustration, and anger. However, the counters to institutional rhetoric fortunately need not be developed in one environment, and through use of media the consumer can be reached and educated in strategies.

A further problem is that consumer education, like war, often carries the participants beyond sane battle lines. The consumer finds himself fighting fire with fire, using aggressive tactics when necessary to win a point. And at what point do the producers and consumers create among themselves such destruction that the battle is no longer worth winning?

There are no easy solutions to this problem of means versus ends. A consumer who discovers that abandoning a car at the dealer's will facilitate service is knowingly engaging in a deceptive act. On the other hand, the consumer stuck with a repair bill of $350 and a still-defective vehicle is left with his integrity and poverty. The only answer is for the consumer to understand the full range of strategies available and let personal values, morals, and the urgency of the situation dictate their use. *The Great American Communication Catalogue* has attempted to synthesize some of the more salient of these strategies.

IGNORANCE OF STRATEGIES

In many of the communication situations in the catalogue the consumer was unaware of common institutional strategies. This consumer ignorance creates an opportunity for a one-sided game in which the dominator is in position to do what he will. Institutional Rhetoric is based upon this consumer inactivity. The consumer who is innocent of the car dealer's ploy of delivering a new car in a dim service area is pleading for destruction. A more subtle example is the layout of a store with the sale items, shelf locations, and lighting all calculated to increase your grocery bill. There is nothing quite as satisfactory as countering a car dealer by insisting on a sunlit delivery or following a strict grocery list in the supermarket. The result may be just a happier life.

FEAR

Another factor in complete domination of the consumer is the inexplicable terror often created by a producer. We observed teachers intimidating students through grades, tire salesman screaming about integrity, and the Princess frightening her boyfriend. Still other situations such as job interviews normally are dominated by the employer because of fear. However, many of the situations in the catalogue revealed the consumer as irrationally fearful because of misconceptions as to the capability of punishment by the producer. No one can dominate or even play evenly if unduly in fear of retribution.

CONVENIENCE

An additional factor that affects dominance is the consumer's willingness to sacrifice it for convenience, rather than to be burdened with active participation. The faculty member who never attends budget meetings risks being dominated by those members who do attend. The same rule applies to any communicator who abstains from reading package labels, street signs, or who turns over the power of attorney to someone else. To play evenly means bothering to participate, and attempting to complain without having made an effort is not only fruitless but often demeaning.

FANTASY

A problem with may producer-consumer relationships is the consumer's willingness to believe in producer fantasies. An effective communication program often creates images for consumers that are not real and can range in cost from a 39¢ can of soup to a $25,000 plot of swampland. The soup maker who claims a product is "close to homemade" is suggesting an earlier world when dedicated cooks used wood-burning stoves, raised fresh vegetables, and labored over the soup all day. A factory-manufactured soup is far removed from that nostalgic image in taste and care. Even more manipulative are the cheap, mail order advertisements selling the fantasy that a $1.98 bottle of "living fluids" will add four inches of bosom. And, of course, the big league of fantasy makers includes the pyramid sellers who promise instant millions for the holder of a distributorship and the land hustlers who paint pictures of "fertile land, hard by gentle streams and gracious trees." An effective producer often understands that some consumers are more susceptible than others to the lure of sudden gains and easy riches. An effective consumer understands that most of the world's possessions cost dearly; easy promises should be investigated and usually ignored.

RISK

Finally, it is clear from *The Great American Communication Catalogue* that few communication strategies are more effective than calculated, escalating risk. In most examples, the producer-consumer relationship was severely altered by one or the other taking dramatic risk. A risk can work, because an institution is unprepared to deal with aberrant behavior or because the risk so suddenly changes the situation that an appropriate institutional response is delayed ("I know you've got a room full of out-of-round tires").

The problem in all risk strategies is knowing when the risk is out of proportion to the gain. Is losing your car worth a $350 repair settlement? How do you make those judgments? The only answer is knowing all the possible strategies, weighing the consequences, and then selecting from the choices. And fortunately, the events themselves accumulate, and with experience—you get smarter.

FRUSTRATION

An understanding of the strategies of the producer-consumer relationship is essential for each participant to function without stress. Too often consumers find themselves not able to respond intelligently to manipulation. How often do they claim "a great deal" in order to rationalize a one-sided beating? Or, what of the consumer who continually searches, asking, "Should I buy?" when frozen with indecision? The consumer who makes hasty decisions, strikes back emotionally, and heckles due to frustration and anxiety is in the long run of little benefit to the legitimate producer. The producer-consumer transaction ought to be marked by civility, understanding, and mutual respect. This condition can be managed only when both participants understand the strategies and counters now used in desperation.

THE NEXT CATALOGUE

This catalogue, by necessity, presents a societal relationship between institutions and consumers that resembles armed combat. Most rational people must call for a better way—a new, more open, communication catalogue. Perhaps someday we all will tire of the games, and we will level with one another. It will be a pleasure to write that version.

In the meantime, consumers must try to understand how Institutional Rhetoric affects their daily lives. To understand the strategies of cereal media and to counter their mainpulation is a step toward creating a more receptive communication system.
The next institutional attempt to communicate may be more facilitative because of the principle of "enlightened self-interest."

THE FINAL CLEARANCE BIBLIOGRAPHY

On Cultural Communication

> BOORSTIN, DANIEL, *The Image: A Guide to Pseudo-Events in America,* New York: Atheneum, 1971. The author analyzes how Americans have produced exciting events from formerly nonexistent occurrences. A shopping center grand opening is an excellent example of this phenomenon.
>
> BROWN, JOE DAVID, *Paper Moon,* New York: Signet, 1971. A fictional account of a 1930's hustler and a little girl who move through the South, fleecing widows and avaricious farmers.
>
> HERZOG, ARTHUR, *The B.S. Factor,* Baltimore, Md.: Penguin Books, Inc., 1974.
> A clever study of how Americans have confiscated and used language to obscure truth.
>
> REIN, IRVING J., *Rudy's Red Wagon: Communication Strategies in Contemporary Society,* Glenview, Ill.: Scott, Foresman, & Co., 1972. A book that discusses cultural communication from put-ons and obscene language strategies to making it in dissent and in owning a country dance hall.
>
> WEISS, RICHARD, *The American Myth of Success,* New York: Basic Books, Inc., 1969.
> An insightful discussion of the origins of the success and positive mental attitude philosophy in America.

On Getting Rich

> CAPALDI, NICHOLAS, *The Art of Deception,* New York: Donald Brown, Inc., 1971.
> A philosopher's analysis of the methods of manipulation from Aristotle to modern strategies.

the final clearance bibliography

GOLDENSON, ROBERT M. (ed.), *The Franchise Guide,* Princeton, N.J.: Resource Publications, Inc., 1969. A collection of America's latest franchise bargains, beginning with AAMCO Automatic Transmissions and ending with World Bazaar. If those prospects fail to excite the reader, information on page 133 reveals the method to buy into the Miss America Teen-Ager Contest, Inc.

MURPHY, JOHN (ed.), *Secrets of Successful Selling,* New York: Dell, 1969. An account by five crackerjack salesmen on how to sell plenty of merchandise. In this book the reader will learn how to get around objections, how to think big, and how to turn setbacks into stepping stones.

RIGGS, BOBBY, with McGANN, GEORGE, *Court Hustler,* New York: Signet, 1974. A discussion of hustling strategies by one of America's foremost proponents. The best section covers Bobby's tips on winning at tennis and is helpful to neophyte tennis strategists.

On Spending Your Money

MELVILLE, JOHN (rev. by Jefferson Morgan), *Guide to California Wines,* New York: E.P. Dutton and Co., Inc., 1972. There comes a time in your success when a bottle of Ripple is no longer good enough for a Great American Triumph. This book tells you how to order wine like a connoisseur.

NELSON, WALTER HENRY, *The Great Discount Delusion,* New York: David McKay, Inc., 1965. A discussion of how discount stores have systematically forced out the small-store owners by selling only fast-moving merchandise cheaply and ignoring slower-moving models and customer service.

PURDY, KEN, *Ken Purdy's Book of Automobiles,* Chicago, Ill.: Playboy Press, 1972. A book recommended for those readers who plan to do so well that they can afford $100,000 Dusenbergs.

SMITH, ADAM, *The Money Game,* New York: Random House, 1968. Smith reveals how big-time investors in the stock market can get fleeced. An admonition to small-time investors of how investment games are played.

STEVENS, PAUL, *I Can Sell You Anything,* New York: Peter Wyden, Inc., 1972. A warning to consumers on how advertisers try to influence decisions. Stevens discusses such popular campaigns as Ben-Gay's "When you hurt, it helps," to Ex-Lax's "Have a good day tomorrow."

TYMON, DOROTHY, *America Is For Sale,* Rockville Centre, N.Y.: Farnsworth Publishing Co., Inc., 1973. In this book a citizen can discover how land developers use manipulation to sell worthless land. If you own a ranchette in New Mexico, you might want to trade it for a swampette in Florida.

On Other Catalogues

EMMET, VORIS and JOHN E. JEUCK, *Catalogues and Counters; A History of Sears, Roebuck and Company,* Chicago, Ill.: University of Chicago Press, 1950. The definitive history of the world's largest catalogue company.

HERNDON, BOOTON, *Satisfaction Guaranteed; An Unconventional Report to Today's Consumers,* New York: McGraw-Hill, 1972. An account of how the first major catalogue company turned around its faltering divisions and began to compete successfully again with Sears.